EXPLORE
HAMPSHIRE

Front cover photograph
Hampshire Farm Museum
Upper Hamble Country
Park

Back cover photograph
The Royal Oak Public
House at Langstone on
the Solent Way and The
Wayfarer's Walk

Explore Hampshire
Its Coast, Countryside, and
Heritage
By John H. Holder and
Barry Shurlock

Third Edition

Copyright © Hampshire
County Council 1986

Published by
Hampshire County
Recreation Department

Designed by
Michael Goddard
Design Assistant
David May

All photographs except
where stated by
John H Holder

Distributed by
Countryside Books
3 Catherine Road
Newbury, Berks.
Telephone (0635) 43816

Produced through
MRM (Print Consultants) Ltd
76 South Street,
Reading, Berks.

ISBNO 0 948176 02 4

E X P L O R E

HAMPSHIRE

ITS COAST, COUNTRYSIDE
AND HERITAGE

JOHN H. HO

BARRY SHUR

PLACES TO VISIT
THROUGHOUT THE YEAR
INCLUDING CITIES,
SHIPS, COUNTRY PARKS,
CASTLES AND COUNTRY
HOUSES

PUBLISHED BY HAMPSHIRE COUNTY COUNCIL RECREATION DEPARTMENT

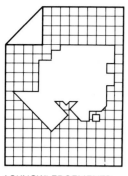

GENERAL INFORMATION

ACKNOWLEDGEMENTS

The authors would like to express gratitude to John Chapman, David Aston, and Keith Rushforth for their help writing the pages on the New Forest, Marwell Zoological Park and the Hillier Arboretum.

Grateful acknowledgement for help with illustrations is made to Portsmouth City Council, the National Trust, The Department of Environment, Mr. Murray Davidson, the Beaulieu Estate, Mr. Butler Kearney, the Broadlands Estate, Southampton Common Studies Centre, Longdown Dairy Farm, Naval Ordnance Museum, Spit Bank Fort,, Paultons Park and Bird Gardens, the Butser Ancient Farm Trust, among many others.

The authors would like to thank the many people who have helped with advice and comments during the preparation of the book:

John Holder would like to express particular gratitude to the designer, Michael Goddard, for his dedication to Explore Hampshire and his enthusiastic collaboration during many long hours spent planning the book.

Finally, John Holder wishes to thank his family for their encouragement, and support in writing this book.

Every endeavour has been made to check that information given is correct, and the publishers would be grateful for further information which may be included in future editions of this guide.

EXPLORE HAMPSHIRE has been planned to help you get the most out of your visits and travels around the county.

Where possible we have given details on who owns or manages the sites and properties included, for anyone who would like more details.

Further information is available from:
Hampshire County Recreation Department,
North Hill Close, Andover Road,
Winchester, Hants SO22 6AQ
Telephone (0962) 64221 and
Southern Tourist Board,
Town Hall Centre, Leigh Road,
Eastleigh, Hampshire SO5 4DE
Telephone (0703) 616027

There is also a comprehensive network of Tourist Information Centres, many of which are open throughout the year (those marked ★ are only open during the season). Their telephone numbers are given below:

Andover ★: (0264) 24320
Beaulieu: (0590) 612345
Eastleigh: (0703) 614646 Ext 3067
Fareham: (0329) 221342
Farnborough: (0252) 513838
Gosport ★: (0705) 522944
Havant: (0705) 480024
Hayling Island ★: (0705) 467111
Lyndhurst (and New Forest) ★: (042128) 2269
Petersfield: (0730) 63451
Portsmouth: The Hard (0705) 826722
Clarence Esplanade, Southsea: (0705) 754358
Continental Ferry Terminal ★: (0705) 698111
Romsey ★: (0794) 512987
Rownhams Service Area, M27 Westbound ★ (0703) 730345
Southampton: (0703) 221106
Winchester: (0962) 68166, 65406 (weekends only)

The 'Price Guide' given for each attraction is simply a guide to the cost of entry.

Cost for a family, 2 adults and 2 children at time of publication:

A. Less than £1
B. £1 - 2
C. £2 - 4
D. £4 - 6
E. £6 - 10
F. £10 or more

Prices may change in the future but the guides should remain a useful pointer to which are relatively dear and which are relatively cheap. As the most expensive sites offer a complete day out with special attractions, the classification is no indication of value for money.

Where parking is known to be free this is mentioned, elsewhere car drivers may have to allow for this further expense.

Comments on suitability for the handicapped and how long to allow for a visit have in most cases been based on how people cope in practice and the advice of the owners and managers.

Information on publications etc. is included to indicate what is available to help you during or after your visit.

Advice on where to eat is given to help families. It has not been possible however to include mention of pubs and inns with gardens or family rooms which can be found near some sites.

Public Transport - Services are subject to frequent changes and visitors should carefully check the bus services, especially outside the main towns.

Bus information is obtainable from:

Portsmouth	0705 696911
Southampton	0703 22635
Winchester	0962 52352
Basingstoke	0256 464501
Aldershot	0252 23322

In most cases nearby railway station have been mentioned. Some may involve more than a short walk but could be used to make visits combining cycle rides and train journeys.

Rail information can be obtained from:

Southampton	0703 229393
Basingstoke	0256 64966
London	01-928 5100

It should be pointed out that at the time of publication Bursledon Windmill is a project which we can look forward to exploring but is not 'open' yet. Southwick Brewhouse and the Naval Ordnance Museum are open only by appointment.

Events - Every year there are many private gardens open to the public, and a wide variety of special events including a very large number of guided walks. For information contact Hampshire Recreation Department.

FOREWORD

It gives me pleasure to welcome this third edition of 'Explore Hampshire'. In its short life this Hampshire County Council publication has become a best seller and has inspired similar guides to other parts of the country.

'Explore Hampshire' has been well used. For thousands of Hampshire residents and their guests it has brought many days of enjoyment.

This third edition now has many more attractions. There is also, for the first time, a useful directory to live entertainment in and around the County.

A few of the new entries are an indication of museums in the making, and readers may need to make individual arrangements for a visit or watch out for 'open days'. Others are opening for the first time in 1986, like Wolvesey Castle, Whitchurch Silk Mill and the new Sealife Centre at Portsmouth. Throughout the book our wealth of military heritage, linked now by the special Defence of the Realm Theme, is clear to see.

The enormous variety of attractions revealed in its pages is an indication of the health of our County's growing leisure service industry. It also shows how conservation and preservation of our heritage can lend valuable support to our drive for economic prosperity.

I am fully confident that armed with 'Explore Hampshire', readers will find much happiness for years to come.

F.A.J. Emery-Wallis
Chairman of the Southern Tourist Board

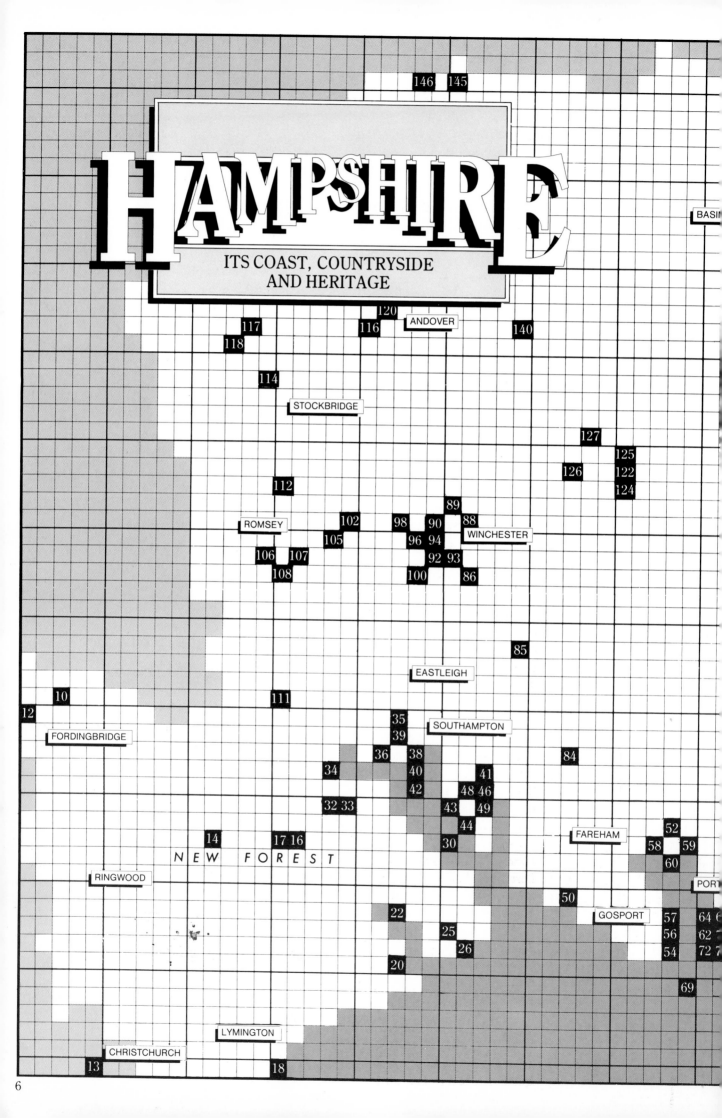

HAMPSHIRE

ITS COAST, COUNTRYSIDE AND HERITAGE

BASIN

146 145

120 ANDOVER
117 116 140
118

114

STOCKBRIDGE

127

125
126 122
124

112

89
ROMSEY 102 98 90 88
105 96 94 WINCHESTER
106 107 92 93
108 100 86

85

EASTLEIGH

10 111
12
FORDINGBRIDGE 35 SOUTHAMPTON
39
36 38 84
34 40
42 41
32 33 48 46
43 49
44
14 17 16 30 FAREHAM 52
N E W   F O R E S T 58 59
60
RINGWOOD PORT
50
22 GOSPORT 57 64 6
25 56 62
26 54 72 7
20
69

LYMINGTON

CHRISTCHURCH
13 18

6

CONTENTS

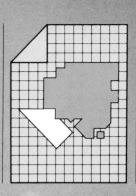

THE NEW FOREST AREA

Bucklers Hard Village
Photo: Beaulieu Estate

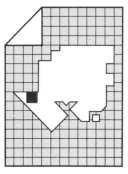

BREAMORE HOUSE
& COUNTRYSIDE MUSEUM

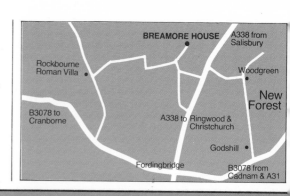

Like so many of the great houses of the reign of Elizabeth, Breamore (pronounced Bremmer) was built in the form of an E. The red brick structure was later extended with a wing at the back and nowadays the entrance is no longer through the middle stroke of the E. Otherwise, the sight we see today as we walk across the park can

Breamore House -
Countryside Museum -
Carriage Museum
(Sir Westrow Hulse Bart)

Breamore
Near Fordingbridge,
Hampshire
SP6 2BY
Telephone
Downton (0725) 22270

Price Guide - D
(Includes house and two museums)

Car Parking
Free

Handicapped
Museums suitable: Ground floor of house only.

Party Visits
Educational resources
Tours of Countryside Museum in mornings by appointment

Publications etc.
Leaflets and guidebooks

Where to eat
Tea-bar
Suitable picnic area in car park adjoining countryside museum

Time to allow
2 - 3 hours

Open
April - September
Every afternoon (except Monday and Friday)
Open all Bank holidays

Public Transport
Bus Services -
Wilts and Dorset buses at least every hour from Salisbury and Bournemouth to Breamore village, Tuesday - Saturday (every 2 hours on Sundays).

Nearby Attractions
Rockbourne Roman Villa and Woodgreen Village Hall (by appointment only)
Telephone Downton (0725) 22288 or 22469
Price Guide - A

Avon Tyrrel
(National Association of Youth Clubs)
Lutyens House
Visitors welcome by appointment
Telephone (0425) 72347

Open Good Friday to mid October, Bank Holiday Mondays and Sundays

Moyles Court Nr. Ellingham
(Manor House School Trust)

16th century house re-modelled in the restoration times. Former home of Dame Alice Lisle

Visitors welcome by appointment
Telephone
Ringwood (042 54) 2856

have changed little from the view four hundred years ago when it was constructed.

The tour gives visitors a chance to see the wood-panelled Great Hall, 85 feet in length, with a splendid collection of late 16th and 17th century portraits and fine tapestries. From the windows there is an unspoilt view across the Avon valley to the Forest. Other rooms on the ground floor show an interesting contrast between the stark simplicity of the 16th century and the greater comfort and elegance of the 18th century, a contrast which will also be noticed in the bedrooms upstairs: in the north wing heavy oak furniture, great four-poster beds and simple plastered partitions between the rooms, but in the Georgian bedroom on view there is fine carved walnut, with rich embroidery and family portraits.

A special feature is the kitchen, hung with ranks of copper pans and a remarkable beer barrel on wheels marked "Waste not, Want not", from

which the kitchen staff served themselves. The house is all the more remarkable when one learns that there was a severe fire in 1956 which ruined much of the interior.

In the nearby carriage museum, set in the old stable block, is a display of the fire-fighting equipment often kept for such private houses until the first world war. The museum has carts and coaches, drags and chaises but the 'star' is the "Red Rover", the last stage-coach to run on the London to Southampton road which was so busy until the railways were built. Part of the stable is still kept as a tack-and-saddle room.

Not far from the house a path leads across the park to the Parish Church, a simple flint building that is one of Hampshire's best Saxon churches, thought to be a thousand years old. On the walls is an attractive display about life in the priory, which stood near the mill on the Avon. Its canons farmed the estate for four centuries.

'HOW TO GET THERE'

From Southampton, or New Forest, follow M27, or A336 to Cadnam Roundabout, then B3078 (through Brook). At Bramshaw road fork left, sign-posted to Fordingbridge. At Godshill turn right into Woodgreen village, then across the valley to the A338. Turn right, and then left following signs to Breamore.

1.			4.	
2.	3.	5.		6.
				8.
		7.		

1. House seen from across the Park
2. Dining room
3. Steam traction engine
4. Cottage Interior
5. Wheelwright's shop in Countryside Museum
6. Boots, in Carriage Museum
7. Breamore Church
8. Tractor in the Countryside Museum

1,6,7: Mike Goddard
2,3,4,
5,8: Breamore Estate

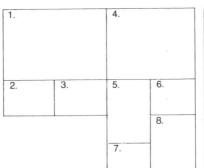

Breamore Countryside Museum has been built in recent years in a large walled garden on the edge of the park. Near the entrance is a maze which involves 1200 feet of brick path. The design is based on the shape of the five-bar gate and was the winning entry in the Great British Maze competition, organised in 1983 by *The Sunday Times*. The museum is large and very well organised and the displays are spread among several buildings connected by sheltered walks. Many of the tools and equipment used before the days of petrol or steam are laid out to illustrate, season by season, the work in field and pasture. Some recall a life of hard labour and others show how mechanical aids improved efficiency, if not the condition of life of the villagers. The changing design of the plough, better equipment with which to harvest the wheat and root crops, as well as machinery from old barns, all portray country work through the year.

Another building contains a labourer's cottage of some fifty years ago, without running water or electricity, which has been rebuilt so faithfully that the kettle on the stove seems about to boil for tea. Here other village 'workshops' have been re-created and look as if the blacksmith, or the wheelwright (among others) had stepped outside a moment before. A recent addition is the bootmaker's shop, complete with all the tools used by this craftsman. A modern barn has a large collection of vehicles which show the impact of steam power, and later petrol, on farming. There are horse-drawn wooden waggons, heavy traction engines and a large group of tractors, spanning the years from world war I.

Within the walls of the former garden are a variety of farm animals including rare breeds of sheep, poultry and goats. The track across the park leads past the house and, as a public footpath, climbs gently up to the downs, passing close to another Breamore maze, the Saxon mizmaze on Gallows Hill. Because the mill is provided with a causeway the Forest is easy to reach beyond Woodgreen. The lane across the valley provides a useful short-cut to avoid the crossing at Fordingbridge.

Before returning home visitors may enjoy a look at "The village-on-the-wall", a set of murals in the simple village hall of Woodgreen. This was painted in the 1930s when little more than a farm and a collection of cottages made up the parish. The whole gives a fascinating picture of country life fifty years ago seen through the eyes of two young students from the Royal College of Art.

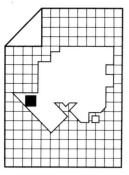

Rockbourne Roman Villa and Museum

(Hampshire County Council)
County Museum Service,
Chilcomb House,
Bar End,
Winchester, Hants.
SO23 8RD
Telephone:
Winchester (0962) 66242
Rockbourne (07253) 541 and 445

Price Guide - B

Car Parking
Free

Handicapped
Suitable with exception of toilets

Party Visits
By arrangement
Tours available

Publications etc.
Leaflet and guidebook

Where to eat
Suitable picnic area on adjacent land

Time to allow
½ - 1 hour

Open
Good Friday - 30th June and 1st September - 31st October:
Monday - Friday, 2 - 6pm,
Saturday and Sunday,
10.30am-6pm
July and August: Every day,
10.30am - 6pm

Public Transport
Bus service -
Wilts and Dorset buses run from Salisbury and Bournemouth to Fordingbridge, then local bus to Rockbourne, Monday - Friday, limited service.

Nearby Attractions
Breamore House

Top   Reconstruction of the villa during the fourth century, drawn by Nigel Fradgley

Below left   Skull in museum display

Right centre   Cottage in Rockbourne village

Bottom right   Mosaic

Villa: *Royal Commission on Historic Monuments, Crown Copyright reserved*

Mosaic: *Hampshire County Museum Service*

Skull: *Bridget Hillyard*

ROCKBOURNE
ROMAN VILLA

Rockbourne Roman Villa was discovered during the last war by a farmer who was hunting rabbits on his land, and excavations over the last 20 years have proved it to be one of the largest known villas in the South of England. The earliest part of it was an Iron Age settlement and it is probable that its British occupants adopted Roman ways shortly after the conquest, replacing it with a small four-roomed stone house. This in turn was replaced by a great single-storey mansion with more than fifty rooms, as well as farm buildings to store a plentiful supply of food from many outlying farms of the large estate. The main residence was grouped at one corner of a three-sided courtyard. The villa even had two separate bathing suites, both with at least half-a-dozen rooms. Many of the bathing rooms close to the main house have been identified: dressing rooms, hot plunge rooms, steam rooms and others for cold plunges. Hypocaust pillars of the underfloor heating system can be seen and also the room with the furnace.

The domestic and farming wing had rooms where the grain was stored, the corn ground by hand and some of it malted. There was also a smithy. The water-supply came from wells which have been discovered and excavated.

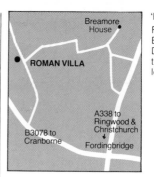

'HOW TO GET THERE'
From Fordingbridge, take B3078 (to Cranborne and Damerham). At Sandleheath turn right. Villa approx 1 mile on left.

Rockbourne and Breamore both lie on the edge of an area of superb unspoilt countryside which spans the borders of Wiltshire, Dorset and Hampshire: Cranborne Chase and the Downs, which form a broad belt from the Dorset coast up to Salisbury and the Plain. From Rockbourne numerous footpaths radiate to other picturesque villages such as Whitsbury, Breamore, Martin and Damerham. Near Martin some of the fine ancient downland has been preserved as a National Nature Reserve. The harsh life of the old shepherds of this area during the last century was brilliantly described in the masterpiece by W.H. Hudson, *A Shepherd's Life*. The principal character, Shepherd Bawcombe, was based on an old friend of his who lived at Martin.

The most attractive finds have been a series of mosaics, two of which are on display. They are covered each winter to prevent frost damage. The site has a museum of finds, the fruit of many years of digging. There is a model reconstruction of the villa, skeletons found in the different rooms, lead pipes and building materials, dedication stones and tools used by the farmers and carpenters. There are also many bronze objects and a good collection of the pottery which was made close by in the New Forest.

Close to the archaeological site stands a prominent monument raised in 1828 by the East India Company to honour their servant, Sir Eyre Coote, who returned to buy the local estate. Sir Eyre had successfully besieged Pondicherry, the corner-stone of French India on the coast of Madras State, which changed hands many times again but remained French until this century.

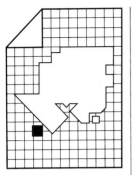

Redhouse Museum and Art Gallery, Christchurch

(Hampshire County Council)
County Museum Service,
Quay Road,
Christchurch,
Dorset.
BH23 1BO
Telephone
Christchurch (0202) 482860

Price Guide - A

Car Parking
Nearby

Handicapped
Unsuitable

Party Visits
By arrangement

Publications
Leaflet

Where to eat
Extensive gardens provide a suitable picnic area
Cafes in town nearby

Time to allow
½ - 1 hour

Open
All year Tuesday - Saturday all day and Sunday afternoons

Special projects
Archaeology galleries under construction

Public Transport
Bus services -
Frequent service from Bournemouth to Christchurch (daily). Wilts and Dorset buses every 30 minutes from Lymington and hourly from Salisbury, Monday - Saturday (every 2 hours on Sundays) B.S. Old Town Hall - 5 minutes walk).
Rail Services -
Christchurch Station
Trains from London via Southampton

Nearby Attractions
Next to Christchurch Priory.
Town Trail leaflet available at Museum
Hengistbury Head (Ferry service from Mudeford)

Top	Natural History Gallery
Below	House from the garden
Illus.	Hampshire County Museum Service

CHRISTCHURCH MUSEUM
"THE RED HOUSE"

It may seem strange to include in a book on Hampshire a museum in neighbouring Dorset, but the Red House has for ten years been in the care of Hampshire County Council, bequeathed by the Druitt family who had from Victorian times been dedicated to the creation of a museum of Christchurch. Their achievement is a very fine regional collection which records domestic life,

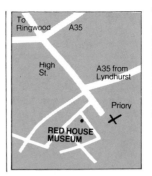

'HOW TO GET THERE'
From New Forest take A35 (Lyndhurst to Bournemouth). At the end of the by-pass turn left into Christchurch High Street, continuing down Church Street, then right into Church Lane. Quay road is on left and car-park at end, by the Priory Church.

the occupations of the poor in the workhouse. Some examples of these minute products are displayed in the museum. There are several ground-floor rooms filled with household goods for lighting and cooking, as well as tools and toys. In a large fire-place can be seen the old iron equipment for boiling and roasting in the days before ranges were available. A costume gallery covering the fashions of 1865-1915 was recently opened. Its latest model is a land-girl of the First World War.

The museum has a small aquarium with some of the freshwater fish of local waters and another room has many examples of archaeological evidence of the different prehistoric cultures of Wessex through to Roman times: flints and axes, pottery and burial remains. A new geology gallery includes a fine display of the Tertiary fossils found in the cliffs to the east of Christchurch.

There is also a fine natural history gallery which shows the great richness and variety of the area around Christchurch: the unspoilt Avon Valley, natural heathlands nearby, marshes on the coast and the superb coastal open space of Hengistbury Head enclosing the harbour which is fed by the Stour and Avon rivers. The birds, animals and vegetation of each habitat are beautifully depicted in lifelike dioramas matched with photographs and diagrams which tempt one to explore for oneself.

The grounds of the old workhouse have been turned into most attractive gardens of which the museum staff are justly proud, and there is an art gallery which shows the work of local artists as well as artists of national repute.

geology and natural history, as well as the industrial activity of the area.

The building which the family owned and turned into the museum has its own fascinating history, for it was built in the shadow of the splendid Norman priory church in 1767 as the Parish work-house by the Churchwardens and Overseers of the Poor. Christchurch was not a wealthy town, since most of its inhabitants relied on fishing and smuggling for their livelihood and late 17th century plans to make the Avon navigable, and Christchurch a port for Salisbury, came to nothing.

One specialised product of the region was very finely worked 'fusee' chain used in clock-making, a cottage industry which became one of

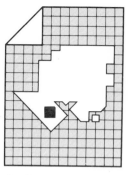

New Forest

Tourist Information Centre
(Summer only) in Lyndhurst car park.
Telephone
Lyndhurst (042 128) 2269

Forest Camping Information
and Forestry Commission
Telephone
Cadnam (938 27) 2888

Pitches have to be booked
ahead during Spring Bank Holiday.
Sites vary from equipped to informal.
Camping is restricted to the official sites.

Youth Hostels
At Burley
Telephone Burley (04253) 3233
At Norleywood, near Lymington
Telephone East End 220

Car Parking
130 car parks with picnic facilities for visitors.
Picnic fires and stoves are not permitted.

Nearby Attractions
Gardens open to the public at Minstead, Boldre and Bransgore.
Horse-drawn wagon rides at Lyndhurst, near Balmer Lawn.
Telephone Lymington (0590) 23633
There are trail publications for walks by the Ornamental Drives at Boldrewood and Rhinefield, and at Oberwater near Brockenhurst. There is a deer enclosure in Boldrewood Walk and a Reptiliary near Holidays Hill Camp-site west of Lyndhurst.
Queens House, Lyndhurst
(Forestry Commission)

Medieval Manor House extensively rebuilt. Includes the Verderers court of 1388 which has deer antlers and 'Rufus stirrup'. Traditional courts can still be witnessed.

Open by appointment
Telephone
Lyndhurst (042 128) 3141

Top, 1   Anses Wood
Below
Left, 2   Ponies at Godshill
Below
Right, 3   New thatch
           near Gorley

1. 2. 3.   Michael Goddard

THE NEW FOREST

Throughout Britain today relics of the past are disappearing under the tide of development, yet in the New Forest it is still possible to step off a modern highway straight into a landscape which has changed but little in a thousand years, an ancient Royal forest where forest laws and forest rights still determine the shape of everyday living and where the authentic spirit of medieval England can be sensed at every turn. The very look of this unique place is the result of its history.

The New Forest was created by decree of King William I and enclosed in about 1079. Today the perambulation, or legal boundary, of the Forest encircles 145 square miles and of this just over two-thirds is under the management of the Forestry Commission which inherited the Crown's rights and responsibilities in 1924. Woodland accounts for less than half of this area, the remainder consisting of open and unfenced forest waste, heath, bracken, gorse and grass.

In medieval times a forest was simply a tract of countryside designated for the conservation of beasts of the chase, chiefly deer, and as a reservoir for hides and meat. The importance of royal hunting forests to the economy of the times is shown by the severe restraints placed by the dreaded forest law on the freedom of unlucky forest dwellers. As a result of the progressive reduction in woodland which had taken place since the Bronze Age through clearances, pastoral agriculture virtually ceased in "afforested" areas. The aim was to preserve the coverts which harboured the deer and supplied their food, and the King's sport was protected by savage penalties for unlawful hunting. Perhaps most important of all, in terms of future developments, local husbandmen were not allowed to enclose their land lest fences hindered the free run of the deer. The hardship that this caused was recognised and rights were granted for domestic animals to graze for limited periods on the open forest. These are the rights of pasture registered by Act of Parliament which today allow ponies and cattle from properties holding common rights to wander freely over the unfenced parts of the New Forest. There are other Forest rights of lesser importance still surviving but only to a limited degree.

By the 15th century the use of wood, the principal raw material of the age, had so increased that supplies of timber for building and fuel were feared to be at risk. Thus began the long history of inclosure of large tracts of the Royal forests for tree planting, which swiftly grew in importance as a source of revenue as the sovereign's preoccupation with hunting diminished. These inclosures had the effect of reducing the land available for the exercise of grazing rights and led to many disputes between the Crown and the Commoners. These disputes were largely resolved by the New Forest Act of 1877 which called a halt to further inclosure of open forest waste and consolidated the timber inclosures as they exist today.

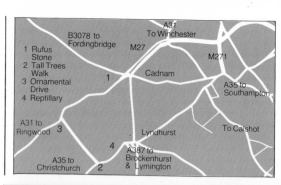

1 Rufus Stone
2 Tall Trees Walk
3 Ornamental Drive
4 Reptillary

The New Forest is, however, not a museum but a working community of foresters and farmers, shopkeepers and smallholders, commuters and country-lovers. There are many local events which the visitor will enjoy, the most notable being the New Forest Agricultural Show, held in the last week in July at New Park, and the open-air pony sales near Beaulieu Road Station in April, August, September, October and November. Model aircraft are flown at Beaulieu airfield on fine Sundays, and model power boats can be seen at Foxhills Pond near Stoney Cross. There are horse-drawn carriage drives through the Forest under the auspices of the British Driving Society, and of course this area is a paradise for riders. The New Forest attracts thousands of visitors, most of whom arrive by car, and there are

'HOW TO GET THERE'

From Winchester, A33 to Southampton links with M27 to Cadnam, then A337 to the south of the Forest or B3078 to north. From Portsmouth, M275 and M27 to junction 8 at Hedge End. Then A3024, turn left into B3033 to cross Itchen Bridge (toll). Follow signs to Docks and Western Esplanade to join A36, and A35 to Lyndhurst. For Ornamental Drives take A35 out of Lyndhurst.

It is the earnest wish of all those who live and work in and for the Forest that visitors should enjoy this national treasure to the full. In return they ask their guests to observe one or two ground rules:

Let ponies eat their natural food not yours! Feeding them draws them to the roads where they cause accidents to themselves and others. Never stand between a mother and her foal!

Leave litter in your car or pocket! Be careful with cigarettes and matches at all times; fires are not permitted.
Close all Inclosure gates.
Park only in car parks provided not on the roadside or in gateways.

numerous car parks and picnic places provided near to lakes, streams, lawns, heaths and woods. Many roads are unfenced but ditches have been dug to prevent the over-running of the open forest by vehicles. Camp sites are provided, some well equipped and others more informal, where both tents and caravans are welcome.

It is the great diversity of scenery combined with the freedom to walk at will that draws most people to this area. The open forest is as near a natural landscape as it is possible to find in southern Britain. It has indeed been shaped over the centuries by grazing and browsing animals, and one of its greatest charms is the closely cropped turf of the myriad lawns which lace the streamsides. It contains a great variety of terrain: purple heather moorland and yellow gorse thickets ask for the colour camera; self-sown Scots pines march across the wide skyline; the watercourses frequently share their route to the sea with peat bogs, often tangled with alder and willow. Its greatest glory is known as the Ancient and Ornamental Woodland; over eight thousand acres of oak, beech and holly which have been relatively undisturbed for centuries.

The Inclosures are managed woodlands from which high-quality timber is produced as it has been for centuries. Thinning, felling, planting and natural regeneration has created a diversity of scenery unequalled in these islands. Of particular interest are the substantial stands of plantation oak planted in the early 1800s for the Royal Navy but never needed after the coming of ironclads. Both the timber inclosures and the open forest teem with wild-life and are the refuges of many rare species of plants and animals which have largely disappeared elsewhere in lowland Britain.

The village of Lyndhurst is the centre and capital of the New Forest. Even before the Conquest it was a royal manor and it remains the home of the forest administration. The Forestry Commission occupies the Queen's House at the top of the High Street, a Stuart building on the site of the first manor house. Next to it is the Verderer's Hall where the New Forest Verderers sit in open court every two months on a Monday at 11am. The Verderers have always been part of the hierarchy of the Forest; today their duties are mainly administrative, controlling the health of animals, grazing and rights of common, and encouraging the conservation of the Forest as a whole. They still retain a judicial responsibility and can try offences against the New Forest Byelaws.

Really to enjoy the New Forest and to get the most out of it, the visitor needs to be armed with some information beforehand. By far the most comprehensive and useful guide is *Explore The New Forest* published by HMSO and obtainable from all local bookshops.

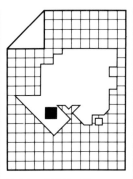

Holidays Hill Reptiliary
(Forestry Commission)
New Forest Forestry
Commission,
The Queen's House,
Lyndhurst,
Hampshire,
SO4 7NH
Telephone (042128) 3141

Price Guide - Free

Car Parking
Nearby

Handicapped
Suitable, though cell walls are
three feet high

Party Visits
By arrangement only

Publications
Leaflet

Where to eat
A wide choice of places in
Lyndhurst

Time to allow
½ - 1 hour

Open
Daily, 8am - 8pm

Public Transport
Bus Service - Every 2 hours
from Southampton and
Bournemouth
Monday - Sunday and
Summer Sundays. (B.S. Bank
Turning)

The Rufus Stone
(Forestry Commssion)

Price Guide - Free

Car Parking
Nearby

Handicapped
Suitable

Time to allow
15 minutes

Open
At all times

Public Transport
Bus Service - Every 2 hours
from Southampton and
Bournemouth daily.
Additional buses from
Lyndhurst on Monday -
Saturday. (B.S. Castle
Malwood).

Nearby Attractions
Breamore House
New Forest
New Forest Butterfly Farm
Longdown Dairy Farm
Rhinefield Ornamental Drive
National Motor Museum
Buckler's Hard

1. The reptiles are contained
within several low-walled cells

2. Adder

3. The Rufus Stone

1,2,3. Tony Nutley

HOLIDAYS HILL REPTILIARY
& THE RUFUS STONE

The New Forest is a unique reservoir of wildlife which is particularly well known for its reptiles. Snakes and their ways are part of the forest folklore typified by local characters such as 'Brusher' Mills, who gained an astonishing reputation in the last century for his skills at handling adders.

With the exception of the wall lizard, which is an introduced species, the New Forest contains every species of British reptile. All of these can be seen in complete safety at the Holidays Hill reptiliary. There are adders, grass snakes, slow worms, the three species of newt, the common toad and frog, and two rarities - the sand lizard and smooth snake, the latter first identified as late as 1859.

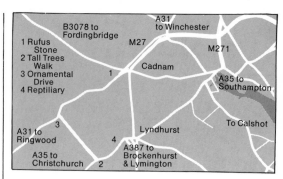

The animals are contained in low-walled open cells where they live and breed in micro-habitats created to give the special conditions they require. The smooth snake, for example, is a creature of sunny heathland in the vicinity of damp ground where plenty of lizards and small mammals are found. These it consumes after killing by suffocation, occasionally using coils like a boa constrictor.

The smooth snake is now only found in small numbers in a few places in Hampshire, Dorset and Surrey. The sand lizard is even less common and is on the point of extinction in the New Forest. To keep up the population, these creatures have been bred at the reptiliary and returned to the wild.

Situated amongst the beautiful trees of the forest, the reptiles are most likely to be seen at the reptiliary on a sunny day. Then you may see specimens of the 'all-black' melanistic adder sliding through vegetation, or catch sight of a grass snake climbing one of the small trees in its cell.

THE RUFUS STONE

The New Forest owes its very existence to hunting, and even today three hunts are permitted. The Rufus stone is a reminder of the days when Norman kings and their noblemen spent long days in the saddle in pursuit of deer, and occasionally wolf and wild boar.

The event marked by this monument, the killing of King William II ('Rufus') in August 1100, is one of the most mysterious in the history of England. It is known that William Rufus was pierced through the heart by an arrow and that his body was subsequently carried on a cart to Winchester – where his tomb can still be seen, in the cathedral. His brother Henry, though not the rightful heir, is known to have ridden to Winchester to claim the keys of the king's treasury, and then to have continued to London, where he was crowned three days after his brother's death.

But whether Rufus was murdered or killed in a hunting accident, as two of his kinsmen had been, will probably never be known.

Even the location of the 'stone', dating from 1745 and replaced in the last century by the present metal casting, is in doubt. One compelling theory suggests that Rufus was in fact killed a few miles from Beaulieu, where the earliest known hunting lodge was built. Certainly the oldest written account of the site of the king's death, by the topographer Leyland, refers to 'Thorougham', which is the original name of Park Farm, near Beaulieu.

A pub close to the Rufus Stone has taken its name from the man who is said to have fired the fatal arrow, Sir Walter Tyrrell, who later fled to France.

BS

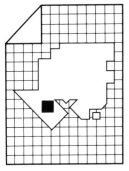

Rhinefield Ornamental Drive
(Forestry Commission)

New Forest Forestry
Commission
The Queen's House,
Lyndhurst,
Hampshire,
SO4 7NH
Telephone (042128) 3141

Price Guide - Free

Car Parking
In two locations on the Tall
Trees Walk

Handicapped
Suitable for short sections
near the car parks

Publications
Leaflet

Where to eat
Picnic sites at both car parks.
Rhinefield Lodge Hotel, a
short distance along the road
to Brockenhurst. A wide
choice of places in Lyndhurst
and Brockenhurst.

Time to allow
1-2 hours for the longest walks

Open
At all times

Public Transport
Bus Service - Every 2 hours
from Southampton and
Bournemouth. Monday -
Saturday and Summer
Sundays. (B.S. Knightwood
Oak)

Nearby Attractions
New Forest Butterfly Farm
Longdown Dairy Farm
Holidays Hill Reptiliary
The Rufus Stone
National Motor Museum
Buckler's Hard

Car Park amongst the Tall
Trees.

*Hampshire Recreation
Department*

RHINEFIELD ORNAMENTAL DRIVE
& THE TALL TREES WALK

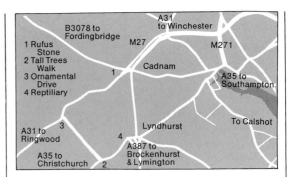

1 Rufus Stone
2 Tall Trees Walk
3 Ornamental Drive
4 Reptiliary

The decision of a forest nurseryman in the middle of the last century to make an avenue has given us one of the finest stands of tall trees anywhere in the country. They were planted along what was then a track wich led to a predecessor of today's Rhinefield Lodge, traditionally the home of the Keepers of the Forest. Several of the specimens at Rhinefield are the tallest of their kind in Great Britain, notably a Redwood which is at least 42 metres (137 feet) high and more than 14 feet in girth.

These fine trees towering above the forest floor now form a setting for the Tall Trees Walk,

a trail of about a mile and a half which has been laid out with explanatory plaques by the Forestry Commission. The path, which has been well gravelled, runs in a narrow loop up one side of the avenue, across the former track, now metalled, and down the other side.

Forty-eight trees standing alongside the road have been numbered and can be identified by reference to a locally available Forestry Commission leaflet. The most frequent species at Rhinefield is the Douglas Fir, a tree which reaches a height of 300 feet in its native North America and has topped 150 feet in the forest.

There are also specimens of the Indian Cedar or Deodar, a larch-like Himalayan species that traditionally was used in the building of temples and palaces in its native land. But perhaps the most amazing tree along the Tall Trees Walk is the Wellingtonia, a pyramid-shaped tree that in California lives to an age of 3000 years!

The Redwood, another tree from the west coast of America, is easily recognised from its distinctive red bark, which in the New Forest provides nesting sites for goldcrests.

In one part of the walk, close to the Black Water car park, can be seen a re-creation of a section of the inclosure boundary which was made in 1700, following a special Act of Parliament to fence off the Vinney Ridge Inclosure for the

planting of young oak and beech. Its five-foot ditch and six-foot bank, topped by an oak pale, formed a formidable barrier to protect the trees by keeping out deer, cattle and ponies.

Some of the work of the normal forest is apparent along the trail, including a plot of 'forest grown' sessile oaks which have been regularly measured for growth since their planting in 1859. These trees have been set in a group close together to force long straight trunks.

At one point along the Tall Trees Walk is a bomb crater, a reminder that during the Second World War German incendiaries rained down on the forest in an attempt to destroy its valuable product: during this period more than 12 million cubic feet of timber went towards the war effort.

Shorter trails run from each of the two car parks situated at opposite ends of the main walk. At the northern end is the Brock Hill Walk, which is only a quarter of a mile long and runs through woodlands of oak and beech. To the south is the Black Water Walk, a three-quarter mile path through woodland by the side of an aptly named stream.

Half-a-mile further on is Rhineland Lodge Hotel, built as a grand country home in the 1880s with the aid of a gift of £250,000 given to a daughter of the family which owned Eastwood Colliery in Nottinghamshire, portrayed in the novels of D.H. Lawrence. She married a naval lieutenant and Walker-Munros, as the family became, lived at Rhinefield until the 1950s. Their lives were filled with controversy: without foundation they assumed the 'Lordship of the Manor of Rhinefield' and became so estranged from the community that both the lieutenant and his wife were buried in a remote copse.

The house has been restored and refurbished as a luxury hotel and restaurant. BS

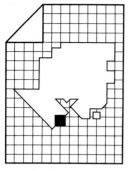

Hurst Castle
(English Heritage)

Keyhaven,
Milford-on-Sea,
Hampshire,
Telephone Milford-on-Sea
(059-069) 2344

Price Guide - B

Car Parking
Free

Handicapped
Unsuitable

Party Visits
No arrangement needed

Publications etc.
Guidebook

Where to eat
Cafe/tea-room (Summer only)

Time to allow
1 - 2 hours

Open
All year (except 24 - 26 Dec,
1 January and first Monday in
May).
Open every day
October-March, 9.30am - 4pm
weekdays, 2-4pm, Sundays.
March-October, 9.30am-
6.30pm, weekdays, 2-6.30pm,
Sundays

Public Transport
Bus Service –
Wilts and Dorset buses run
every hour from Bournemouth
and Lymington to Milford-on-
Sea Monday-Saturday, (every
2 hours on Sundays).
(B.S. Milford-on-Sea) 3 miles
walk
Rail Service –
Stations at Lymington and
New Milton

Nearby Attractions
Beaulieu
Buckler's Hard

Hurst Ferry Mid-May to
October 10-6, also Summer
evening cruises to Yarmouth
from Keyhaven, and Needles
cruises. Telephone New
Milton (0425) 610784 or
Milford-on-Sea (059 069)
2500.
Lymington-Yarmouth ferry,
telephone Lymington (0590)
73050. Local summer cruises
from Lymington, telephone
(0590) 74899

The Solent Way
A detailed guidebook with
relevant sections of the
Ordnance Survey is available.
See also p.24

HURST CASTLE
& THE SALTERNS COAST

Tides drifting from the west have gradually shifted huge quantities of shingle up the English Channel into the mouth of the Solent, building up the banks of Hurst Beach two miles out towards the Isle of Wight, leaving a gap of less than three-quarters of a mile. The result, Hurst Spit, is dominated by a large castle and two lighthouses. At the side of the taller free-standing lighthouse the building is still preserved in which the keepers used to produce their acetylene gas by mixing carbide and water. There are also old coastguard houses, and at one time there were fishermen's cottages and even a pub, doubtless once crowded with members of the local garrison who guarded the castle until as late as the last war.

The earliest part of Hurst Castle dates from the 1540s, for it was one of a large number constructed all round the English and Welsh coasts when the threat of invasion by France was very real. With the work at Hurst, together with new castles at Southsea, Yarmouth, Calshot and Cowes, the Solent was to be made secure against attack. Their effectiveness was soon put to the test when the Isle of Wight was invaded and part of the French fleet, poised opposite Portsmouth, is said to have attacked Lymington and left it in ruins in 1544.

A century later, Charles I was held prisoner here for a short time before his trial and execution. The small Tudor tower and bastions in which he was kept have since been incorporated into a Victorian fortification of the 1870s and an earlier pair of lighthouses had to be replaced as a consequence. From the castle roof-top, or from the beach below, there is an outstanding view across to Fort Victoria Country Park, Colwell and Totland Bays, Headon Warren and the National Trust's cliffs overlooking the Needles. Here, out of the wind under the castle walls, is surely one of the best vantage points for watching the nearby passing ships and boats. The waters can be decidedly dangerous, for the changing tides create almost the effect of a whirlpool near to the Spit.

Getting to Hurst Castle involves either a long wearing tramp on the shingle from the car park at the Milford end, or a ferry trip from Keyhaven (which is only possible in the summer months). In summer there are also occasional trips on the Keyhaven ferry across to the Isle of Wight. The tiny village of Keyhaven is perhaps the only Hampshire village which has survived on the coast; fortunately it has not been overwhelmed by marinas. The Avon Water, fed from the New Forest bogs near Burley, has been filling the Solent behind the Spit for some 10,000 years, while from mediaeval times local men have built up seawalls to reclaim the saltings which are left exposed when each high tide retreats.

The coastal footpath along the seawall from Keyhaven to Lymington is a section of the Solent Way, a long-distance path for anyone wishing to explore the shores of Hampshire. However, as a means of walking between Lymington and Keyhaven the path is not ideal, for the seawall twists and turns in a way that makes sense only when the Salterns' origins are remembered. At different times the walls have

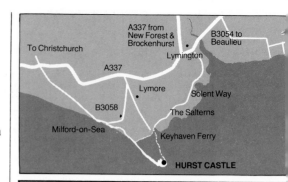

'HOW TO GET THERE'

To Hurst Caste from Lymington take A337 (New Milton Road) and turn left at Everton, B3058 sign-posted to Milford-on-Sea. Soon on left take small lane through Lymore to Hurst and Keyhaven.

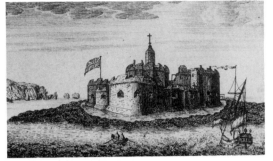

Top   Engraving of Castle
Above   Hurst Castle Ferry
Bottom   The Lymington
left   Saltern marshes
Bottom   Boat moored in
right   creek amongst
         marshes
Right   Salt pans, drawn by
         Rowlandson in
         1780

Engraving: Hampshire County
          Records Office
Salt Pans: Henry E.
          Huntingdon Library
          and Art Gallery

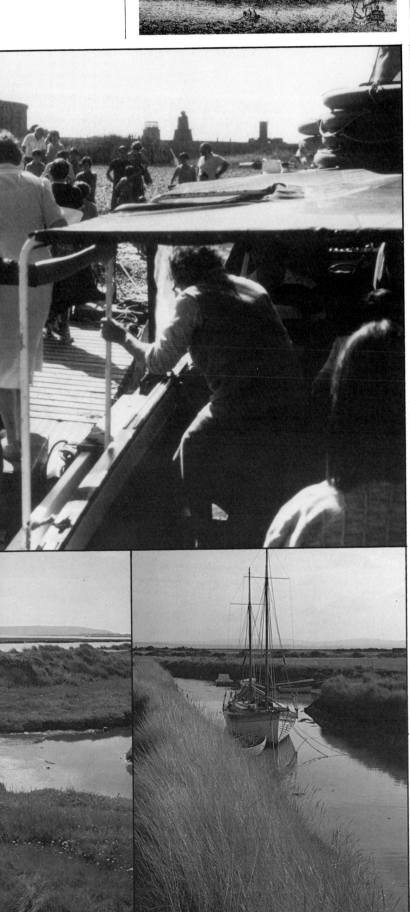

been pushed out and joined up to create what was once one of the country's great industrial centres – the Lymington Salterns. These consisted of shallow ponds supplied with sea-water through systems of dykes, with windmills to pump the brine to the many boiling houses or 'pans'. The inlets and waterways across the marshes were once busy with the comings and goings of the coastal sailing ships bringing in coal and collecting the salt. The business died in the 1840s through competition from salt mines in Cheshire when land transport became easier. Almost certainly it survived so long because of its proximity to the great market for salt, the Portsmouth Dockyards, where vast numbers of barrels of salted meat and food were prepared for shipment to the fleets all over the world.

It is a good idea when exploring these marshes to follow the example of other walkers who will be found carrying binoculars, for the salt marshes and shingle beaches are especially important as a breeding site for the very attractive terns which in the summer months arrive from as far away as Southern Africa or even the Antarctic. The mudflats, exposed at low tide, are hunted by many different species of waders feeding on enormous populations of shell-fish and worms. Around the platforms created by the grass-like *Spartina* can be seen the Brent Geese in winter grazing eelgrass and green seaweeds. One of the most celebrated ornithologists who wrote about this coast was the wildfowler, Colonel Peter Hawker, whose life in the mid-19th century was dedicated to shooting game and any rare birds he saw on the marshes. Fortunately, the detailed diaries he kept make a classic record of the local bird life a century and a half ago.

Parking is available at the Lymington end of the path, near the Royal Lymington Yacht Club and town swimming pool, or at Keyhaven Village. The path follows a very contorted course, and as a footway is rather uneven.

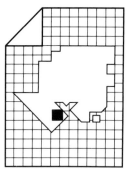

Buckler's Hard
(Lord Montagu of Beaulieu)

Buckler's Hard,
Beaulieu,
Hampshire.
Telephone
Buckler's Hard (059063) 203

Price Guide – C.
Admission charge covers car
parking and entrance to
Maritime Museum and restored
cottage interiors

Car Parking
Nearby

Handicapped
Ground floor only of Maritime
Museum
Village pathways are gravel

Party Visits
By arrangement
Educational resources
Visits with guides
Tours available

Publications
Leaflet and guidebooks
Trail

Where to eat
Cafe
Licensed restaurant/bar on site
Picnic site

Time to allow
2 hours

Open
Easter – September 10am -
6pm
September – Easter 10am -
5pm (except Christmas Day)

Public Transport
Bus Services –
Southampton – Buckler's Hard
(in summer only)   111
Hythe – Beaulieu (40 minutes
walk away)   112
Rail Services –
Nearest station, Beaulieu Road

Nearby Attractions
Beaulieu
New Forest
Butterfly Farm

BUCKLERS HARD

The hamlet of Buckler's Hard is a unique and surprising place. Its setting is without parallel in Hampshire and, although it attracts two hundred thousand visitors each year, it remains unspoilt. Local estates have resisted the pressures and the temptation to allow heavy marina development and most of the small number of boats on the river are on swinging moorings, changing direction with each tide. Today the Agamemnon Boatyard is the only slight intrusion on the otherwise perfect rural scene.

Car parks for the village are out of sight but close at hand, together with a tearoom and maritime museum. The first impression of the street is surprising; less than two dozen cottages, each with a uniform brick front, face each other across a simple wide green. This, in the 1720s, was to be the start of 'Montagu Town', a port to rival Southampton and Lymington, which was to be based at first on refining sugar-cane from a West Indian colony. Perhaps fortunately, the scheme failed, for an expedition to take over the island of St. Lucia on behalf of the ambitious Montagu, the second Duke, was defeated by French troops.

Twenty long years of inactivity followed until the building of the *Mermaid* in 1745, a 24-gun ship for the Admiralty. From the very start one family named Adams was intimately involved and remained so for a complete century. They lived in the Master Builder's house, close enough to the five local slipways for careless workmen to be called to the window for reproof. The founder, Henry Adams, lived to be 91 and built 43 ships, providing more men-of-war for the Admiralty than any other private shipbuilder in the country.

Building for Navy contracts was a hazardous business, for delays were penalised and inflation could reduce profits. Smaller vessels were usually built at the same time as larger boats, to make use of offcuts of wood and to raise capital as work proceeded. The village Maritime Museum and the guidebook explain more of the fascinating story of how the New Forest timber was sawn and built into the 'wooden walls'. A spectacular model shows the launching of H.M.S. *Euryalus* in 1803, a ship which fought at Trafalgar and at Buckler's Hard they also built the *Agamemnon*, which was Nelson's favourite ship and his first command. It was during this time that Nelson met Lady Hamilton at Naples. *Swiftsure*, built here and *Agamemnon* also were at Trafalgar.

The village Maritime Musuem contains a number of Nelson items, and another feature of the museum is a large collection of meticulous models of the ships constructed on the local slips around Buckler's Hard. There are also displays on the epic travels of yachtsman Sir Francis Chichester, who used the Beaulieu River as a base when he became the first man to sail round the globe single-handed. The charts he used on the 160-day voyage can be seen, showing daily records of his position and the 'completion of the circle' at a point in the South Atlantic near the Tropic

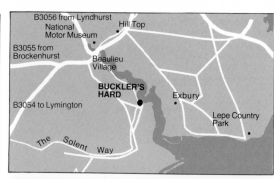

'HOW TO GET THERE'
From Lyndhurst, B3056 through
Forest down to Beaulieu.
Continue on by-pass, not
through village, and then turn
left. Village sign-posted.

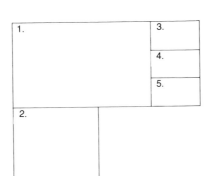

1. Model of the village 1803 *1,3,4, 5: National Motor Museum*
   with the 'Euryalus' and
   the *'Swiftsure'* on the
   slipways
2. Buckler's Hard village
   from the quayside
3. The New Inn, part of the
   life-size display in the
   Maritime Museum
4. The inn-keeper and his
   customers
5. Cottage interior

of Capricorn. Beyond the museum has been constructed the two-and-a-half century old 'New' Inn and labourers' cottages, brilliantly re-creating the daily life and interiors of the village in the 1790s. In the Inn villagers play cards and visitors warm themselves by the fire, including one of the Salt Officers who checked on the tax returns of the saltern workers. Of the two contrasting cottages one, which is threadbare, belongs to James Bound, a simple labourer, and the other, much more comfortable, to Thomas Burlace, a skilled shipwright with a reliable income, during war-time at least. At the bottom of the street, part of the Master Builder's house has also been re-created to show Adams discussing his building plans, and visitors can look into the room through the window.

The Montagu Estate hope one day to be able to reconstruct the shipbuilding activity and to carry out archaeological investigation of the site, for evidence of the old industry can still be seen in the quays and sloping ground between the river and village, much of which has not been disturbed in this century. The last time any boats were built was more than forty years ago, when motor torpedo-boats were constructed. As part of a major conservation programme many of the cottages

have been renovated. Opposite the museum is a tiny one-room shop and there is even a minute wood-panelled chapel further down the street. The Master Builder's house is now a successful restaurant and hotel, with public bars and, in summer, buffet lunches. Clients can use the hotel car park.

In summer, the village has its own river bus, *Swiftsure*, which gives visitors the opportunity to enjoy a half-hour trip on the water. There are also cruises from Southampton and Portsmouth to the village. Another way to explore the river is along the riverside walk between Beaulieu and Buckler's Hard. This goes past Bailey's Hard, where there was once shipbuilding, and a brick-works whose products were shipped to ports around the coast. The path begins in Beaulieu near the Fire Station behind the Montagu Arms.

One strange fact about the Beaulieu River, dating back to the Abbey's foundation, is that its ownership is private and not, as is usual, Crown property.

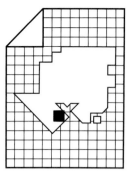

Beaulieu - National Motor Museum, Palace House and Gardens
(Lord Montagu of Beaulieu)

John Montagu Building,
Beaulieu,
Brockenhurst,
Hampshire,
SO4 7ZN
Telephone
Beaulieu (0590) 612345

Price Guide - F

Car Parking
Free

Handicapped
Fully equipped

Party Visits
By arrangement
Educational resources for
schools and tours

Publications etc.
Leaflet and guidebook
Displays and audio visual
shows

Where to eat
Cafe
Licensed Restaurant
Suitable picnic area nearby
including picnic tables on site

Time to allow
4 hours

Open
Every day (except Christmas
Day). Open at 10am, closed
at 5-7pm, depending on the
season

Public Transport
Bus Service -
Wilts & Dorset buses every
2 hours from Lymington.
Through bus from
Bournemouth and Poole,
Monday - Saturday. Special
services from Bournemouth,
Lymington and Southampton
on summer Sundays.

Nearby Attractions
Buckler's Hard Village and
  Maritime Museum
New Forest Butterfly Farm
Lepe Country Park
Exbury Gardens

BEAULIEU
& THE NATIONAL MOTOR MUSEUM

Anyone planning a visit to Beaulieu should try to allow the best part of a whole day to enjoy the National Motor Museum, Palace House and the Abbey ruins, as well as the attractive gardens and many amusements for children. Each year there are also numerous special events. The whole site of Beaulieu has been carefully planned to lead away from the woodland car park along gravel paths to the Information Centre, and from this a gently sloping path runs down to Palace House and the nearby abbey ruins.

Lord Montagu of Beaulieu has gathered together the country's best collection of cars and vehicles to form the National Motor Museum. Even visitors with little interest in motoring will discover that the museum is an outstanding one which is both colourful and educational. The collection began in the early fifties with just two or three veteran cars in the rooms of Palace House. Today there are old buses, commercial vehicles, record-breakers and the vintage Rolls of the wealthy, as well as many of the more typical cars in which our parents or grandparents first took to the road in the decades since the first world war. There are also displays of veteran motor-cycles and even special exhibits by manufacturers about the history and present-day technology of the varied components, materials and fuels needed to keep our modern society on the move. A recent addition is 'Wheels', an exhibition of the social history of motoring seen from a specially designed 'pod' which twists and turns as it conveys visitors past a succession of dioramas. At one point a blast of cold air emphasises the rigours of early motoring! All these exhibits are displayed in a vast building of impressive modern architecture, with galleries looking over the exhibits and even into the workshops. A monorail passes through the building at roof-level starting near the Information Centre and skirting Palace House, which is beautifully situated. Across its lawns, which are a thick carpet of daffodils in spring, is the picturesque reed-fringed mill-pond filled by rising tides as well as by the Beaulieu River.

The "Palace" is an unusual house which incorporates the abbey's substantial gate house, scene of stormy encounters as well as of generous alms-giving: it stood well away from the main cloisters. Although later converted into a house which was visited on occasions by James I none of its owners lived there until the 19th century. The present rambling grey-stone chateau-like building was planned in the 1870s, in such a way as to retain the old gateways and their simple fanned vaulting. The rooms on view include drawing rooms and dining halls; perhaps the most interesting among the works of art are the portraits of members of the complicated family link between the Wriothesleys, who took over the abbey, and the present owner, the Third Baron Montagu of Beaulieu. There is also in the house a collection of stuffed birds that have been shot on the estate since the 1870s.

A short walk from the house to the east are the cloisters and other remains of the abbey, established by King John and dissolved during the reign of King Henry VIII,three centuries later. The abbey with its monks and lay brothers, and its

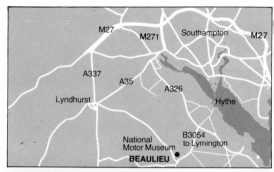

often extravagant abbots, has a fascinating and even dramatic history. It was the Cistercians who gave the site its fitting name "Beautiful place". Despite their order of silence, simplicity and withdrawal from the world, and especially independence of government, the abbots often served the Crown and in turn depended on royal grants. Little remains of their great church except the cloister, the door and two buildings. In one the monks slept in a large dormitory (used now for banquets), while downstairs was the hall in which ate the lay brothers who worked at the abbey and its scattered granges. This room now contains an excellent museum about monastic life and the historic past of Beaulieu, including fine models.

'HOW TO GET THERE'
From M27 Cadnam roundabout
take A337 down to Lyndhurst. In
town follow one-way system
onto A35 in Southampton
direction, then turn right onto
B3056. Entrance to Museum on
left short distance before
Beaulieu village.

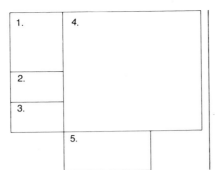

1. 'Wheels' display
2. Bluebird - part of the display of World Speed Record breakers
3. Auburn Supercharger, 1935
4. Palace House with part of the original Abbey gatehouse
5. Looking across the Cloisters to the Domus, once the brothers' apartments

2,3: Alan Cassedy
1,4,5: National Motor Museum

Visitors can also enter the parish church which was adapted after the Dissolution from the hall in which the monks silently ate their simple food while one of them read from the scriptures. Steps in the wall up to the pulpit are still there to be seen. Only traces remain of the many other buildings, where the food was cooked, the estates administered, the infirm cared for and the library kept, though a great deal of the abbey's history is known. One surprising feature of Beaulieu was its right of sanctuary, which meant that criminals on the run could be harboured within the walls of the Great Close which enclosed the buildings and nearby fields. Some were even joined by their families to start a new life safe from the authorities.

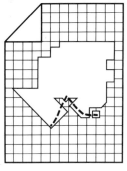

The Solent Way
Price Guide - Free

Car Parking
Milford-on-Sea -
Seafront (parking tickets)
Limited free parking by Sturt
Pond Bridge

Emsworth -
Car park in South Street

There are numerous car parks
at other places along the route,
including: Beaulieu, Hythe,
Southampton, Netley,
Hamble Common, Warsash,
Hillhead, Lee-on-Solent,
Gosport, Portsmouth,
Southsea, Farlington
Marshes (by sea wall), and by
Langstone Bridge.

Publications etc.
Leaflet
Guidebook
Video on show at Heritage
Centre, Royal Victoria Country
Park

Public Transport
Milford-on-Sea:
Bus services -
Bournemouth -
Lymington 123, 124

Rail service -
New Milton Station,
4 miles away

Emsworth:
Bus service -
Portsmouth-Emsworth 16

Rail service -
Emsworth Station

Attractions En Route
Hurst Castle
Buckler's Hard
Beaulieu: Abbey and National
　　Motor Museum
Historic Southampton
　　Tudor House Museum
　　Maritime Museum
　　Gods House Tower
　　Southampton Hall of
　　　Aviation
Southampton Art Gallery
Netley Abbey
Royal Victoria Country Park
Titchfield Haven Nature
　　Reserve
Naval Ordnance Museum
Royal Navy Submarine
　　Museum
Portsmouth and Southsea
　　H.M.S. *Victory*
　　Mary Rose - Museum
　　　and Ship Hall
　　Warrior 1987
　　Royal Naval Museum
　　Spitbank Fort
　　Old Portsmouth
　　D-Day Museum
　　Royal Marines Museum
　　Eastney Pumping Station
Farlington Marshes

The Solent Way
beside the Beaulieu
River

*Photo: County Recreation
Department*

THE SOLENT WAY

'One of the pleasantest things in the world is going a journey.' - William Hazlitt

The Solent Way is a 60-mile journey that passes along one of the richest and most varied coastlines in the country. Starting at Milford-on-Sea to the west of Lymington, it uses three ferry crossings in threading its way to the former fishing village of Emsworth on the Sussex border.

The first part of the walk runs along the mile-and-a-half length of Hurst Castle Spit and then takes to the wilds of the former salterns at Pennington and Woodside. Skirting the southern limits of the New Forest, the path passes through woodland and farmland on its way to Buckler's Hard, where part of Nelson's fleet was built, and then continues to Beaulieu Abbey. The activities of the Cistercian monks who worked these lands until the Dissolution more than 400 years ago have left many traces in addition to the ruins themselves, including a huge fish-pond at Sowley and the towering ruins of a grange barn at St. Leonards.

Beyond Beaulieu, the Solent Way crosses bleak heathland on its way to Hythe, once a maintenance centre for BOAC flying boats, where

the first ferry crossing takes it into the heart of Southampton's dockland. Hereafter, the path hugs the shoreline all the way to Emsworth, via ferries at Hamble (a one-man operation) and Gosport.

Although the route passes through several built-up areas, there are lengthy stretches where it is surprisingly remote. A long quiet stretch atop the low cliffs that stretch beyond the Hamble River at Hook and Brownwich gives way to a populous, mile-long promenade at Lee-on-Solent, which is followed by the desolate shingle of Browndown.

After crossing the narrow mouth of Portsmouth Harbour, close by *HMS Victory* and the *Mary*

Follow the Country Code

Enjoy the countryside

and respect its life and work.

Rose, the path passes the fortifications and sally-port of the old town and runs along the entire length of the seafront at Southsea. It then follows the edge of Langstone Harbour, a huge expanse of mudflats and shallow water, fishing boats and sea birds. At the top of the harbour is a nature reserve, Farlington Marshes, where a wide variety of wildfowl and waders can be seen, particularly during the winter. At this time of the year, vast numbers of birds fly down from the north: for example, it is estimated that three per cent of the entire world's population of dark-bellied geese winter in this one area.

One of the attractions of the Solent Way is that it is dotted with museums and other attractions that enable the walker to break his journey, if he wishes. Many of these places are described in detail elsewhere in this book; Beaulieu, Southampton, Gosport, Portsmouth and Southsea - they all provide opportunities to add to the pleasures of walking by learning about the heritage of Hampshire's coast. The Solent Way may be walked in six easy, day-long legs, allowing plenty of opportunity for sightseeing. But a fit walker could easily cover the ground in three days, while the stroller can take up the route at one of the many points which can be reached by car.

Ideally, the Solent Way is best not rushed: time should be allowed to watch the comings and goings of boats, to explore the marine life - and perhaps even linger for a spot of fishing!　BS

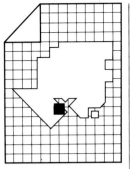

EXBURY GARDENS

Each spring one of England's really outstanding gardens is open to the public on the eastern boundary of the New Forest at Exbury. Here in the 1920s and 1930s Lionel de Rothschild established within natural woodland a collection of rhododendrons which is now probably the greatest in the world.

For many years after the first world war hundreds of men dug the ground, laid pipes for the supply of well water, and planted acre after acre of rhododendrons, azaleas, magnolias and camellias. Fortunately, the earlier owners of Exbury had left a legacy of great cedars, Wellingtonias, a few beech, and mature woods of oak and pine. Lionel de Rothschild's further plantings made more than a wonderful arboretum, for this is no simple display of individual trees but a grand stage for one man's outstanding contribution

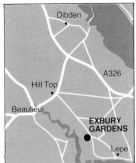

'HOW TO GET THERE'
From Southampton, A326 to Dibden Purlieu then B3054, sign-posted to Beaulieu. Turn left by Royal Oak Public House at Hilltop down road sign-posted to Exbury. Gardens 3 miles.

fascinate gardeners and naturalists alike. However, a visit is just as likely to be enjoyed by non-gardeners, simply for the natural atmosphere, and the magnificent scale of planting.

Among the fine walks possible is one which winds through the woods from the house, round a trio of ponds, to the Winter Garden. Many of the paths which interlace the broad banks of rhododendron offer attractive views across the Beaulieu River.

Exbury Gardens
(Edmund de Rothschild)

Exbury,
Near Southampton,
Hants.
SO4 1AZ
Telephone
Fawley (0703) 891203

Price Guide - E

Car Parking
Free

Handicapped
Suitable

Party Visits
No booking needed
Tours available

Publications
Leaflet
Brochure

Where to eat
Cafe - on site
Picnic tables on site

Time to allow
2-3 hours

Open
8th March - mid-July, daily
10am - 5.30pm.
Plant Centre, March -
November.

Public Transport
Bus services - Every 30 minutes from Southampton to Blackfield Monday - Saturday (every hour on Sunday) then a 2.5 mile walk.
Wilts & Dorset buses run approx. every 2 hours from Lymington to Hill Top Monday - Saturday then a 2.5 mile walk.
Hampshire Bus run special buses on Spring Sundays from Winchester and Romsey to Exbury.

Nearby Attractions
Lepe Country Park

to the world of beauty and colour. To many hundreds of natural species of rhododendron he added a further four hundred and fifty hybrids created at Exbury.

There are many other beautiful flowering shrubs and outstanding trees which will

There is a small plant centre offering trees and shrubs from the extensive nurseries of the estate. The Gardens are open between March and mid-July, but the peak of flowering occurs throughout May.

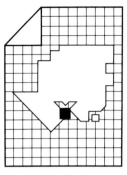

LEPE AND CALSHOT COUNTRY PARK

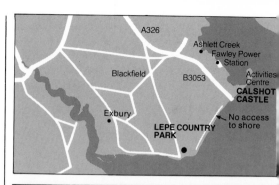

Lepe Country Park
(Cadland Estate and
Hampshire County Council,
Recreation Department)

Exbury,
Hampshire
SO4 1WD
Telephone
(Office) Winchester
(0962) 64221
(Ranger) Fawley
(0703) 899108

Price Guide - Free

Car Parking
Nearby
Charge from Easter to end
September
Out of season, free

Handicapped
Suitable

Where to eat
Cafe and Licensed
Restaurant on site.
Picnic and barbecue site
bookable on request.

Time to allow
1 - 2 hours

Open
All year

Public Transport
Bus services - Every 2 hours
from Southampton to Lepe
Beach on Sundays (on
Monday - Saturday buses run
to Langley, then a 2 mile
walk).
Buses run every hour from
Southampton to Calshot
Beach on Monday - Saturday
(every 2 hours on Sundays)

Calshot Castle
(English Heritage)
Telephone enquiries:
(0892) 48166

Price Guide - B

Car Parking
Nearby

Handicapped
Not suitable

Party visits
Welcome

Where to eat
Cafe
Kiosks on beach

Time to allow
1 hour

Open
March - October,
9.30am-6.30pm, weekdays,
2pm-6.30pm, Sundays

Nearby Attractions
Beaulieu
Longdown Dairy Farm
New Forest Butterfly Farm
Bucklers Hard
Exbury Gardens
New Forest

Lepe Country Park is ideally situated for gazing at those on the water, whether they have the advantage of size and power, or little more than a wind surf-board and the art and skill to exploit wind and tide. This is due to the closeness to shore of the channel to which yachts must keep to get in and out of the Beaulieu River; for almost a mile and a half they must cling to the shore. Anyone wishing to see yachtsmen facing a real challenge should be here when the tide is rushing out and the wind is blowing from the west; ideal conditions to get out into the Solent, but very difficult for anyone needing to get back to their mooring upstream!

Here can be found one of the few sandy beaches of Hampshire, although low tide reveals a muddy foreshore, and it is all the more pleasant for having neither sea wall nor beach huts. There are three car parks, one on the shore and two behind, but the Country Park is also accessible by bus for a service runs here from Southampton during the summer.

Coastguard cottages at Lepe and at Needs Ore (across the Beaulieu River), as well as at Lymington and Hurst, are solid evidence that both smuggling and its control were important activities in the 18th and 19th Centuries. Cadland, behind Lepe, was notorious, one part even being called "Lazytown" because the inhabitants were seldom ever seen out of bed in daytime. At one time there was a village at Lepe, which has disappeared, and until the 18th Century a regular ferry service to Cowes. From mediaeval times this was the meeting place for the militia when warning beacons were fired on the Isle of Wight and inland. From here soldiers were carried over the water to stengthen the island defences against invasion. Ships were once built on Lepe beach, including a 50-gun vessel, the *Greenwich*, launched in 1784, and 15 years later at the time of the Seven Years War a '64', the *Europe*. The finished hulls were towed by men in rowing-boats to Portsmouth Dockyard, where they were fitted with masts and other equipment and provisioned.

On the beach, beneath the attractive cliffs fringed with pine trees, is a convenient cafe, and the whole park is ideal for picnicking on a summer day. Along the beach is a relic of the war-time dock where parts of Mulberry Harbour were constructed out of concrete caissons (hollow blocks), which were floated across the Channel after D-Day to form part of a ready-made invasion harbour on the Normandy beaches. The site is at

the far end of the Lepe beach, which has a shore-line about three-quarters of a mile long. An alternative walk for visitors, which is only practicable at low water, is a path to the west in the direction of Inchmery.

The Country Park continues with a further half-mile of beach at Calshot where the shore has a different character. It can only be reached from Lepe by road, since the shore between is an NCC Grade 1 site with no public access. Here a long line of huts stretches from below the wooded cliff eastwards, along part of the Spit which has been heavily developed in this century. From the beach at Calshot and the paths behind the Spit one has a fine view across one of the most crowded sailing waters in the world. There are few places in Hampshire with such a fascinating past or which offer so much to see and to do. The beach is

'HOW TO GET THERE'

From Southampton take the A35 to Eling, then the A326 to Holbury and turn right to Lepe through Blackfield. For Calshot continue on A326 past Fawley. From Beaulieu take B3054 to Hilltop turn right and follow the road through Exbury.

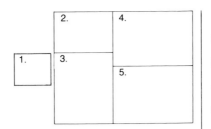

1. Preparing for the Schneider Trophy Race
2. Shore between Lepe & Exbury
3. Learning board sailing at Calshot
4. Lepe Country Park during Cowes Week
5. Seaplanes return to Calshot Castle at a Schneider Trophy reunion

1: Southampton City Council
3: The News, Portsmouth

always very popular in summer and many of the huts have such individuality that one could say they add to the local character rather than spoil it.

This is an ideal spot to watch the water traffic of Cowes Roads and Southampton Water. The deepest channel is very close to the Spit so that gigantic tankers, some nearly a quarter of a mile long, pass within a hundred yards. A mile out from the beach is the light ship *Calshot*, which marks the deep-water channel, and beyond is a shallow bank named the Brambles. The channel turns to run parallel with the shore, and even the ferries to the Island have to follow an abrupt zigzagging course, while the largest vessels have to be guided at very slow speed by Trinity House pilots.

With such a commanding position at the entrance to Southampton Water it is surprising that Henry VIII was the first to site a fort here, but no record or trace exists of any earlier castle. Henry, who had himself experimented with cannon ranges and elevations at Southampton, must have realised that his artillery's one-mile range was enough to secure the mouth of the Water, and the round castle, built with masonry and materials shipped from nearby abbeys, was ready within eighteen months of Beaulieu's suppression. The castle is open to the public. A prominent feature beside the castle is the coastguards' crows-nest, an impressive building 110 ft. high. From here, with their powerful binoculars, they can see over the hangars and nearby cliffs at Lepe, keeping watch, co-ordinating rescue services and looking out for pollution. Their weather reports are a familiar item on local radio. Beneath the tower is the Lifeboat Station, only one of many local rescue services.

For all this the real fame of Calshot arose from its service as a Naval sea-plane base which began in 1913, two years after the first successful sea-plane had flown in the United States. After experimenting with sea-planes Calshot aircrews flew them in defence of the English Channel in the first world war, especially helping to watch for the new submarines. Between the wars, with larger and larger planes requiring even more crew training, the Air Station grew in size.

Worldwide attention was fixed on the Solent when Calshot, now in R.A.F. hands, played host in 1929 and 1931 to the sea-plane races for the Schneider Trophy, which was won by record-breaking planes built in Southampton by Supermarine. The final race of 1931 was flown without competition and gained the Trophy permanently for Britain with another world record of 407½ m.p.h. Designed by R.J. Mitchell, these marvellous machines were to be developed into the Spitfire that played such a crucial part in the defence of Britain 40 years ago.

In the last war Calshot was thought too vulnerable to attack and was used for repairs only. Since then, sea-planes have been out of fashion. The great jets and helicopters, long-range reconnaissance planes, and even satellites do much of the varied work for which they were once used. In 1961 the base at Calshot was closed, the last sea-planes having departed some years earlier. The hangars and many of the buildings were adapted by Hampshire County Council for use as a large sports centre where courses can be taken in sailing and cruising, sea-canoeing, and environmental studies. The larger hall has a ski-slope, an indoor cycle race-track and a climbing wall. Courses long and short in these and many other recreations are available not only for schools, but also for families and individuals.

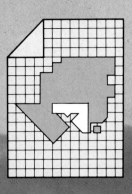

SOUTHAMPTON AND ITS WATERSIDE

The River Hamble
Photo: Terry Southwell

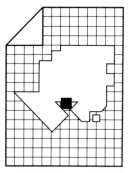

Southampton Water

Ideal view point for Southampton Water is the tower of the Royal Victoria Country Park Heritage Centre, Netley

The Solent Way
The route continues from Beaulieu village up the B3054 to Hilltop, where the way bears north across Beaulieu Heath to Hardley. A quiet lane then leads into Hythe where the ferry can be taken to Southampton. Unfortunately there is no Sunday service but local buses to the city are an alternative.

Tourist accommodation
For information contact the New Forest District Council. T.I.C. Lyndhurst car park Telephone (042 128) 2269

Local Cruises on Southampton Water are operated by the Hythe Pier and Ferry Company, telephone Hythe (0703) 843203, and Blue Funnel Cruises who operate also from Portsmouth/Southsea and Buckler's Hard, telephone Southampton (0703) 223278

SOUTHAMPTON WATER

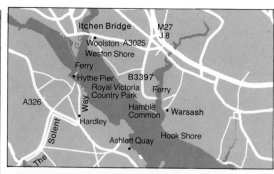

If one could choose a time and a means to enjoy Southampton Water it would certainly be high up on the deck of one of the ocean liners sixty years ago, viewing the pleasant greenery of its still unspoilt shores. It has to be admitted that today the local waterfronts show a different face, although one that is certainly still full of interest. The infant industries of aircraft manufacture and oil refining have since grown and turned the shores into one of the important centres of British industry.

In 1921 the foundations of the Atlantic Gulf West Indies Refinery (AGWI to the locals) were laid outside the Saxon village of Fawley on the western shore of Southampton Water. Built originally to supply fuel to ships using the port, and bitumen for road construction to meet the ever-increasing needs of the motor car, it is today the largest refinery in the United Kingdom and the centre of a complex of petrochemical and energy industries. In the late twenties the Anglo-American Oil Company, later known as Esso (the British affiliate of Exxon which was started as the Standard Oil Company by J.D. Rockefeller) acquired this small refinery and in 1951 completed a newer and much larger edition. Since then, the refinery has grown in size and complexity, and today with its chemical manufacturing employs over 2,000 staff. The refinery's raw material, crude oil, is brought through the vast marine terminal, which handles some 14 million gallons of oil every day, in some 3,000 ship movements a year including the V.L.C.C's (very large crude carriers). About 25 per cent of the refinery's output is distributed by sea and almost all the remainder is sent out by pipeline to other chemical companies and energy industries that have grown up in the shadow of the refinery, and to terminals outside London, as well as to Staffordshire and Avonmouth.

The huge oil-fired power station nearby, which was built in the 1960s to take advantage of the easy supply, is now running much below capacity because of the high cost of oil and the reduced use of electricity. A second station, nearer Southampton, was the first British power station to be designed to use oil or coal fuel. The scientists working at Fawley and Marchwood for the C.E.G.B. have done much research on wave power, and the possibilities for extracting "free heat" directly from the earth's crust by pumping water down specially drilled wells.

During the exciting years before the first world war, several of Hampshire's flying enthusiasts started small-scale works around Southampton Water, beginning an industry which soon spawned seaplane bases and aircraft building at Hamble which continues to this day. In September 1913 Winston Churchill, then First Lord of the Admiralty, had his first experience of flight here in a small biplane and, quickly realising the potential of this new war weapon, helped to boost the Naval Wing of the Royal Flying Corps which had just arrived at Calshot. Until the 1960s the whole of the Water was designated an aerodrome. As the flying-boat era came to an end

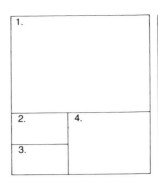

the local expertise in developing novel forms of transport was not wasted, for within a year of the last flight, to Madeira in 1959 the world's first hovercraft flight was made down Southampton Water.

Despite the successful growth of these modern industries along the shores there are still a variety of places to enjoy walking or to relax, perhaps watching with binoculars the continuous movement of ships up and down the estuary. One of the best vantage points outside Southampton is the Royal Victoria Country Park, and from here it is possible to walk to Hill Head along the coast, crossing the Hamble River by ferry. By the mouth of the river, at Hamble Common, there is another fine coastal view point, directly opposite the Fawley oil refinery and its terminal. Another of Henry VIII's castles once stood here to guard the approaches to the river, but little of it can be seen today.

A quite different marine prospect can be enjoyed from the 100-year-old pier at Hythe which was built to upgrade the ancient ferry-crossing. Surprisingly, some of the ferry service's busiest days were during the first world war when the people of Southampton, their Common taken over by the army, flocked to the New Forest on Bank Holidays. The electric railway which saves passengers a long walk (2,000 feet) was added in 1922 and had been built originally for use in a mustard-gas factory in the West Country. The ferry unfortunately no longer runs on Sundays, but on other days it is a convenient and enjoyable way to join the buses which run to Beaulieu, Lymington, Exbury, Lepe and Calshot.

From Fawley village a small lane drops down to Ashlett Quay where an old pub and a green can be found by a large tide mill, with its millpond nearby; tankers at berth provide a striking background. From here there is a short coast path of about a mile-and-a-half, which passes at the foot of the power station to Calshot Spit. Offshore are tidal saltings and mudflats which are protected as a local nature reserve, particularly for waders and many other birds which exploit the rich invertebrate and fish life of these estuarine shores.

Anyone wishing to get out on the water will find a good choice of boat tours operating each summer: there are trips from Southampton, from Hythe pier, and from the Hamble River. Visitors to Southsea, Portsmouth and the Isle of Wight also enjoy longer excursions to Southampton Water, while there are also scheduled ferry crossings to and from the Island, as well as short cruises from Southampton to Buckler's Hard. The best land view of Southampton Water is from the new platform recently built inside the dome of the chapel at the Royal Victoria Country Park.

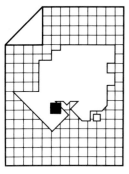

THE NEW FOREST BUTTERFLY FARM

Opening its doors for the first time in the summer of 1981 the Butterfly Farm is beyond doubt Hampshire's most enchanting and imaginative tourist attraction, a covered tropical garden filled with free-flying butterflies and moths from around the world. This is probably Britain's first purpose-built 'indoor safari park' for these beautiful creatures, which were so common a generation ago but now are reduced to small numbers. We have just fifty-nine species in Britain; but at the Butterfly Farm it is possible to enjoy up to seventy species, including some of the world's largest such as the Owl Butterfly from Central America and the Atlas Moth from India, with wing spans of 8" and 10", respectively.

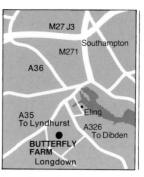

'HOW TO GET THERE'
From M27 take M271 down to Redbridge then A35 out of Southampton in direction of Lyndhurst. Take turning on left sign-posted Longdown. Farm is short distance on left.

together, how some species make long migrations, whilst others only live for a few days or weeks. The relationship of our 'blues' to the ants is one of the most curious stories in nature. The Butterfly Farm, a vast greenhouse, is warmed by solar heating and its atmosphere is maintained at a high humidity. Visitors, safely behind glass, can also watch tarantulas, scorpions and a superb

New Forest Butterfly Farm
(New Forest Butterfly Farm Ltd.)

Longdown,
Near Ashurst,
Southampton,
Hampshire,
SO4 4UH.
Telephone
Ashurst (042129) 2166

Price Guide - E

Car Parking
Free

Handicapped
Full facilities

Party Visits
By arrangement
Educational resources

Publications
Leaflet and guidebook
Displays

Where to eat
Cafe on site
Picnic tables on site
Picnic area 100 yards from farm

Time to allow
1 - 2 hours

Open
1st April-31st October
Every day 10am-5pm

Public Transport
Bus Services-
Buses approx. every hour from Southampton and Lymington to Colbury on Mondays to Saturdays (every 2 hours on Sundays) then 1 mile walk
Also special high Summer Sunday buses direct from Southampton

Rail Service:
Lyndhurst Road Station
(2 mile walk)

Wagon Rides
Short 20-minute rides daily, 11am-4pm. On selected days and during school holidays, longer 50-minute rides

Nearby Attractions
New Forest
National Motor Museum
Buckler's Hard

New Forest Butterfly Farm

Left, 1	View of building
Top Right, 2	American Swallowtail
Upper Right, 3	Monarch or Milkweed
Lower Right, 4	Red Legged Tarantula
Bottom Right, 5	Red Admiral

The enterprise is more than just a chance to watch and photograph the spectacular colours and patterns: visitors may have the unique experience of walking through clouds of butterflies. The Butterfly Farm also provides a fascinating introduction to their biology and strange life-cycles, as well as the problems of conservation. It is particularly exciting to see every stage in the cycle: butterflies mating, eggs being laid, then hatching into growing larvae and caterpillars eventually spinning cocoons. Most visitors are unlucky if they miss the small miracle of a butterfly emerging to unfold its wing and fly for the first time.

At Ashurst on can learn much about the other strange aspects of the world of butterflies: how only blue males and brown females pair

natural living bee-hive in a hollow oak tree, as well as other insects such as praying mantis, locusts and a colony of leaf-cutting ants from Trinidad. Outside is a delightful reed-fringed pond stocked with several species of dragon-fly.

We are all concerned about the lack of butterflies in the countryside and so it is good that the enthusiastic staff here are able to give advice on plants which will encourage butterflies to breed in and visit our gardens.

Wagon rides through the beautiful woodlands of the Longdown Estate are also available at Ashurst. Specially restored drays, drawn by Shire or Clydesdale horses, operate regularly.

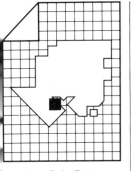

Longdown Dairy Farm
(Longdown Management Ltd)

Deerleap Lane,
Longdown,
Ashurst,
Southampton SO4 4UH
Telephone (042129) 3326

Price Guide - C

Car Parking
Nearby

Handicapped
Much of farmyard is suitable

Party Visits
By arrangement (28th March -
31st October)
Guided tours provided

Publications
Guidebook

Where to eat
Cafe and picnic area provided
for visitors to the New Forest
Butterfly Farm nearby

Time to allow
1 - 2 hours

Open
28th March - 31st October.
Sundays, 11am-5pm, and
every day during school
holidays and Bank Holidays
between these dates

Public transport
Bus services -
Bournemouth - Southampton
(B.S. - Ashurst P.O.) X1
Lymington - Southampton
(½ mile walk) 56a, 56
Rail service -
Lyndhurst Road Station
(2-mile walk)

Nearby Attractions
New Forest
New Forest Butterfly Farm
Holidays Hill Reptiliary
The Rufus Stone
Rhinefield Ornamental Drive
National Motor Museum
Buckler's Hard

Left, A visit to Longdown

Right, Milking time

1, Barry Shurlock

2, Longdown Dairy Farm

LONGDOWN DAIRY FARM

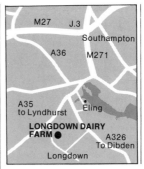

'HOW TO GET THERE'
From M27 take M271 to
Redbridge, then A35 out of
Southampton in direction of
Lyndhurst. Take turning on
left sign-posted Longdown.
Farm is a short distance on the
left.

So many people used to lean over the gate and ask questions about Longdown Farm that the owners decided to open it to visitors and mark out a tour of the buildings. The result is a delightful place where children can get close to a wide variety of animals and see the workings of one of the most up-to-date farms in the country.

The prize exhibits are Baldwin, a Hereford bull - said to be 'a big softie' - and a herd of pedigree Friesian cows. But there are also many other animals to be seen, including rabbits, chickens, geese and goats. Feeding of the animals by visitors is permitted and bags of suitable food are on sale.

The farm also holds some unusual animals, notably a small number of 'Iron Age' pigs, which are a cross between a wild boar and a Tamworth pig. Originally bred by the Cotswold Farm Park for the Butser Ancient Project, these primitive looking animals are still relatively wild. A more docile strain is being bred at Longdown for the production of a low-fat, 'delicacy' type of pork.

address of the farm. Cows which are about to produce their calves at Longdown can be seen in the farm's Sick Bay and Maternity Unit.

Young calves are taken from their mothers at two days of age, then fed colostrum for five days after which they are fed with an 'automatic mother' in the Calf Unit. This is a device rather like a hot-drinks machine in which dried milk powder is mixed with water and delivered at the right temperature to a 'teat on the wall'.

Those calves which are earmarked to maintain the main herd are first reared to the age of two-and-a-half and then ready to become 'dairy followers', when they join the other cows and start breeding.

The main aim of the small three-man team who work the farm - herdsman, stockman, and tractor driver - is to manage a dairy herd for profit. But Longdown is a farm where a real concern for the welfare of animals is also apparent, while visitors are made extremely welcome. All aspects of modern dairy production are on show, from calving to milking. A display in the Information Centre shows how a cow's output of milk builds up to a peak over a ten-month period and then slowly declines, after which she is not milked (the proper term is 'goes dry') until her next calf has been born two months later.

Maiden heifers at Longdown are first served by the Hereford bull, since the resulting 'white-faced' Hereford cross Friesian calves are relatively small and easily delivered. They are fed on beef nuts and hay and reared for beef. Calves produced in subsequent years are pedigree Friesian stock from artificial insemination and are all formally called Deerleap after the name of the herd, which in turn takes its name from the

A popular event with visitors is the afternoon milking, which starts at 3pm and continues for two-and-a-half hours. (This is actually the second milking of the day: the first takes place at 5am!) During this period 150 Friesians are milked automatically in the parlour, where fourteen cows at a time stand in a herringbone pattern of 'standings'. As each cow is milked it is fed according to its yield - usually about 1200 gallons per year - a measured amount of food being delivered down a chute. The correct amount is calculated by a computer, which is actuated by the herdsman keying in the cow's number branded on its rump.

The computer is, in fact, an essential part of the management of Longdown Dairy Farm. It helps to plan each cow's milking cycle and calving and works out the most cost-effective mix of food from that available on the farm. It even prints out an 'action list' so that the herdsman can plan veterinary visits and other matters. Working a day that starts at 4am and runs to 9.30pm, he certainly needs all the help he can get! BS

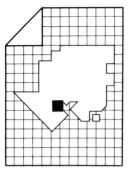

ELING TIDE MILL

L ong before there were oil refineries and power stations millers knew how to take advantage of the power of the tides, as well as of rivers and the wind. Today, from perhaps hundreds which once used the tides, only three working mills survive, two in England and another in Wales: Eling is the only known tide mill still producing flour in Western Europe. After several years of dedicated work by volunteers, government trainees and professionals, the Eling water-wheels are turning again and even grinding corn to produce the mill's own 'Canute' brand of flour.

T he mill stands on a causeway over Bartley Water which rises near Minstead, crosses the New Forest and meanders around Totton. The causeway not only provided a bridge to Eling and the other Waterside villages but it was also used to trap the waters at high tide, which are held up for an unusually long period because of the unique double tides of Southampton Water. The critical devices in such a mill are the sluice gates, or sea

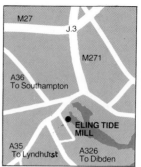

T here is a small museum display at the entrance to the mill which includes photographs of the work of restoration carried out with such devotion and enthusiasm over the years. There are also occasional displays on aspects of local history such as shipbuilding and brewing. The beauty and power of the old mill can be best seen and appreciated from the height of the bin loft, where corn is tipped into a hopper and released down to the mill's grinding-stones on the 'stone' floor. The water turning the great wheels below supplies the power to work the heavy stones, as well as to lift

hatches, which allow water to fill the millpond and then close as the tide drops. The water can then be let through the mill to turn the wheels.

M illing at Eling started in the 14th century but the present building was constructed about two hundred years ago by Winchester College, who were lords of the manor and owned the mill until 1975. By Victorian times the mill was a thriving business and the local quay had warehousing, as well as a malt kiln in which germinating barley was dried for use by brewers. Sailing ships and barges were loaded and unloaded at the quay. But eventually shiploads of wheat came across the Atlantic to be milled by steam-driven machinery in the main ports and this threatened small-scale milling. A booklet about the mill describes how the business survived for more than fifty years until the worn-out machinery finally ground to a halt after the last war.

sacks of corn from the ground floor to the bin loft at the top of the building.

O ne advantage for the tenants of Eling Tide Mill used to be the toll that they were able to take from users of the causeway. Today it is collected by the New Forest District Council.

V isitors can see the equipment working if they time their visit right. The low tides are four hours in every eight, but only once or twice a week is there a demonstration, so it is advisable to telephone for information or watch out for publicity. There is a well-stocked sales counter where the products of the mill can be bought.

A car park is available on the south bank, near to Eling Church, where there is also a water-front picnic site. The most pleasant way to arrive at the Mill is certainly from this direction rather than through the built-up centre of Totton.

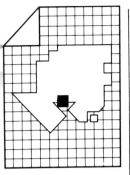

Southampton Common Studies Centre
(Southampton City Council/
Southampton Common
Studies Centre Association)

Cemetery Road,
Southampton,
Hampshire SO1 2NM
Telephone
(0703) 36094

Price Guide - Free

Car Parking
Nearby

Handicapped
Suitable

Party Visits
By arrangement
Guided tours by day and night

Publications
Guidebook (published by The
City of Southampton Society),
booklets, monthly newsletter,
quarterly magazine

Where to eat
Pubs nearby, picnic site at
north-east corner

Time to allow
Minimum 2 hours

Open
Centre:10am-5pm, Sunday -
Friday, 2pm-5pm, Saturday
Common: at all times. (N.B. It
is advisable for young
children to be accompanied)

Angling
Free on the Ornamental Lake
in the north-east corner.
Southern Water Authority
licence required.

Public Transport
Bus Services-
Frequent services from city
centre daily. Every 30 minutes
from Winchester and
Eastleigh Monday - Saturday
(hourly on Sundays).
Connections from city centre
from Southsea, Fareham,
Bournemouth, Gosport,
Salisbury and Lymington

Nearby Attractions
Southampton Hall of Aviation
Tudor House Museum
Maritime Museum
God's House Tower
Southampton Art Gallery

Investigating wild life
in one of the ponds on
Southampton
Common. (V. Appleby)

SOUTHAMPTON COMMON
AND STUDIES CENTRE

In the heart of Southampton, only half a mile from the Civic Centre, is an extensive area of semi-wild grassland and woodland that has belonged to the city and its citizens since Anglo-Saxon times. Once an asset on which commoners grazed their cattle, it is now a quiet delight for strollers and naturalists. It also hosts the Southampton Show each year in the summer and provides a place where anglers can fish and toddlers can paddle.

Covering an area of 365 acres - almost half the size of Central Park, New York - the common is large enough to contain a wide range of activities, but in recent years it has perhaps been most used by naturalists, who have surveyed its wildlife and flora in great detail. The hub of their work is the Southampton Common Studies Centre on the southern edge of the area. Newcomers are strongly advised to view the displays here and to talk to the staff before exploring the common.

A wide range of inexpensive publications has been produced, including booklets on trees, birds, bats, 'minibeasts' (insects), fungi and

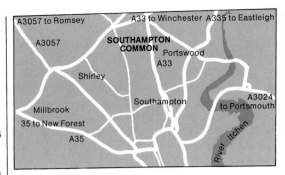

Overall, more than 350 species of plants have been recorded on the common, including seven species of orchid. About a hundred species of birds have been seen, including rare visitors such as the Goldeneye. Many common birds are breeding residents, together with relatively rare regulars, such as the Cirl Bunting, Coal Tit, Treecreeper and many others. There is a small breeding population of ducks, geese and swans on one of the four ponds on the common, Cemetery Lake, at the south-western corner.

The bats of the common have also been studied by naturalists, who monitor these creatures with a 'bat detector' - a modified transistor radio that shifts the frequency of the sound emitted

orchids. Special events are organised throughout the year, such as the hugely popular night walks, when the habits of nocturnal creatures such as amphibians and bats are observed.

One feature of the Studies Centre to whet the appetite of any young naturalist is the animal room, where a changing menagerie of common creatures and exotic strays can be seen. There is a butterfly cage where emerging insects are kept, a colony of red ants, and a tank where voracious ways of the dragonfly larva (it eats small newts!) can be studied. Also on view are lizards, slow worms, frogs and toads, including 'Ena', currently a teenager, but expected to live to the grand old age of 40.

from the ultrasound to the audible range. In this way, bat enthusiasts can tell the distinctive 'Chowp-wip! Whowp-wip! Dwat! Dwawt! Chowp-brrrrr...!' of the Little Pipistrelle from the 'Chionk-chionk-chionk! Brrrr-p!' of Daubenton's Bat.

Also available at the Studies Centre is an historical map of the common, which can make a stroll an exercise in field archaeology. Successive encroachments of the cemetery, the former race-course, the former cattle pound, the site of the Court Leet and traces of the military encampment of the two World Wars - all these and many other features are there for the eye to see.

BS

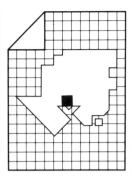

OLD SOUTHAMPTON
& GOD'S HOUSE TOWER

Today, the casual visitor to Southampton has to use some imagination to relate the present-day centre, with its modern precinct and great stores, to its past as one of England's ancient cities and one of Europe's greatest ports, for the shopping centre has grown outside the historic heart of the town well away from the old quays. A problem common to any historic town is that we can hardly realise how very small cities were when still contained by their mediaeval walls and ditches, as Southampton was until the beginning of the 19th century.

Until two centuries ago the prospect and surroundings of Southampton changed little and ironically, the first major development, in 1804, was the building of a grandiose sham-gothic castle on the site of the original Norman stronghold. Since that date change has certainly been rapid. Until that time the city occupied a small corner of land between the Itchen and the Upper Southampton Water. The transformation gathered pace in the next forty years, when the local fields were crossed by the railway and colonised by houses.

The muddy banks by the Itchen to the east were reclaimed for docks. There were also changes made to the west, though these were much later. What had been the west wall, with the high tides of West Bay lapping at its foot, can still be seen in several sections with its turrets and towers, but between the wars West Bay was reclaimed and the wall left stranded well inland. Luckily, the bombing in World War II, which destroyed so much of Southampton, left the old defences unharmed.

The best way to learn about the substantial medieval remains of Southampton is to join one of the various tours conducted by voluntary guides at frequent intervals throughout the year. One of these, led daily during the season, explores the western half of the mediaeval city where the ancient (and modern) castles stood. Visitors can walk along the old fortifications and enter the underground vaults of some of the oldest houses. The tour and a number of other walks are described in booklets and leaflets which can be bought from the Information Centre in Above Bar. The 'Bar' is the Bargate, one of three gates which have survived, where all tours start. It was progressively improved until essentially completed in its present form following a disastrous raid on the town by the French in 1338 during the Hundred Years War. It is probably one of the finest town gates in Britain. Temporary exhibitions on Southampton's history are arranged

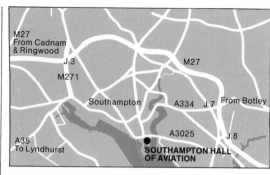

'HOW TO GET THERE'

(To the Bargate) Follow road signs to town centre, and near Civic Centre, follow one-way system into Portland Terrace. Car-parks sign-posted.

(To God's House Tower) From Civic Centre take Western Esplanade to dockside and Town Quay. Museum at eastern end of Winkle Street, which runs behind dockside.

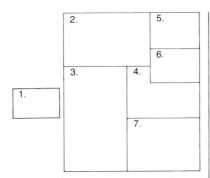

1. The City walls before reclamation of the former bay
2. The Bargate
3. Ancient building in Bugle Street
4. Section of old walls near the Bargate
5. God's House Gate and Tower from an old engraving
6. Bargate in 1830s
7. The High Street before the First World War

1: Hampshire County Records Office
6,7: Southampton City Council

here by Southampton City Museums. Southampton is very fortunate in have four museums housed in mediaeval buildings, each of which is worth a visit in its own right.

GOD'S HOUSE TOWER

This ancient building stood at the south-eastern corner of the town walls, straddling the ditch outside the eastern wall which was used as a tidal mill-pond. It also formed part of the ill-fated 18th century canal which was to connect the town with Salisbury. The building itself was erected to house the town gunner and the dangerous business of making gunpowder. The tower, which for safety stood outside the crowded mediaeval streets, is the earliest surviving artillery bastion in Europe, dating from 1430 AD.

The museum display tells the story of archaeological discoveries not only from the old mediaeval town but from its predecessor, Saxon Hamwic, which looked out over the west bank of the Itchen on the land north of the new tollbridge. This was discovered in one of the most important excavations of its kind, and has proved to be the earliest planned town in England, even the start of urbanisation in these islands. The Saxons landed in Southampton Water near Calshot in 495 and defeated the Britons some twenty years later. The town grew up as a trading community and was well established by 700. The trenches have revealed pottery, quern stones, gold coins, axes and swords, and even an iron-smelting furnace. The port's trading links were with the Rhine where wool was exported, but the Vikings eventually cut the trade routes and by 900 Hamwic was a ghost-town. However, even Hamwic had a forerunner, further upstream across the river on the east bank: Clausentum, a crowded Roman port, much of whose story has yet to be discovered.

Even though Southampton has been the most important commercial port on the south coast - at least since Roman times - it has had a very chequered history. Though wars have often been good for Portsmouth, they have all too frequently afflicted the fortunes of Southampton: its story until recent times has involved a continual ebb and flow of resident foreign trading communities whose supply routes have been cut, their markets captured, their homelands troubled with war or their presence simply resented. Indeed, the return of the rejected Italians with the French fleet in 1338 at the beginning of the Hundred Years War was so very bloody and disastrous that the port was ruined for years, and the town in decline for a century. It was only after this catastrophe that the open western side of the town was fortified with the walls and towers which stand to this day.

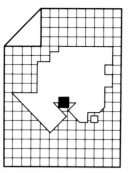

Tudor House Museum
(Southampton City Council)

Bugle Street,
Southampton,
SO1 0A.
Telephone
Southampton (0703) 24216

Price Guide – Free

Car Parking
Nearby

Handicapped
Ground floor accessible to
wheelchairs

Party visits
By arrangement
Educational resources
Tours available

Where to eat
Suitable picnic area outside
Tudor Merchants Hall nearby

Time to allow
1 - 2 hours

Open
All year Tuesday - Friday
10am - 5pm
Saturday 10am-4pm
Sunday 2-5pm

THE TUDOR HOUSE MUSEUM

This timber-framed building in the heart of old Southampton is one of the few surviving examples of a fairly large town house of early Tudor times. Three separate houses were knit into the present museum, which has its own re-creation of a Tudor garden; a small oasis of peace in the middle of a busy city. Inside is a superb collection of bygones which are displayed to form complete period rooms.

The main part of the house was built by one of Henry VII's wealthy customs officials, Sir John Dawtrey, and after his death it was owned by Richard Lyster, who became Chief Justice.

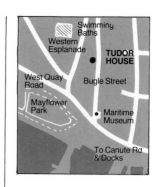

'HOW TO GET THERE'

From west – Follow A36 to West Quay Road or Western Esplanade. Large car park by Public Swimming pool. Access to museum through small gate in medieval wall.
From east and north, (A33 or Itchen bridges) follow signs to Docks, and Town Quay. Swimming baths car-park access from West Quay Road

When the town walls were built in 1360 the Norman building was only provided with extremely small 'windows' to seaward. These were in fact gun-ports, the earliest known in Britain, and were intended to take small primitive

The great Front Hall and the bedrooms above may have been built on to an existing Banqueting Hall, which has a splendid oak panelled ceiling and what looks like a minstrel's gallery.

In the basement beneath are the remains of earlier mediaeval buildings of the mid 12th century, and several interesting cellars which are not open to the public.

From the garden one can see part of a Norman house, which overlooked the town's West Quay and belonged to a merchant. Built between 1150-1175, it has a rare fireplace and chimney and has been described as one of the best examples of its period surviving in Britain. Although used until this century it now has no roof or upper floor.

cannon as protection against attack from hostile ships.

The restoration of the garden, which was laid out in 1980, owes much to the enthusiastic support of the Friends of Southampton's Museums. It has patterns of coloured earth, knot garden flowerbeds, low clipped herb hedges, painted railing trellises, pergolas and arbours.

The Tudor House was opened as Southampton's first museum in 1912. The present-day displays include a Victorian parlour, numerous household items from the kitchen and scullery and, perhaps most delightful, a child's bedroom at the top of the house which is crowded with toys.

Top, 1	Tudor House in the 1890s before the timbering was added
Lower Left, 2	Victorian Child's bedroom
Lower Centre, 3	Interior view of room downstairs
Lower Right, 4	Restored Tudor garden

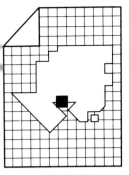

SOUTHAMPTON ART GALLERY

Southampton Art Gallery
(Southampton City Council)

Southampton Art Gallery,
Civic Centre,
Southampton,
Hampshire,
SO9 4XP.
Telephone
Southampton (0703) 832769

Price Guide - Free

Car Parking
Nearby

Handicapped
Suitable (Ramps, lifts,
wheelchairs and disabled
toilets are present)

Party visits
By arrangement

Publications
Gallery catalogue

Where to eat
Suitable picnic area at Watts
Park

Time to allow
1 - 3 hours

Open
All year

Public Transport
Bus Services -
Regular bus services from
Bournemouth, Romsey,
Winchester, Newbury, Oxford,
Lymington and Portsmouth
(daily), and from Salisbury and
Gosport on Monday -
Saturday
Rail Services -
Southampton Station
(10 mins. walk)

Nearby Attractions
Tudor House Museum
Bargate
Wool House
God's House Tower

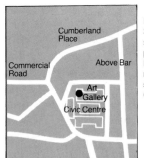

'HOW TO GET THERE'
Follow road signs for
Southampton Central railway
station, or Civic Centre. Car
parks off Inner Ring Road and
Havelock Road, and limited
meter parking on nearby
streets. Entrance to Gallery in
Commercial Road.

During the depression of the thirties, Southampton remained relatively prosperous because of its successful port activities, and some of the wealth was invested in the ambitious Civic Centre, the pride of which is a marvellous set of spacious art galleries. Although they were bombed soon after completion in 1939, restoration was achieved and in the 1950s and 1960s with the help of a considerable private bequest the gallery built up a collection of works of art that is now one of the finest in the south outside London. The gallery is

Southampton Art gallery is outstanding for the way its small staff help visitors and especially young ones to enjoy and understand the collections, with numerous information sheets and leaflets for adults and quizzes for children as well

remarkable also for the range of activities and events organised by its staff.

The collection includes paintings by some of the most famous artists: Van Dyck, Gainsborough, Turner and Reynolds. There are pictures by the pre-Raphaelites as well as the French Impressionists including Monet and Renoir. The display also includes fine ceramics and sculpture and a lively programme of exhibitions, usually two different ones at once, with shows of photographs, prints, drawings as well as crafts and industrial design, enabling visitors to keep up-to-date with the latest trends in art. The gallery provides a chance to enjoy works of art such as a beautiful Italian mediaeval altar piece or works by modern artists such as Lowry and David Hockney.

as comfortable seating, so nobody need suffer from 'gallery feet'.

There are also school and holiday projects, films every Sunday afternoon, workshops and talks and even popular crafts courses. In the modern foyer is a well stocked and very tempting art shop which has a wide range of post cards, reproductions, posters, slides, calendars and greetings cards. Work by local craftsmen is also kept in stock. Local residents can subscribe to the Print Loan Scheme and borrow up to twelve original prints each year.

Hampshire is clearly fortunate to have such a valuable and lively art gallery. The building has a lift to the upper floor so visitors in wheelchairs are just as free to enjoy themselves.

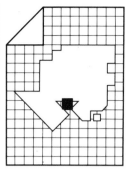

Maritime Southampton

Tourist Information Centres
Telephone
(0703) 221106/
223855 Ext. 615

The Solent Way
continues from the Town Quay
past God's House Tower, the
Dock gates and Tourist
Information Centre in Canute
Road to the new Itchen
Bridge. There is then a further
mile or so through Woolston,
past the Vosper Thornycroft
shipyard to Weston shore. An
alternative to this stage of the
walk is provided by several
bus services out from the city
centre. The walk continues
alongside the beach to Netley
Abbey ruins and Royal
Victoria Country Park. The Way
then continues to Hamble
Common, a short walk from
the village, where there is an
all-year-round ferry to
Warsash.

Harbour Cruises
are organised by Blue Funnel
Cruises, telephone
Southampton (0703) 223278

Ferries
To the Isle of Wight, (Car and
Hydrofoil) Red Funnel
Sevices. Telephone (0703)
222042

**Wool House Maritime
Museum**
Southampton City Council
Town Quay

Price Guide - Free

Car Parking
Nearby

Handicapped
Ground floor access for
wheelchairs

Time to allow
1 hour

Open
Tuesday - Friday 10am -5pm
Saturday 10am - 4pm
Sunday 2 -5pm
Closed for lunch 1 -2pm

Maritime Southampton

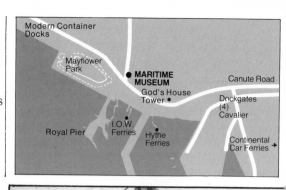

Southampton's Maritime Museum, in the 'Wool House', once inside the town walls, now faces the seafront by the Royal Pier. This magnificent building was a warehouse built for the monks at Beaulieu Abbey in the early 15th century to store wool, their main source of revenue, which was exported from the nearby quayside to the Continent. It now houses a collection of mementos of local maritime history. Here one can see models of many of the ships which were built in Southampton or which used to be a common sight along the waterfront, from the biggest and most famous liners such as the *Queen Mary* down to one of the Cowes ketches which continued trading locally right through to the present century, carrying coal to the local riverside works and corn and flour to the many tidal mills. The magnificent model of the *Queen Mary* is 21 feet long. The museum also contains papers and souvenirs of the recently discovered *Titanic*, which sailed from Southampton on her ill-fated maiden voyage in 1912. A fascinating exhibit tells the story of a Hythe firm which developed high-speed craft for the Air Force and the Royal Navy between the wars. One of the servicemen involved in testing the boats was the enigmatic T.E. Lawrence.

Upstairs can be seen the wonderful joinery of the mediaeval timbered roof which has been especially lit. Downstairs, a crowded display includes the engine of one of the old paddle steamers, a traditional diving suit, models of dredgers and cranes, and photographs of some of the luxurious steam yachts built at Southampton eighty years ago, in an age which seems so far from our own. Dominating the displays is a great model of the docks, 27 feet long, that shows the port in its hey-day of the 1930s.

Visitors should not miss the chance to take a boat tour around the docks from the quayside close to the Royal Pier and the Hythe ferry landing; these one-hour tours take place several times a day and include a commentary. Guided tours of Old Southampton's shoreline are also available during the summer months; these end on the new Itchen Bridge which was completed in 1976. From its peak height of 80 feet above the river there is a fine view over the port and the town below. This immense structure replaced a floating bridge built in 1836; one of the surviving bridges has been converted into a restaurant on the Woolston side.

Usually one cannot visit the Docks for security reasons, but Southampton Corporation have arranged a conducted tour by bus all round the town which includes a visit to the modern

container port, which can otherwise only be seen at a distance from the out-of-town motorway to the west.

Close to the Maritime Museum stands the Mayflower Monument, which records that it was from Southampton on August 5th 1620 that the *Mayflower* and *Speedwell* set sail to America carrying some of the Pilgrim Fathers, harried by King James I, who were to become the first settlers across the Atlantic. The ships ran into trouble and had to turn back to Plymouth, the *Mayflower* eventually arriving 3,000 miles away with just 101 passengers on November 11th 1620. The memorial in Southampton was erected in 1913 and includes many tablets placed by descendants of the New World settlers. Nearby another intriguing monument records the heroic deeds of a nurse on a sinking British ship. The Royal Pier was built in 1833 to serve the growing number of

'HOW TO GET THERE'

For Wool House Maritime Museum) From near Civic Centre and bus station, on foot walk down Above Bar Street to High Street turning right through to Castle Way, and into St Michael's Square by the Tudor House Museum. Walk down Bugle Street. Museum on corner by Town Quay.

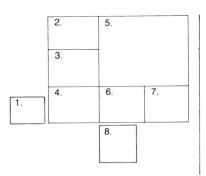

1. The docks in the early days of steam ships
2. Modern container handling
3. Southampton International Boat Show
4. Hythe Ferry setting off across Southampton Water
5. *Mayflower* and the departure of the Pilgrims from Southampton
6. View of gallery, Maritime Museum
7. *Miss Britain III*
8. Plaque on Memorial to Mary Anne Rogers

1: Hampshire County Records Office
2: British Transport Docks Board
3: Artman Exhibitions
5: Harvey Barton
7: Southampton Maritime Museum

Clement Attlee in 1951 has been demolished. Ironically its superbly efficient design was used as a basis for some of the passenger terminals that were built at Heathrow, and of course Heathrow's gain was Southampton's loss.

From the full height of the Itchen Bridge there is a magnificent view west over the Docks or north up the Itchen. (To appreciate the view one should walk the bridge, for stopping a car is forbidden). The private Northam riverside quays started to develop in the 1780s despite opposition from the Corporation who were losing their customary charges. Early in the century the town was 'dying with age' as Defoe reported. In 1734 Hope said "There is little trade in the town and if it had not been much frequented for bathing and drinking the salt waters they would have very little commerce except among themselves". Naval shipbuilding took place, but with little success, as a string of businesses failed, until after 1803 when there followed twelve years with seventeen vessels launched at Northam and others nearby. Pleasure craft for the rich, paddle steamers, dredgers, bridges, tugs and mail ships followed through the century.

Many of the last, and very fine, sailing ships from the 1870s and 1880s were built to the south of the present bridge site at Woolston. Within twenty years the building of some of the first Supermarine flying boats was beginning near the same spot: "boats that fly rather than aeroplanes that float", and the same site was used later to create the Spitfire.

To the south the view is dominated by the Docks: the Princess Alexandra (1842) used mostly by cross-channel ferries today; the Empress Dock beyond (1890), traditionally the landing place for bananas and fruit; the Ocean Dock (1911) to the right or west, where the great liners including the Cunard *Queens* docked and beyond this stretching into mid-stream the built-up quays carrying the very modern Queen Elizabeth II terminal opened by Her Majesty in 1966. Here stands the Port and Signal radar station fitted with batteries of radar screens, which provide continuous surveillance and navigational information over the port area and its seaward approaches, controlling the 'traffic' and its 'parking' from a windowless room!

Each year in September the Southampton International Boat Show is staged in Mayflower Park by the docks. From small beginnings in 1969 this has now grown to be a major event in the boat and yachting world.

steamers, which began to make an appearance in the 1820s on the ferry routes to the Isle of Wight and Northern France. The pier was opened by the 14-year-old Princess Victoria and became a popular promenade, but sadly is now closed.

Near to the Town Quay can still be seen some of the buildings used by the commercial flying boat services which grew from the pioneering flights in 1919. Southampton played an important part in the history of commercial air flight as larger planes were developed for the Empire Air Mail Scheme. These carried small numbers of passengers to the ends of the Empire, including Australia in eight days and Hong Kong in seven. In 1950 such BOAC services came to a sudden end. Even in the 1960s twenty-two passenger liners called regularly at Southampton. Today the *Queen Elizabeth II* and *Canberra* are still seen occasionally but the Ocean Terminal opened by

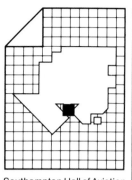

SOUTHAMPTON HALL OF AVIATION

Southampton Hall of Aviation,
Incorporating the Mitchell
Museum
(R.J. Mitchell Memorial
Museum Ltd)

Albert Road South
Southampton,
Hampshire SO1 1FR.
Telephone
(0703) 35830

Price Guide - C

Car Parking
Alongside Museum

Handicapped
Suitable

Party Visits
Tours by arrangement

Publications
Guidebook

Where to Eat
Cafe
Eating places and pubs
locally

Time to allow
1 - 2 hours

Open
Tuesday-Saturday, 10-5,
Sunday 12-5

Public Transport
Bus Services -
Frequent buses from
Southampton city centre and
every hour from Eastleigh,
Fareham and Gosport,
Tuesday-Saturday.
(4 buses from Eastleigh
on Sundays).
Rail Services -
Southampton Station,
20 minute walk.

The Spitfire Society is based
at the museum. Contact:
Group Captain David Green,
chairman and founder.

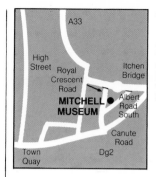

'HOW TO GET THERE'
Signposted from the centre of
Southampton. Make for Dock
Gate No.2. From Woolston,
cross Itchen Bridge and bear
left into Saltmarsh Road,
which leads to Albert Road
South.

For nearly half a century between 1909 and the late 1950s the Solent was an important centre of aviation. During this period, entrepreneurs and local boatbuilders designed and manufactured a host of seaplanes and flying boats and tested and operated them in the sheltered waters of the Hampshire coast. Many of these aircraft played an important part in the early history of military and civil aviation, but the most celebrated of them all

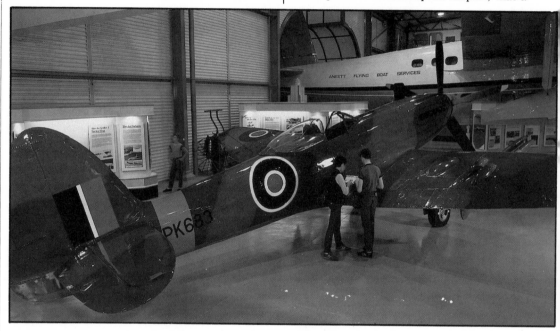

is undoubtedly the Spitfire. Indeed, the inspiration to set up this museum came from a local wish to record the life and achievements of the Spitfire's designer, R.J. Mitchell.

Purpose-built to house a collection of aircraft and extensive displays about aviation in the Solent area, the museum stands in the Eastern Docks area of Southampton, almost opposite the site of the Supermarine Works at Woolston where 'R.J.', as he was universally known, produced a succession of outstanding aeroplanes between the wars. These included such models as the Seal and Seagull, produced in large numbers for the RAF and the Royal Australian Air Force, and the famous Southampton flying boats.

After serving an apprenticeship in his home town of Stoke-on-Trent, R.J. Mitchell joined Supermarine's as a young man at the end of the First World War. Within a short time, still only 24 years of age, he became Chief Designer and was able to use his extraordinary talents to develop novel design concepts that led from the relatively slow biplanes of the time to streamlined monoplanes capable of travelling at more than 400 mph.

Much of the impetus for this progress came from the famous Schneider Trophy races, which in 1931 were finally won outright for Britain with a twin-float seaplane, the Supermarine S6B. A similar aircraft, the S6A, flown in the Schneider Trophy races in 1929, is on display in the museum.

The Spitfire itself came from the lessons learned in competing for the Schneider Trophy, though it was not until 1936, from the site of the present Southampton Airport, that a prototype was first flown. Designed by R.J. Mitchell in response to an Air Ministry specification, the Spitfire became the backbone of RAF Fighter Command during the last war, more than 22,000 aircraft being produced in many variants. The Mk 24 model on show in the museum was the last of the line.

At the same time that military aircraft were being pushed to the limits of the petrol engine, civil aviation was also developing in the Solent area. The British Marine Aircraft Navigation Company and the owners of Southampton Docks, the London and South-Western Railway, formed Imperial Airways and in 1923 set up a regular service between Woolston and the Channel Islands. By 1940, when the company became the basis of BOAC, Short Empire flying boats were operating regular passenger and mail services to many parts of the world, including Africa, Australia and North America.

The centre piece of the museum, a Sandringham flying boat (so large that the hall had to be built around it!), gives some idea of the style of travelling in these early days, though it was never operated locally. Visitors can climb onto the flight deck of this magnificent relic or sample the comforts of the cabin. Perhaps opposite, you may imagine, is a colonial civil servant and his family returning to Africa, a steward serves drinks, and after a day's travelling you can look forward to a stopover at a luxury hotel and some sightseeing.

Photo: Southampton Hall of Aviation

BS

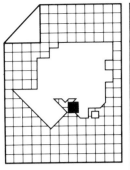

NETLEY ABBEY

Netley Abbey
(English Heritage)

Netley,
Southampton,
Hampshire
SO3 5GF
Telephone
Hamble (0703) 453076
or (0892) 48166

Price Guide -
Free

Car Parking
Free

Handicapped
Suitable

Party visits
Welcome

Publications
Guidebook

Time to allow
1 - 2 hours

Open
All year (except 24-26
December, 1 January,
May Day Bank Holiday)

Public Transport
Bus services -
Hampshire Bus run 2 buses
on hour from Southampton to
Netley Abbey on Monday-
Saturday (every 2 hours on
Sundays)
Rail Services -
Netley Railway Staion (1 mile
walk)

Nearby Attractions
Royal Victoria Country Park
Upper Hamble Country Park
and River Hamble
Bursledon Windmill
Hampshire Farm Museum
Southampton Hall of Aviation

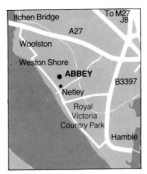

Mediaeval monastic communities sometimes produced offshots; and so it was that in 1239 monks from Beaulieu came ashore to establish Netley Abbey as a daughter foundation to their own across the water. It was, however, set up at the behest of one of the Bishops of Winchester, and built with the support of King Henry III. Paradoxically, impressive as Netley's remains are, comparatively little is known of the abbey's three hundred years. It does seem though that the abbey was not a success financially, and that it gave rise to no other communities.

'HOW TO GET THERE'
From Southampton, cross new Itchen bridge to Woolston then follow signs to Weston shore and Netley.
From M27 (junction 8), follow signs for A27 roundabout and then B3397 (to Hamble). Netley Abbey sign-posted to right.

daily meeting of the monks. On another side of the cloister can be seen the kitchen and warming house, the only place where the monks could have a fire. This side ot the cloister was altered to make

In 1536 the estate was granted to Sir William Paulet who converted the nave into a private house which was occupied until 1700. Paulet, responsible for building many of the Solent castles ordered by Henry VIII, built one at Netley in the abbey grounds. All traces of his own mansion have disappeared but the castle still stands and is still privately occupied to this day. Since the middle of the 18th century the abbey ruins have attracted visitors from far and wide.

It is a beautiful sight, for much of the church's walls and windows still survive and the south transept is particularly impressive. This part of the abbey had been adapted by Paulet as a Great Hall with a screened-off kitchen. Nearby stands the Chapter House where the business and organisation of the abbey were carried out at a

a gateway for Paulet's new house, and the hall where the monks ate was torn down.

Nearby is what is thought to have been the abbey's sanatorium, where the sick were cared for and the monks were bled regularly for their health's sake. Close by was the special room where invalids were allowed to eat meat, which was otherwise forbidden in the monk's diet; strangely enough, birds such as pigeons were not regarded as meat.

Another feature of interest is the separate house for the abbot, who sometimes had to provide accommodation for the king and for the ecclesiastics who were travelling or even on a visit of inspection. Each of its two floors had a hall, which was the main room for eating, a chamber for sleeping, and a chapel.

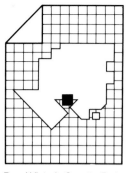

Royal Victoria Country Park
Hampshire County Council

Recreation Department,
Netley Abbey,
Southampton,
Hampshire
SO3 5GA
Telephone
Southampton (0703) 455157
Winchester (0962) 64221

Price Guide - Free

Car Parking
Charge in summer

Handicapped
Suitable
Free car parking passes

Party visits
Tours available by
arrangement

Publications etc.
Leaflet and guidebook
Trails on site. Exhibition
and Solent Way video in
Heritage Centre (former
chapel)

Where to eat
Cafe/tea-room on site
Picnic tables on site

Time to allow
1 - 2 hours

Open
Every day of the year

Public Transport
Bus services -
Two buses an hour from
Southampton, Monday-
Saturday, every two hours on
Sunday
Rail Service -
Netley Railway Station
(½ mile walk)

Nearby Attractions
Hamble Common,
Netley Abbey ruins

ROYAL VICTORIA COUNTRY PARK

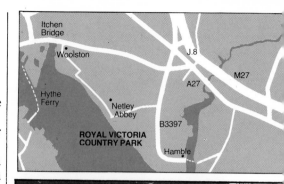

In 1980 the gates of the Royal Victoria were opened to the public for the first time in more than 100 years, for this was formerly the site of Britain's most famous military hospital, built after the Crimean War. Huge crowds had gathered to see Queen Victoria when she laid the foundation stone in 1855, just as the Crimean War came to an end. Now, strange to say, the site must look rather as it did when the first stone was laid, for nearly all the buildings have been removed and the grounds are wide open for enjoyment.

There is a long beach thick with sea shells, one of the most pleasant on Southampton Water, while behind it are more than 100 acres of grassy open spaces and terraces, some of them used as sports fields by local clubs, and all beautifully surrounded by cedars and other exotic trees. There are also attractive woods, one of them sheltering a military cemetery of such character and charm that this alone is well worth a visit. It is said to hold 700 graves, dating from the First World War. Visitors can usually enjoy watching at close hand a great variety of small craft out on the water, for at one corner of the Park is a sailing club, one of the few which run courses throughout the year to teach new members the sport.

The centre point of the site is a surprisingly large church with a high dome, one of the best known landmarks of Southampton Water. It is now used as a Heritage Centre and contains a permanent exhibition of the history of the Royal Victoria and the Solent coast in general - at peace and war. The reminiscences of those who once worked at the hospital, or were treated there, are being collected on tape. The chapel itself, which was interdenominational, was said by one chaplain to have an 'uniquely picturesque congregation'. The chapel tower is being renovated as a viewing platform.

Prominent though it was, the chapel was just a small section of the hospital, whose main buildings were a quarter of a mile long, making it probably the longest building in the world in its early days. It became notorious even before completion because of staunch opposition to its design from Florence Nightingale, following her appalling experiences of military hospital life in Turkey. However, the building was completed because of Queen Victoria's determination and for the remainder of her long reign she was a frequent visitor to its wards. Probably the worst aspect of the building was the design of the seemingly end-less corridors which looked out over the nearby water while the patients lay in sunless rooms facing the backyards where the orderlies had their barracks.

Each winter wounded and sick troops were brought in troop ships and hospital ships from every part of the Empire around the world. Some were landed directly on the hospital's long pier but most arrived by road or ambulance train from the docks. At the back of the courtyards the Royal Victoria had its own station and branch line railway, which came into use at the time of the Boer War. Many of the returning invalids were

cared for by the nursing sisters who now came to be trained in increasing numbers at Netley. The laboratories were one of the leading centres of medical research, especially in the field of tropical disease, and its staff were involved in the setting up of the Red Cross Organisation.

The First World War put immense strain on the staff at Netley, which was designated the No. 1 base hospital. A huge Red Cross camp was built in the grounds with treatment rooms of all kinds and even operating theatres in the huts. All this was swept away after the war ended.

One of the few surviving buildings on the site is an attractive timber recreational hall, the Y.M.C.A., put up in the early days of World War II

'HOW TO GET THERE'

From Southampton cross new Itchen bridge to Woolston, then follow signs to Weston shore and Netley. Country Park entrance at far end of village street, past 'The Prince Consort' public house.
From M27 (junction 8) follow signs for A27 roundabout and then B3397 (to Hamble). Turn right as to Netley Abbey (signposted). At bottom of Station Road turn left.

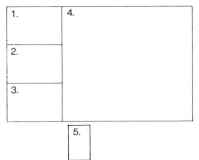

1. Cyclists in the Park
2. Part of Heritage Centre Exhibition
3. The Hospital Pier, demolished in the 1950s
4. Aerial view of the site
5. Cemetery Stone

4: *Eastleigh Borough Council*
3: *Royal Army Nursing Corps*
1: *Mike Goddard*
2: *Hampshire Recreation Department*

and first used by soldiers evacuated from Dunkirk. The American Forces later took over the Royal Victoria and are supposed to have driven along the corridors in jeeps. The old buildings were used much less in the following years and were said to be too expensive to maintain by the 1960s. The Empire had gone and the Victorian monster was demolished. The last moment of excitement came with the discovery of the very first Victoria Cross, which had been laid under the foundation stone.

A full history of the hospital and the part it played in army life in the days of the Empire is told in a richly illustrated souvenir booklet on sale at the Park Centre, which has been created in the Y.M.C.A. building. Royal Victoria is now a fine place for walking and picnicking, or just sitting by the beach. Its level roadways are particularly pleasant for cycling or even roller skating! The Park Centre has a tea-room and an open-air 'pavement' cafe. The Solent Way passes through the Park before crossing (on a permissive path that may occasionally be closed) through the grounds of the British Aero-Space factory at Hamble. The Way emerges onto Hamble Common and then by a lane enters Hamble itself. A ferry boat crosses the river throughout the year and allows walkers to continue to Hill Head from Warsash. For most visitors the Country Park will be sufficient to explore, and they will find few spots which are more ideally enjoyable than this.

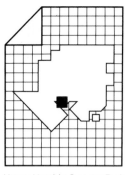

Upper Hamble Country Park and Hampshire Farm Museum (Hampshire County Council)

Recreation Department,
Pylands Lane,
Bursledon,
Southampton,
Hampshire
SO23 8DH
Telephone
(Ranger) Bursledon (042121)
2534
(Office) Winchester (0962)
64221
(Farm) Botley (04892) 87055

Price Guide - Free
Farm - B

Car Parking
Charge
Free at Farm

Handicapped
Partially suitable (disabled
toilet and gravelled paths),
otherwise depends on
condition of paths

Party Visits
By arrangement

Publications etc.
Leaflets
Guide
Trails on site
Guided walks available

Where to eat
Picnic tables on site
Cafe at Museum

Time to allow
2 - 4 hours

Open
Every day of the year
Farm 10-6 during season
check for winter opening

Special Events
Programme of demonstrations
held at weekends

**Friends of the Hampshire
Farm Museum**
Membership gives free
admission, a quarterly newsletter and occasional social
events such as a Harvest
Supper

UPPER HAMBLE COUNTRY PARK
& HAMPSHIRE FARM MUSEUM

For most visitors the Hamble River is typified by the boatyard and packed marinas seen from Bursledon Bridge - the sort of scene depicted in the BBC series *Howards Way,* which was filmed hereabouts. But this vibrant world of expensive yachts stops, of necessity, at the relatively low A27 road-bridge. Above are the quiet muddy reaches of the upper river and Country Park. Here the native trees and wildlife of the ancient drowned tributary flourish, though the trees have been depleted by generations of working. It is left to the under 'storey' and ground cover, the flowers and bushes, to prove their long history.

The woodlands between Botley and Bursledon have been used in many ways over the years. In mediaeval times Venetian galleys were rowed up the Hamble to collect ash, which was locally harvested. To this day the ash is still one of the best woods for making oars for which the Venetians must have had a great need. For centuries large areas were coppiced for firewood, much of it being carted to Southampton. In Victorian days the woodlands along the Hamble were almost ravaged to supply a chemical works producing alkali and smelting iron near the Hamble river-mouth, and more recently large parts were cleared for gravel-pits and brickworks.

During the last war a Navy camp was built where Marines were gathered for training and eventual departure for the Normandy invasion. The whole of Southern England bristled with camps set up for this short-lived but critical moment, but *HMS Cricket,* as the camp was known, must have been ideal with its water-front and leafy camouflage Here motorised landing-craft commandos of the 606 Flotilla arrived in the early summer of 1944. The officer commanding *HMS Cricket* was killed two days after landing on the beaches.

The park has a long shoreline and is a place of great beauty. There are grassy riverbanks and tide-filled creeks as well as long views up and down stream. From Botley, where the narrow river was once harnessed by a large mill, down to the motorway the Hamble is perhaps as unspoilt as the Beaulieu River. With each high-tide there is room to manoeuvre small craft but few explore here apart from boats from a YMCA Centre at Fairthorne Manor, scouts and youths groups or members of the Activities Centre for the Handicapped, which is in the Country Park.

Five hundred years ago these waters were used as a collecting ground, or 'road' for the King's ships when not at sea, and since then sailing ships and many others have been left to rot and disappear eventually in the mud. At low tide some of their skeletons can still be traced. One was the greatest vessel of her day, *The Grace Dieu,* built in Southampton for Henry V in 1418, which still entices archaelogists 540 years after sinking. Although built like a Viking longship she was as large as the *Victory!* She was leaking badly even as she was towed to the Hamble for fitting and stores and there she stayed until twenty years

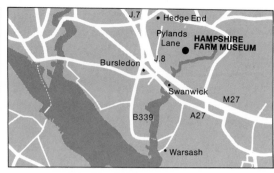

later when she was struck by lightning and caught fire, remaining to this day in the mud opposite the park shore.

Youth camping on a site run by the Scouts is carried out in the park, which also includes the Queen Elizabeth II Jubilee Activities Centre for the Disabled. Here people with every kind of handicap are able to relax and to learn or practice many sports including archery, sailing and riding.

HAMPSHIRE FARM MUSEUM

Farmyards where chickens roam and dung stands in a pile have virtually disappeared from the English countryside. This is one of the reasons that Manor Farm, Botley, has been preserved: it is a living record of an era of farming beloved by many and fast becoming a distant memory. To walk around the farmyard at the Hampshire Farm Museum is to go back in time. Norfolk Black Turkeys, now a rare breed, peck amongst the debris, sows and their young wallow in the sties and there are hens everywhere - such traditional breeds as Rhode Island Red, Leghorn and Light Sussex. The cattle, too, are the now-rare Shorthorns, while the stable block is occupied by Janey the shire horse.

The aim of the museum is to show farming as it was during 1850-1950, a period when the horse gave way to the tractor and farming with chemicals began, yet farms were mostly owner-run in relatively small units. During the 19th century cattle and cereals were important at Manor Farm, together with coppicing and timber, mainly for naval use. In the early part of the present century, horses for the growing town of Southampton were bred and reared here. Today, the museum staff still run it as a farm, albeit of small acreage, growing wheat, hay and root crops for the animals. The great Timber Barn was thatched with wheat straw grown on the farm - it took the entire product of 4 acres . . . and a little more!

Manor Farm is now situated in a relatively remote position, at the end of a long winding lane in the far eastern corner of the Upper Hamble Country Park. At one time, however, it was at the centre of Botley, which later grew up a mile to the north. The present farmyard contains the remains of the former parish church, now used for exhibitions, which was progressively abandoned in favour of a more central church built in 1836. William Cobbett, who farmed less than a mile away, cruelly caricatured 'The Botley Parson', Richard Baker, in his *Rural Rides.*

The antiquity of the farm site is reflected in the present farmhouse, which derives from a mediaeval open hall. Much of the house is open to

'HOW TO GET THERE'

From M27, exit at Junction 8 and follow signposts. Museum is reached via the entrance to the Upper Hamble Country Park. From Southampton, take A3024 or A3025 to A27 and turn left at large roundabout at approach to Bursledon, signposted to Hedge End. Country Park is in Pylands Lane, on right after passing under the M27.

visitors and contains reconstructions of domestic life on the farm - a kitchen and iron range, a sparsely furnished bedroom and a scullery complete with a huge mangle. Other buildings of the original farm also house displays, including dairying in the former cowshed and farm machinery in the cart shelter. One particularly interesting exhibit is an early tractor, a Titan of 1919, of a type shipped from the United States to improve productivity during the First World War. The great Red Barn, once used to store corn - especially during the Napoleonic Wars - has been converted to a visitor's centre; it includes a small theatre where a film about the farm is regularly shown.

The original farm site has been added to and expanded to show a range of other typical farm buildings, including a large 18th century barn on staddle stones, a typical Hampshire structure which came from Longstock in the Test valley. Nearby are two craft workshops, which have also been saved from demolition and brought to Manor Farm. The forge came locally from Hedge End, and was last used in the 1950s. The wheel-wright's shop, provided with plenty of window space for this most exacting of crafts, was discovered in Nether Wallop, near Stockbridge, complete with tools left from the 1920s.

The old crafts are regularly demonstrated at Manor Farm. Indeed, as well as making 'a day out', the Hampshire Farm Museum provides an opportunity to observe at first hand the traditional methods of farming. Special events are held at weekends and enable specialists to discuss the finer points of their crafts with visitors. The demonstrations cover sheep shearing, reaping and corn dolly making, threshing and hedging, hurdle making and other traditional activities. BS

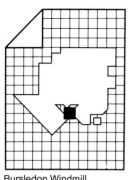

BURSLEDON WINDMILL

On high land overlooking the Hamble River and the Solent stands the brick tower of a mill which is almost unique. Although it only dates from 1813, the fact that it has been in decay for more than a century has, paradoxically, helped to preserve enough of its wooden machinery to provide a pattern for reconstruction. By contrast, most other similar mills had their original mechanism replaced by cast-iron construction in the second half of the last century.

Bursledon is one of about 120 windmills that were once worked in Hampshire, but only five of these have survived in any form and only Bursledon can be restored. The efforts of the Hampshire Buildings Preservation Trust and the Friends of Burseldon Windmill over the past few years have ensured that the mill is now safe from further decay. It can be viewed from time to time on Open Days and will be opened to the public regularly within a year or two.

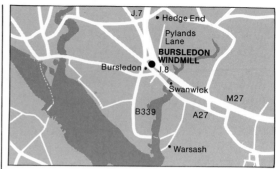

Recently the cap and the internal machinery of the mill have been restored by craftsman Jim Lewis, using similar hand tools to those of the original millwrights and following the plans of mill expert John Reynolds. The 'clinker' construction of the cap is similar to that of a boat, which is very appropriate for a place like Bursledon, which has long been known for the skills of its shipwrights.

When the mill is once more restored to a condition in which it can grind corn, to earn its living, the sails will turn a wooden windshaft set in the cap at an angle and fashioned from an oak trunk two feet across and 18 feet long. Attached

Like all tower mills, the windmill at Bursledon had its great sails turned into the wind by rotating the cap at the top into the required position. This was done by hand, using an endless chain gear and wheel, which means that the mill was already rather old-fashioned when it was built, for the 'fantail' - a sort of mini-windmill to steer the sails - had been invented for more than 60 years. Its sails were also outmoded, since they were furled and unfurled by hand, according to the strength of the wind. More convenient methods of doing this with 'shutters' date from the 1770s, and a few years before the mill was built a semi-automatic method of adjusting the area of the sails had been devised.

to this great timber is the brake wheel, a large wooden cog-wheel to which is applied a brake to bring the mill to a standstill. This wheel engages with a smaller cog at the top of a shaft running vertically through the tower, thus transmitting power to a large cog-wheel at the base of the tower. This, in turn, drives three sets of millstones lying above it.

When Bursledon windmill is fully restored it will once more be used to grind flour. A staddlestone granary and a barn have been rescued from elsewhere in the country and re-erected on the site. Visitors will be able to inspect the mill machinery or view displays of the mill and milling in the barn.   BS

1.   New wooden bevel
     gears.
2.   The Working Windmill
     1872.

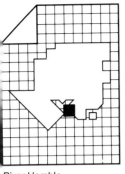

River Hamble

For enquiries about the river telephone the Harbour Master's Office at Warsash tel: Locks Heath (048 95) 6387 or the County Recreation Department, Winchester, tel: (0962) 64221

Visitors guide available free from Harbour Master's Office.

River Trips
Blue Star Boats,
The Foreshore,
Hamble
Telephone Hamble
(0703) 453542 or
(04215) 60031

Ferry Information
R.J. Sedgwick
The Hard, Hamble
Telephone Hamble
(0703) 452352

River bank footpath down to Warsash on east bank due to be opened late summer 1986

RIVER HAMBLE

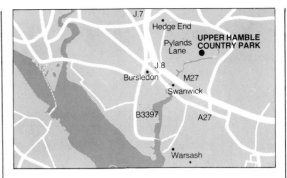

Until 1800 travellers between Southampton and Portsmouth had to take a long detour up to Botley or cross the River Hamble on a small ferry boat near Bursledon. Right up until 1933 travellers and goods-traffic had to stop to pay a toll to cross Bursledon's first small wooden bridge, which was then replaced by the concrete structure still used for the A27 today. Most of the traffic now almost flies over the valley on the M27 with little more than a glimpse of the unspoilt greenery and peace on one side, upstream, and on the other side work-a-day untidiness, and crowded yachts beyond the A27 bridge. The motorist travelling on the old main road can turn either way -towards the boat-parks packed with hundreds of craft, or to the old unspoilt river, still a haven of peace and quiet.

Many ships were built in yards along the river banks through the centuries. The Hamble had a golden age in the decade before Trafalgar, with many warships built under the small cliff near the 'Jolly Sailor' Inn at Bursledon; the yard was named later after Nelson's flagship for the Battle of Copenhagen, the *Elephant,* launched here in 1786.

In the river's repair yards old barges can be found and even relics of operations carried out during the last war. This is a curious world of make-and-mend, of individualists for whom life on board is the only one, however ancient their vessel.

In complete contrast is the big business of building boats and mooring them. The two go hand-in-hand but there are limits to the number of boats which can be kept and used in such a small river. From time to time the channel becomes jammed with traffic.

A ferryman still runs an all-year-round service across the river from Hamble village quayside to a shelter on the bank north of Warsash, continuing a tradition known to date back to the 1500s. From the Hard at Hamble, with its car-park, there is a small company which each summer operates boat trips up the river, into Southampton Water and sometimes over to Calshot Point.

Where can one walk by the Hamble? There are many paths in the Upper Hamble Country Park including one which runs south to Bursledon by the A27 bridge. Another, on the east bank, recently restored, continues down to Warsash. For many years, breaches interrupted the route but repairs of the path have now been carried out to plug the gaps. Whether one explores the river on foot or by boat there is plenty to see. Visitors may like to watch out for some of the historic yachts moored along the Hamble, including *Lulworth,* one of the large yachts built in the 1920s, foil to the 18th century opinion that "anyone going to sea for pleasure would go to Hell for a pastime".

1. Boats on the Bursledon Marina.

2. River Hamble

1: *Hampshire Country Recreation Department*

49

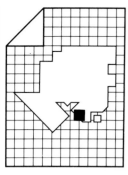

Titchfield Haven Nature Reserve.

Visits on guided tours only. For information about the reserve, and to book visit permits telephone the Naturalist Ranger. Telephone Hillhead (0329) 662145 or Hampshire County Recreation Department Telephone Winchester (0962) 64221

Hook-with-Warsash Nature Reserve

For information, contact same telephone numbers as given for Titchfield Haven Nature Reserve.

Car Parking
Brownwich shore: At Thatchers Copse, follow signs for Meon from Titchfield. Chilling and Hook shore: At end of Hook Lane, off Warsash Road.

Titchfield Abbey
(English Heritage)
Titchfield,
Fareham,
Hampshire
PO15 5RA
Telephone
Titchfield (0329) 43016

Price Guide - A

Car Parking
Free

Handicapped
Suitable

Party Visits
By arrangement -
Phone The Custodian

Publications
Guidebook

Where to eat
Suitable picnic area nearby

Time to allow
Half an hour

Open
All year (except 24-26 December, 1st January, May Day Bank Holiday). March - October, 9.30am-6.30pm, weekdays, Sundays, 2-6.30pm. October - March, 9.30am-4.pm, weekdays, Sundays, 2-4pm.

Public Transport
Bus Services -
Provincial buses from Fareham and Southampton every half-hour on weekdays, every 2 hours on Sunday

Nearby Attractions
Titchfield Tithe Barn (when open for sale of produce)
Fort Brockhurst
HMS Alliance Submarine Museum
Naval Ordnance Museum

HOOK SHORE & TITCHFIELD

The few miles of coastal path between the small village of Warsash and the mouth of the River Meon at Hill Head are the least spoilt on Hampshire's accessible coastline, which is ironic for the Hamble river, where the path starts, has the greatest concentration of yachting in the British Isles. Although the days of great ship building at Warsash have passed it is the location of the College of Maritime Studies, probably Britain's most advanced nautical school, several hundred yards down stream. Even today sail training is part of the education given to the students who are prepared for careers in the Merchant Marine. The college's 80 ft ketch can sometimes be seen off the school's long pier. Its predecessor *Mayona* was lost at sea after winning the first of the Tall Ship races to Lisbon in 1956.

The College of Maritime Studies probably stands close to the site of a wooden tower, one of a pair at the mouth of the Hamble built during the Hundred Years War to protect the river's anchorages. It was here also that until a hundred years ago a factory stood, typical of the beginnings of the chemical industry, which manufactured alkali by distilling wood ash, and heating with salt and chalk. One by-product was charcoal, which was used on site for iron smelting, and the chalk was also used here, together with sea mud for the manufacture of Portland Cement.

South of Warsash, the path crosses the mouth of the Hook river, dammed to make a lake two hundred years ago by William Hornby who had retired in 1803 at 30 as Governor of Bombay, "the Englishman's Graveyard". He cleared an old village to build a palatial mansion surrounded by a fitting park. The Hook river is locally believed to have been a harbour and refuge for ships in gales, as well as a place for ship building and repair.

The low-lying fields adjacent to the coast together with the mud banks, salt marshes and the wooded valley of Hook have been designated a nature reserve. This is an attractive and unspoilt coast with a rich diversity of habitats in close proximity: brackish coastal grazing marshes (formerly salt works and more recently golf links), reed beds and fresh water marsh, valley woodlands, shingle beach, tidal mudflats and shell beds as well as salt marsh. Careful management is required to improve and protect the grassland to replant the hedgerows and woodlands which have been neglected, and to create new freshwater pools. With such a spectrum of plant and animal communities it is an ideal place for the study of ecology and especially ornithology. Much of the reserve can be seen from the nearby Solent Way and two local footpaths which cross it. It could well prove to be the most richly varied of Hampshire's many nature reserves.

Beyond 'Solent Breezes', the County's only coastal caravan park, the path follows a cliff top, behind which lie the fields of Chilling and Brownwich farms. A wartime proposal for a major airport here never materialised but would have combined a new harbour for a sea-plane base with the usual runways of a land aerodrome.

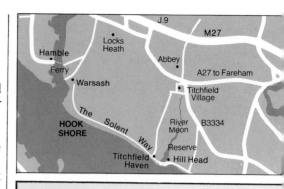

The path continues along the beach to the road and causeway across the mouth of the River Meon, at Hill Head. An important nature reserve has been established here at Titchfield Haven, the estuary of the River Meon. Today it consists mainly of freshwater marshes, dense reedbeds and low-lying marshy fields which attract large numbers of wintering wildfowl. The naturalist ranger shows parties round the reserve which has a variety of observation hides. From these one can watch over specially created lagoons, and enjoy listening to the calls of the numerous birds which gather on well-protected islands.

'HOW TO GET THERE'

From A27 at Sarisbury (near Junction 9 on M27) follow the signs for Warsash. Car parks near Harbour Master's office. Alternative, to Hillhead, follow signs for Titchfield off A27. In village turn right into Coach Hill and left down Posbrook Lane leading to seafront car park. For Titchfield Abbey from M27 (Junction 9) join A27 to east. Near Titchfield turn left, Mill Street, sign-posted to Abbey ruins.

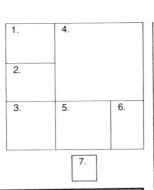

1.		4.	
2.			
3.	5.		6.

7.

1 & 2 Hook shore
3. Reedbeds at Titchfield Haven Nature Reserve
4. Walkway through the reeds
5. Earl of Southampton monument in Titchfield Church
6. Titchfield tithe barn - interior
7. Gatehouse, Titchfield Abbey

3: *Hampshire County Recreation Department*
6: *Hampshire County Planning Department*
7: *Bridget Hillyard Drawing*

After the dissolution of the monastery the church here was converted into a gatehouse for the new owner, Thomas Wriothesley, who also purchased Beaulieu Abbey. The gatehouse still stands with its four-storey, eight-sided towers while in the remaining walls of the nave can be seen smaller and more homely windows inserted to replace the original ecclesiastical windows. The site also includes walls round the abbey courtyard and, marked on the ground, the continuing line of the choir and church; nearby was the Canons' Chapter House and the Library that was once so well stocked.

An engraving of the buildings made in 1733 shows Tudor castellations along the nave, with the turreted towers and decorative brickwork chimneys which transformed the abbey into an elegant home. Unfortunately, most of the house was demolished in 1781.

The principal interest of Titchfield lies in its connections with the Wriothesleys, who were created Earls of Southampton. The first Earl rose to power and wealth, only to be dismissed from office and die in early middle-age. His grandson was Shakespeare's patron, and so some of the great plays may have been acted first here. Tradition has it that the first performance of 'Romeo and Juliet' took place in the superb tithe barn of Fern Hill Farm near to the ruins and the mediaeval fish ponds. Today the barn is regarded as one of the most important structures in Hampshire, a unique timber-framed building which dates back to the 15th century and includes many French features. Its size is also specially impressive, since it is 150 feet long and 40 feet wide.

The ruins are separated from the attractive village nearby by the A27 which by-passes Titchfield, but a visit is recommended if only to see the church which has one of the finest sculptured tombs in Hampshire, made for the second Earl, his father and mother. On the walls of the chapel there is a display about the history of the parish and the church, in which there is much else to be seen and studied.

In mediaeval times the River Meon was, like the Beaulieu and Hamble rivers today, open to the tides, and indeed the town is said to have been a port until 1611 when the third Earl dug a canal, blocked the river-mouth and reclaimed the salt marshes as pasture. This act, which the parish register described as the 'shutting out of Titchfield Haven by one Richard Talbotte's industrie under God's permission' has ever since been celebrated annually with a bonfire night. The canal can still be traced for its towpath is even today a right-of-way, but the navigation was a failure and the port died. The centre of the village has changed little since.

TITCHFIELD

The Abbey of Titchfield was founded by the same Bishop of Winchester as Netley but for a different Order, the Premonstratensian canons who, because of their white habits, were known as the White Canons. The original abbeys were probably very similar, and although much less remains at Titchfield the ruins are very impressive.

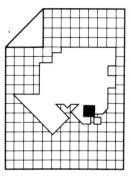

Southwick Brewhouse

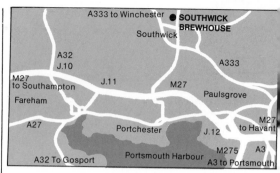

Southwick Brewhouse
(Southwick and Roche Court Estates)

High Street,
Southwick,
Hampshire,
PO17 6EB
Telephone
(0705) 380978 or 376271

Price Guide - B
(Visits by appointment only)

Handicapped
Not suitable

Car Parking
Free - Nearby

Party Visits
By arrangement only.
Guided tours.

Publications
Leaflet

Where to eat
Pubs nearby

Time to allow
1 hour

Open
Any reasonable time by
appointment, with the
exception of Sunday morning

Public Transport
Bus Services -
Portsmouth Corporation
buses from Southsea sea-
front and Commercial Road,
also from Wickham, four
journeys a day, Monday-
Saturday.

Nearby Attractions
Fort Nelson
Sir George Staunton Estate
Havant Museum
Farlington Marshes

Hampshire Buildings
Preservation Trust. Southwick
Brewhouse was restored with
the aid of generous financial
assistance from the
Hampshire Buildings
Preservation Trust.

When brewer George Olding locked up the Southwick Brewhouse for the last time before retirement in 1956 he left behind the workings of a traditional village industry which is now virtually extinct. But he took with him the skill of operating it, for every brew had been carried out 'in secret', with no one present but himself. Nonetheless, when the Southampton University Industrial Archaeology Group and other enthusiasts decided to celebrate the restoration of the works in June 1985, they managed to stage a commemorative brew which led to 300 gallons of fine ale, admittedly with the aid of a retired professional brewer. Alas, this is unlikely to be repeated, for the economics of small-scale brewing and the needs of the Customs and Excise make it an expensive business. Those bottles of Southwick beer are therefore likely to become collectors' items.

leached out and converted to sugar. The resulting liquid, the wort, was drained into a large barrel on the ground floor, the underback. Hereafter the wort was pumped back upstairs to a large copper vessel, where it was boiled for two hours and hops and sugar were added. Spent hops were filtered out in the hopback, which has perforated bottom plates, and after cooling the product was piped to two huge fermenting casks.

After adding yeast the brew formed a head 'like the moon's surface', some of which was raked

The brewhouse was operated to supply an off-licence in Portsmouth and a nearby pub, The Golden Lion. Owned by the Southwick Estates, like much of the village, the pub had sold 'Hunt's Home-Brewed Ales' for a hundred years or more. Its tenants were expected to keep up a high standard, one lease specifing that only 'best Kentish hops' and 'best Welsh coal' were to be used. The coal was needed for the steam engine which supplied power to the various pieces of machinery in the works. It still works and is lovingly cared for by the brewhouse's curator, Tony Dowsett. One of the 'tricks' that George Olding had to remember at the end of the day was to pump up water to the tank so that there would be water there to start the engine and avoid a 'catch 22' situation.

Before brewing could begin the malt (about four 2-cwt bags) had to be cracked in the grist mill on the first floor and the hot water (liquor) got ready. This was performed for the last twenty years of the brewhouse's life by Thomas Carter, a retired farmworker. But he was never allowed to be present when the brewing was in progress. The cracked malt was fed from a hopper (the grist case) into a large circular container, the mash tun, where it soaked for two hours to allow its starch to be

off and kept for the next brew. Brewing usually continued for three to four days, during which the brewer would stir the brew from time to time and take samples. One important task was to enter the specific gravity of the drink in the Charge Book, which was kept on the little desk at the head of the stairs and checked frequently by the Excise Officer. Finally, the finished product would be drawn off into casks on the ground floor.

Southwick Brewhouse, which dates from the early 19th century, was very much a 'make do and mend' affair with a character of its own, but it is typical of the many similar works that once kept the countryside in beer. It also served Thomas Carter well, for part of his pay was 'all the beer he could drink'!

BS

The Southwick Brewer,
George Olding.
(From Secretive Southwell.
Domesday to D.Day) by
G.R. O'Connell

The Mash Tun
Barry Shurlock

THE FERRY BOAT
HAYLING ISLAND

The Ferry Boat,
Hayling Island
Photo: John Holder

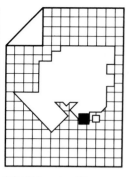

H.M. Submarine Alliance

(Royal Navy Submarine Museum)
H.M.S. Dolphin,
Gosport,
Hampshire,
PO12 2AB
Telephone
Gosport (0705) 529217

Price Guide - C

Car Parking
Nearby

Handicapped
Unsuitable

Party Visits
Tours and educational
resources

Publications etc.
Leaflet
Guidebook
Displays
Audio visual show

Where to eat
Cafe/tea-room
Picnic area at Haslar Road
Pontoon
Picnic tables on site

Time to allow
1 - 2 hours

Open
All year (except Christmas
Day) 9.30am-4.30pm
May be worthwhile to check
in winter

Public Transport
Bus Services -
Every hour from Southampton
to Gosport Ferry Terminus,
Monday-Saturday. Frequent
buses from Fareham, daily.
Provincial buses from Ferry
Terminus, daily.
Rail Services -
Portsmouth Harbour Station
(ferry to Gosport Hard)

Nearby Attractions
Gosport Museum
Royal Navy Museum
H.M.S. Victory
Fort Brockhurst
Naval Ordnance Museum

H.M.S. ALLIANCE ROYAL NAVY SUBMARINE MUSEUM

Just as early submarine pioneers were thought to be incredible, they too would surely find it hard to comprehend that the balance of world power is now daily affected by the offspring of their dreams. The very first submarine to be adopted by the Royal Navy, *H.M. Submarine Torpedo Boat No.1,* generally known as *Holland I,* is now on display in Hampshire at a unique museum which is essential for anyone with the least interest in 20th century warfare.

'HOW TO GET THERE'
From M27 (junction 11) follo
signs to A27 Fareham then
A32 to Gosport. From near
Ferry take B3333, and
immediately left over
Haslar bridge. Alliance
and H.M.S. Dolphin sign-
posted. Car-park near
Hospital entrance.

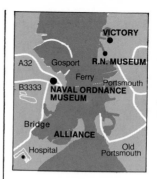

including one of the earliest which was successfu an American foot-pedalled machine of 1776. Ther are photographs of old crews in cramped quarters

It stands at Gosport, across the narrow entrance of Portsmouth Harbour, on the low-lying spit of Fort Blockhouse. This has been a base for submarines since their earliest days at the turn of the century, when they were reluctantly admitted to the Navy. Today, when the role of the submarine is so crucial, it is difficult to imagine the hostility towards these weapons, which were regarded as 'damned un-English' and whose crew were considered pirates who should be hanged in wartime! The first submarines included some curious designs. The Royal Navy Submarine Museum which has been developed by H.M.S. *Dolphin,* the submarine base, has many extraordinary models

collections of skull-and-crossbones flags adopted by crews in World War II, and numerous paintings of wartime episodes. Also on view are the torpedoes which made submarines such a formidable force. There is also a large model of one of the modern Hunter-killer nuclear submarines, half as long again as *Alliance* at 420 feet, with 143 crew compared to 64.

Alliance is displayed out of the water on cradles, allowing doors to be cut into the hull at either end. This makes it very much easier for visitors to embark since there is no need to climb down the usual narrow hatches! Outside, the hull is sleek and streamlined, while inside is an amazing world of pipes and handles, levers and gauges, with sound effects that help to re-create the atmosphere

endured by the submariner. Visitors are shown the workings of the *Alliance* and similar craft in an audiovisual briefing followed by guided tours given by retired submariner guides.

Alliance seems amazingly small for 64 men, and indeed bunks were used in rotation, but she was actually regarded as a spacious vessel. She was completed just as World War II ended, and intended for use in the Pacific War against Japan. She had room for 20 'fish' (torpedoes) and the forward torpedo compartment was large enough for 'community' gatherings. However, she is the oldest R.N. submarine left and the last to have such a purely mechanical interior "decor", newer craft being fitted with laminated plastics. Her service finished in the early 70s. *Alliance*, incidentally, was once caught off the Isle of Wight and beached in a storm.

In 1983 the Submarine Museum acquired 'the greatest discovery in marine archaeology of recent years', *Holland I*. She was the Navy's first submersible vessel and sank in 1913 near Plymouth on the way to the breaker's yard, by which time the Navy had more than 80 submarines in commission.

John Phillip Holland left his native Ireland and emigrated to America in 1873 with one idea in mind - to build submarines to combat the British Fleet which he apparently felt was in some measure preventing Ireland from becoming independent. He eventually abandoned this plan and, after a long struggle, persuaded the American Navy to buy his most successful design at the end of the century. He later sold his design to Britain - for the Royal Navy which he had originally intended to destroy! *Holland I* was duly launched without ceremony at Vickers, Barrow-in-Furness, in 1901 and she served faithfully in the Royal Navy for a dozen years. Although practically all the major navies of the world adopted the same type of submarine at the beginning of the century, *Holland I* is the only surviving example.

In 1982, under the Museum's direction, the wreck was located and salvaged: the little submarine was found to be in outstandingly good condition. She is now being refitted and brought back to her service condition. But even before her equipment is reinstalled visitors get a very good impression of what it must have been like to submerge in those early days. The hull is sound and the single 18" torpedo tube, the splendid Edwardian WC with its mahogony seat and cover, the main engine and main motor are all in remarkably good condition after 69 years on the seabed. The torpedo hatch opened with a slight tug, the steel springs and the petrol engine were free of corrosion and galvanic action had inexplicably not occurred between adjacent bronze and steel components. So baffled are expert materials scientists that it has even been suggested that the *Holland I* just happened to settle in a part of the English Channel where there is an anomalous magnetic field!

Visiting the little 'submarine boat' is a unique experience and after seeing her comparatively huge descendent, H.M.S. *Alliance*, you may wonder what sort of men they were that dared to take themselves below water for the first time in this tiny submarine whose shape, incidentally, foreshadowed the nuclear monsters of today.

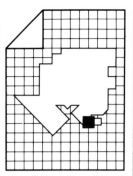

Naval Ordnance Museum
(Ministry of Defence)

Royal Naval Armaments
Depot,
Priddy's Hard,
Gosport,
Hampshire
PO12 4LE
Telephone
(0705) 822351 Ext. 44225

Note: Visitors usually come in
parties, though individuals
can be added to existing
arrangements

Price Guide - Free

Car Parking
Free

Handicapped
Suitable in most areas, but no
suitable toilets.

Party Visits
Guided tours, by arrangement
only.

Publications
Leaflet

Where to eat
Pubs nearby

Time to allow
1.5 hours

Open
Monday - Friday 8-4

Public Transport
Bus Services -
Provincial buses from
Gosport and Fareham every
half-hour on weekdays.
Rail Services -
Portsmouth Harbour Station:
museum reached by ferry and
15-20 minutes walk

Nearby Attractions
Fort Brockhurst
Royal Navy Submarine
Museum
Portsmouth and Southsea
  Old Portsmouth
  Spitbank Fort
  HMS *Victory*
  Royal Navy Museum
  Mary Rose
  D-Day Museum
  Royal Marines Museum
  Eastney Pumping Station

NAVAL ORDNANCE MUSEUM
PRIDDY'S HARD, GOSPORT

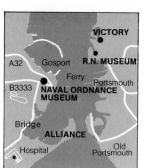

'HOW TO GET THERE'
Leave M27 at Junction 11 for
Fareham and follow signs for
A32 to Gosport. On northern
outskirts of town turn left
at Fort Brockhurst into Elson
Road. Follow signs to RNAD
Priddy's Hard and report at
main gate.

All gunpowder used by the Navy was once stored in the heart of Old Portsmouth, in the Square Tower, a building which still stands. Complaints about the hazards of this practice led to the building of a special depot in a remote area on the Gosport side of the harbour more than two hundred years ago. This is Priddy's Hard, more recently known as the Royal Navy Armaments Depot. Constructed in 1771 on land purchased by the Board of Ordnance from Jane Priddy and the Rev. Thomas Missing, the original buildings have all survived, including the powder magazine, which now houses the Naval Ordnance Museum. The hazards of sparking were so great in a building designed to hold 6000 barrels of gunpowder that the floorboards were held down with timber pegs, which can still be seen.

Priddy's Hard grew considerably during the 19th century, though it held no guns, which were all kept at the Gunwharf, Portsmouth, now occupied by H.M.S. *Vernon*. As the century advanced, new types of armaments developed: round shot gave way to the shell, gun barrels were rifled for accuracy and guns of larger and larger calibres were manufactured. A major influence in this 'arms war' was the advent of the armour-plated ship, led by H.M.S. *Warrior*, soon to be on show at Portsmouth. Later, torpedoes and mines were added to the armaments carried by ships, while gunpowder was supplanted by guncotton, TNT and other explosives.

All these developments, and many more, are demonstrated by the exhibits at the Naval Ordnance Museum. There are early boat mortars, like those commanded by Captain Horatio Hornblower in C.S. Forester's novels, and the rope 'mantlets' that were hung over the sides of ships for protection. There are examples of the large flintlock guns that were mounted on

swivels and used to repel boarders, but inevitably most of the collection is devoted to the much greater numbers of modern arms. There are various types of machine gun, such as the crank-operated Hotchkiss of 1864, as well as much larger items - torpedoes, ant-submarine devices, and mines.

Many small arms, from both the UK and abroad, are also on display, but perhaps the most impressive sight in the museum is the huge breech of one of the 'big guns'. A 15-inch example is on show (the barrel was 54 feet in length), together with a variety of shells, including the largest ever used by the Navy, an 18-inch monster that had a range of 30 miles.

The collection at the Naval Ordnance Museum extends to the present day: a collection of modern missiles includes the scarred remains of a Sea Dart fired from HMS *Coventry* before she was lost in the South Atlantic in 1982.

The recent history of Naval armaments in Hampshire has seen the gradual dispersal of explosives to less populous areas. Priddy's Hard is due to close as a depot in the near future, though armaments will continue to be handled at Frater, Elson and Bedenham nearby, and further afield at Dean Hill, on the Wiltshire borders. Despite the large quantities of explosives held at these places, particularly during wartime, the only major accident occurred in recent times, in 1950, when ships were being loaded with depth charges and 1000-1b bombs at Bedenham Pier above Priddy's Hard. Fortunately, no one was killed, though several people were injured.

BS

Reconstruction of the powder
magazine at Priddy's Hard in
the 18th century

Naval Ordnance Museum

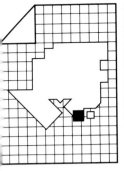

FORT BROCKHURST

In 1858 after a lengthy and heated debate work began on the Palmerston fortifications, a project that turned Portsmouth into one of the most strongly defended places in the world. Three of the great bulwarks then built have now been opened to the public, one from the line of six which ran from Stokes Bay to Fareham, Fort Brockhurst, and two from the further six along Portsdown Hill, named

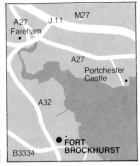

'HOW TO GET THERE'
From M27 (Junction 11) follow signs to A27 Fareham then A32 to Gosport. At traffic lights at junction with B3334 (from Titchfield) turn left. Car-park 50 yds.

Fort Nelson and Fort Widley. One of the sea forts can also be visited.

The story of these Victorian castles and the many other defences around the Solent is the subject of a fine exhibition at Fort Brockhurst, near Gosport. Despite its rather unattractive urban setting between Fareham and Gosport a visit to Brockhurst is well worthwhile. It has in some respects the atmosphere of a mediaeval fortress, for the entrance is across a drawbridge over a water-filled moat which surrounds the whole castle. The keep is a circular building and beyond it is a large parade ground surrounded by the ramparts. Here cannon were placed to

command the local approaches to Portsmouth Harbour in the event of an invasion of Southern England.

The form and positioning of the Fort was designed to defend a large area of ground

across which a powerful enemy might otherwise advance towards the Navy's arsenal, anchorages and dockyards. Building took place during several years of panic after the Crimean War when the French fleet modernised more quickly than our own. Meanwhile in this country a rifled cannon had just been developed, which could double the range of fire to 4½ miles and it was thought inevitable that these former allies would develop the same arms and be able to bombard the naval docks from comparative safety unless new forts were built. Such forts could give protection with limited man power, few guns covering each gap, for at this time the bulk of Britain's army was overseas, spread throughout the Empire.

Widley, Nelson, Brockhurst and the other forts were never even fully armed let alone put to the test, but one could argue that their presence did help to ensure the security and the peace that resulted. Over the years their facilities and accommodation were put to a variety of uses including the reception of soldiers back from the Front in World War I. With models and an audio-visual show, as well as many fascinating historical pictures, the story of the evolution of the defences of Portsmouth is displayed here in a late Victorian army building in the centre of the parade ground. Such forts have a look of invulnerability, for their defeat could only be achieved at great cost and, as in mediaeval castles, the defenders could retreat to the keep and pull up the final drawbridge.

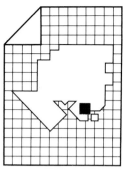

Fort Nelson
(Hampshire County Museum Service)
Military Road,
Fareham,
Hampshire
PO17 6AN
Telephone
(0705) 451155 (Curator,
Havant Museum) or
(0329) 233734/220623

Price Guide - B

Car Parking
Free

Handicapped
Only parts of the fort are suitable

Party Visits
By arrangement
Guided tours

Publications
Leaflet
Guidebook

Special Project
Cannon and artillery on loan from the Royal Armouries, HM Tower of London, are displayed within the fort.

Where to eat
Pubs in Southwick, Fareham or Portsmouth

Time to allow
1 ½ hours

Open
Easter-September,
Saturday and Sundays,
12-4.30

nearby Attractions
Porchester Castle
Southwick Brewhouse and Boarhunt Mill

Fort Widley
(Portsmouth City Council)
Portsdown Hill Road,
Portsmouth,
Hampshire
PO6 3LS
Telephone
Portsmouth (0705) 827261
(Oct.-March)
Cosham (0705) 382133 (April-Sept.)

Price Guide - C

Car Parking
Free

Handicapped
Unsuitable

Party Visits
By arrangement
Tours available

Publications
Leaflet
Guidebook

Time to allow
1 - 2 hours

Open
April-September 1.30-5.30pm
(last tour 5.00pm)
Saturdays, Sundays and Bank Holidays

Nearby Attractions
Porchester Castle
Sir George Staunton Estate

FORT NELSON & WIDLEY
& PORTSDOWN HILL

A suggestion to visit Fort Nelson or Fort Widley as well as Fort Brockhurst, described on the previous page, is no hype, for the contrasts between the two forts that stand on Portsdown Hill above Portsmouth and their lowland counterpart are quite marked. Both forts have been extensively renovated and restored in recent years with the aid of volunteers belonging to the Palmerston Forts Society and others.

At Nelson and Widley there could, of course, be no water-filled moats for their massive brick-built walls stand high up on a dry chalk hill. Yet their purpose was the same, to repulse an enemy approaching on land from the north, and the cannon and the strongest fortifications were directed accordingly. The fear was that the French might be able to force a landing on the coast of Sussex and, equipped with improved mobile guns, quickly sweep round to gain a commanding position on the hill. Such a manoeuvre would have made the dockyard an easy target for the new rifled artillery then available, with its much increased range and accuracy. In contrast to Brockhurst's self-contained circular keep, those of Nelson and Widley are straight-sided and formed sizeable barrack blocks. But the most remarkable feature of both forts is the way in which they were tucked into the natural profiles of the hill, so that despite having deep ditches cut into the chalk they were virtually invisible from the north. Even the chimneys were specially designed to avoid revealing telltale trails of smoke. Notable at both forts are the caponiers, gun positions projecting so as to allow raking fire to be directed along the walls.

It is likely that the generations of hard-living navvies who, having completed the country's canals, then built the new turnpike road system, only to carry on with the railway cuttings and embankments, may have found another two decades of employment on these major projects. Certainly their experience in tunnelling would have been useful, for the highlight of visits to Nelson and Widley is the chance to explore some of the hundreds of yards of deep tunnels through which the gunners were supplied with powder and shells from the underground arsenals.

An equally pleasant part of the tour of Widley is the chance to climb up on the roof of the barrack building for what is certainly the best view of Portsmouth, its harbour and Spithead. One can make out from here other elements of the Palmerston defences. Beyond Portsmouth can clearly be seen the four 'sea forts' which were completed in 1880, twenty years after the emergency had arisen. At the foot of Portsdown Hill stretches another element, the Hilsea lines which were re-fortified and armed so that they could fire at these hill-top forts should they fall. The first lines had been built in 1747 during one of the many periods of war with France during that century.

The tour of both forts is unfortunately difficult for the handicapped, because of steep staircases. Visits can only be made in guided parties.

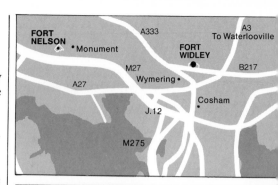

PORTSDOWN HILL

For at least three miles of its seven-mile length Portsdown Hill is open for walkers, with a narrow public open space which runs from near Fort Nelson to Fort Widley and the old main London to Portsmouth Road. Close to this land is the steep south-facing slope which has always been too difficult to plough and has never been suitable for building.

At the eastern end of the open space, near to the A3 London Road and the George Inn, was the site of the first British experiments with telegraphy in 1795, testing the use of telescopic observation of the coded shutter signs. For twenty years during the Napoleonic Wars a hut here was a vital link between London and the Fleet at

'HOW TO GET THERE'

Fort Nelson: Leave M27 at
Junction 12 and follow signs
to A27, Paulsgrove and
Porchester. Turn left onto A27
alongside Holiday Inn and on
outskirts of Fareham turn right
at roundabout, signposted
to Porchester Station. Take
Station Road up long hill and
turn left into Nelson Lane,
which comes out opposite the
Nelson Monument. Turn left,
Fort Nelson car park short
distance on left.

Top: Victorian artillery

Centre: Aerial view of
            Portsdown Hill
            and Fort Widley

Bottom: Inside Fort Nelson

Centre &   Portsmouth City
Top: Council

Bottom: Barry Shurlock

Portsmouth. Contrary to legend, the news of Trafalgar was not passed to London by the telegraph, for by the time of Napoleon's 'Hundred Days' and Waterloo the telegraph had been abandoned. While in operation messages to Portsdown from London were relayed nearly twelve miles from the next hut at Beacon Hill, Harting, which shows the quality of the telescopes used to observe the shutter.

Near the western end of the open down stands the Nelson Monument. This was raised by Nelson's officers and men, who provided a niche at the top which contains a bust of the admiral.

From the crest of the hill near Fort Widley there are views to the north to Butser Hill and the Hampshire downs, across an area once heavily wooded with the Forest of Bere. A public house by the Portsmouth Road, in this area, called 'The Heroes of Waterloo' was the centre of the growth of Waterlooville from 1815. The town was served later by a tram light railway between Portsmouth and Horndean which surmounted the heights of Portsdown. Portsdown Hill is traditionally a popular picnic area for Portsmouth citizens. The hill and its slopes were once crowned with trees and a windmill, and there was a tea-garden for parties to make the most of country excursions. On either side there was fine farmland which William Cobbet had earlier described as the finest corn country producing the earliest harvest: "Here the first sheaf is cut in England". For a century and a half a traditional country fair was held every 26th July on Portsdown Hill until the construction of the forts began in 1862. The beautiful downs were taken over by navvies, the windmill site was cleared to make way for Fort Widley, and the fine trees were cut down.

The view from Portsdown is still one of the most dramatic on the south coast, even though the old wooden ships have gone and the villages at its foot have been lost in the outpouring of the city's growth. In the evening many people enjoy driving along the top of Portsdown Hill to one of the three car parks to enjoy the superb night-time panoramic view of Portsmouth. This is a delightful experience for local people as well as for visitors who enjoy 'looking at the lights'.

With no sheep to graze the turf and keep down the growth of shrubs, it is pleasantly surprising that the slopes have many of the typical and some of the rarer chalk-loving flowers and herbs. Many orchids take up to ten years to mature and die after flowering just once: they should not be picked! The natural history of the hill and many other areas of interest around Portsmouth are described in an excellent Portsmouth Museum booklet by Janet Chamberlain.

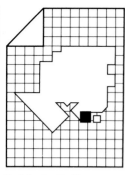

Portchester Castle
(English Heritage)

Near Fareham,
Hampshire,
PO16 9QW
Telephone
(0705) 378291 or
(0892) 48166

Price Guide - C

Car Parking
Free

Handicapped
Partially suitable, grounds and
low levels only

Party Visits
By arrangement, booking with
the Custodian (free school
visits)

Publications etc.
Guidebook
Display

Where to eat
Suitable picnic area nearby

Time to allow
1 - 2 hours

Open
All year except 24-26
December, 1st January and
May Day Bank Holiday
Summer: 9.30am-4.30pm
Winter: Monday-Saturday,
9.30am-1pm, 2-4.30pm,
Sunday, 2-4.30pm

Public Transport
Bus Services -
Provincial buses every half-
hour on weekdays from
Fareham and Southsea,
hourly on Sundays. Hourly
Southdown services to
Portchester from
Southampton, Monday -
Saturday, and from
Portsmouth every half-hour,
hourly on Sunday.
Rail Services -
Portchester Station 1 mile

Nearby Attractions
Fort Nelson
Fort Widley
Southwick Brewhouse
Fort Brockhurst

Harbour Cruises
Organised by Portsmouth
Harbour Ferry Co. Telephone
Gosport (07017) 24551 and
J.Butcher & Sons Telephone
Portsmouth (0705) 22584

PORTCHESTER CASTLE

& PORTSMOUTH HARBOUR

Hampshire's most outstanding ancient monument is without doubt the amazing fort at Portchester which has survived 1600 years. Half a mile of wall, 18ft. high and 10ft. thick, and fourteen bastions still stand, with the keep of the mediaeval castle towering over all. Plans are in hand to floodlight the castle.

Visitors today can leave their cars outside the walls and walk into the ruins through the 'land' gate' by the road or after walking round the shore enter by the 'water gate' on the east side, where there is a fine view across the adjoining harbour. Close to this gate is the church of Portchester, built in the early days of the Norman castle and for a short time a priory for Augustinian canons. Their cloister and buildings ran over to the southern wall but of these nothing now remains, for after twenty years they resettled at Southwick, to the north of Portsdown Hill.

Across the grassy open space within the Roman walls stands the castle which was built first in the reign of Henry I, successor of William Rufus. It was modified and added to through three centuries during which, as one of the largest royal castles, it was frequently visited by kings and queens, sometimes for hunting in the nearby Forest of Bere, sometimes before setting sail for France, sometimes to leave for or return from a Crusade. It was in effect a castle within a castle, which had its own moat and a second gate house defending the entrance to its courtyard, which was dominated by two towers.

Today, it is possible to climb right up to the top top of the keep via steps and wooden floors inserted in modern times. On the way up one can see how previous inhabitants have left their mark, including French prisoners crowded here in the 1790s. Some of the fine carved bonework of the prisoners is on display at Southsea Castle. Kept under appalling conditions, the men were able to use their skills in this way to raise extra money, for there were regular markets for their products.

The lower storey of the Castle Keep has a most informative exhibit on the Roman origins of this and other similar forts. The story of the Roman fort is an exciting one, especially if imagination is allowed some play, for no records survive and we must depend on the findings of the archaeologists and the history of the Roman Empire. Building probably began after the year 280 A.D. when pirate raids from the Low Countries were becoming a severe threat. Not only were ten or eleven castles built around our own coasts at this time but Northern Gaul was similarly protected with half a dozen. One of the consequences of this new building was that for short periods Rome lost control of Britain to the commanders of their coastal forces. Armed with the new forts all along the Channel coast, they defied the imperial forces.

Later, Portchester seems to have been abandoned in favour of Clausentum, Roman Southampton, which would have been an easier harbour for sailing ships. Of all these 'forts of the

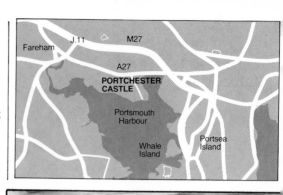

Saxon Shore' Portchester is not only the biggest but it also has the most complete set of Roman walls in Northern Europe. The interior was subjected to a very detailed archaeological excavation in the 1960s under Professor Barry Cunliffe, who has also dug the Roman 'Palace' at Fishbourne and the hill fort of Danebury.

From the top of the great tower of Portchester Castle, or better still from Portsdown Hill, is one of the most outstanding views of the English coast, for below is spread the whole of a great natural harbour and, beyond its narrow mouth, Spithead and the hills of the Isle of Wight. At its narrowest the harbour mouth is just 700 feet wide and 50 feet deep. Tidal races at the entrance can reach speeds up to four-and-a-half miles an hour, so fast that modern yachtsmen are obliged to use their engines rather than fight against the current in a very busy channel.

During mediaeval times, and indeed even in the 18th century, the harbour was quite large enough for the complete Navy to be gathered with great security, many of the smaller ships lying up with ease on mud banks in the shallows. Even today the deep-water channels hold many large warships of destroyer size and above, including aircraft carriers. At the time of the Falklands Crisis in 1982, Portsmouth worked feverishly to

'HOW TO GET THERE'

To Portchester Castle from M27 join A27 at Junction 11 or 12 and follow sign-posts to Portchester. Turn south at roundabout near railway station. Castle sign-posted. From Winchester or Alton take A333 or A32 to Wickham and Fareham, then A27 to Portchester.

1.	4.
2.	
3.	

1. The Castle as it might have appeared in 1415 (by Alan Sorrel)
2. The ruins today
3. Prison hulks in Portsmouth Harbour
4. Aerial view of Portsmouth Harbour

1,2: English Heritage

3: Portsmouth City Council

4: Vosper Thornycroft

prepare ships for the South Atlantic. Such large ships, however, can only enter and leave in the deep, slack water of high tide. In addition to the traffic of large ships at the mouth (including numerous channel ferry movements), the 4,500 acre harbour has some 3,000 small boats, most of them in the upper 'lakes', the channels leading to Fareham and Cosham. In the 17th century, after the closure of the Meon as a portway, Fareham's future as a port looked promising, but today only occasional coasters deliver coal to the quay. The only shipbuilders in the harbour are Vosper Thornycroft, who have one yard at Old Portsmouth and another alongside Portchester Castle. They specialise in fast patrol boats.

Despite the major motorway earthworks which have joined Horsea Island to the mainland, one can still navigate between Portsmouth Harbour and Langstone Harbour, at least in small craft, via the Hilsea and Broom channel. Until the arrival of the railway in 1847 there was just one road bridge across to the island of Portsea, as there still is for Hayling today. Horsea Island, created by hard convict labour from two smaller islands, has a long test lake that was once used for torpedo trials.

Whale Island was enlarged from 10 to 80 acres with the soil dug out by convicts for new basins constructed in the dockyard in the second half of the 19th century. It became the home for *H.M.S. Excellent*, founded in the 1830s to develop trained gunners. The crews of its floating predecessors were the first British sailors to be retained in the Navy in war and peace. Many of the unused and dismasted wooden warships were put to a grim use as prison hulks. The revolution of the American colonies in 1776 stretched prison space to its limits, until the first convicts were sent to Australia from Portsmouth a decade later. However, prisoners were kept in the most barbaric conditions until much later. In 1813 the number of French prisoners-of-war kept on board hulks rose to 10,000 and the ships, most of them French prizes, were moored in long rows in the harbour. Amazingly, while many of these captives, deprived of any activity were reduced to feverish gambling (betting not only their clothes, but meals to come), some spent their time productively, crafting superb model ships and other objects.

In centuries past men from all round the harbour would cross its mud to set eel traps in the channels. Today, despite a good deal of disturbance and pollution the harbour is still rich in marine life, notably large numbers of migrant and over-wintering wading birds. There are also flocks of Brent Geese, which feed on the extensive beds of Eel Grass, our only submarine flowering plant.

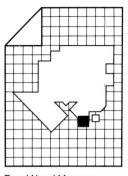

Royal Naval Museum
(Ministry of Defence)

H.M. Naval Base,
Portsmouth,
Hampshire,
PO1 3LR
Telephone
Portsmouth (0705) 822351
Ext. 23868/9

Price Guide - B

Car Park
Multi-storey car park outside
Victory Gate of H.M. Naval
Base

Handicapped
Suitable (ramps are available)

Party Visits
By arrangement
Educational resources

Publications
Leaflet and guidebook

Where to eat
Cafe and tea-room
Suitable picnic area in Victory
arena

Time to allow
1-2 hours

Open
All year (except Christmas and
Boxing Days and some Public
Holidays)
(Sundays, afternoons only)

Public Transport
Bus Services -
Many Inter City coach
services and local bus
services run to Portsmouth
Hard near H.M. Naval Base
Rail Services -
Portsmouth Harbour Station
within a few minutes walk

Nearby Attractions
H.M.S. *Victory*
The *Mary Rose*
D-Day Museum
Sea Life Centre
Southsea Castle
Southsea Beach
Portsmouth City Museum

Royal Naval Museum
& Historic Dockyard

Near H.M.S. *Victory* stands the former Victory Museum, built in the 1920s to house mementos of Nelson, Trafalgar and the Dockyard, and extended to form the Royal Navy Museum by further galleries covering the history of the Royal Navy. These galleries have been developed in adjoining 18th century storehouses.

The upper floor of the Victory gallery and the quayside precinct, the Victory Arena, have many beautiful examples of the special art of the carved figure-head. Two of the principal features on the ground floor of the gallery are the perfectly restored State Barge used at the funeral of Lord Nelson in January 1806, and a large diorama of the Battle of Trafalgar.

The museum has many models of the *Victory* as well as the celebrated panoramic painting of the Battle of Trafalgar by the marine artist W.L. Wyllie, which was hung in 1930 and led to the foundation of the museum. It shows the scene at two o'clock when the battle was at its height. A recorded commentary includes full sound effects.

There are many Nelson family relics; even the story of how they came to be preserved is moving for Nelson was separated from his wife, his mistress Emma Hamilton was to die in poverty and their daughter Horatia never knew her father. In the McCarthy Gallery are gathered many 19th century souvenirs relating to Nelson and his times; this collection was presented by an American lady, Mrs. J.G. McCarthy. The generosity of the presentation is matched by the quality of the display, which consists not only of prints and engravings but also commemorative boxes and enamels, letters by Lord Nelson, miniatures, glass pictures, snuff boxes, engraved glasses, jugs and early books on his life.

The Naval Museum has further galleries which illustrate other periods in the history of the Navy. In the Douglas-Morris gallery there is more about the life of the ordinary sailor of the 1800s, the lesser-known Napoleonic battles and the war fought with America in 1812. Another exhibition entitled "The End of the Sailing Navy", deals with the next half-century, a period when the Navy became more professional and was expanded to serve the worldwide Empire. In the Wyllie Gallery is the museum's latest exhibition "Victorian Heyday" which traces the history of the Royal Navy 1860-1905. Ship models and illustrations trace the development of battleships, beginning with the famous H.M.S. *Warrior*. Other displays include the history of Reserves; Sailors Handicrafts (including woollen embroideries and decorated emu eggs!), Sailors as Folk Heroes and the Navy in Action (including lifelike dioramas of notable battles).

Much relating to the Second World War is also on display, including a set of 45 paintings by David Cobb, which cover most of the major naval battles and incidents of the war, together with a number of lesser known ones. Meanwhile the contrast between the Navy's history and today's electronic age is brought home by relics of the Falklands Campaign and a full-size mock-up of the

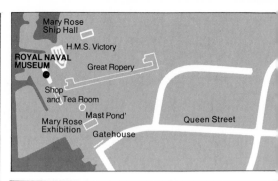

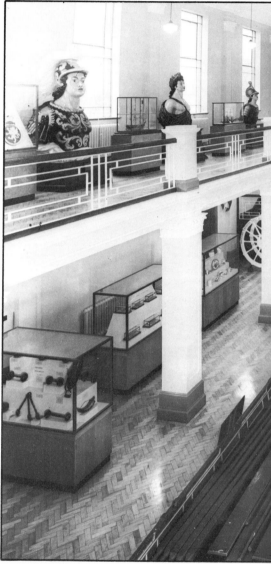

computerized operations room of a frigate which is a feature of the Museum's "Modern Navy Display" housed in a further gallery.

Visitors to the *Victory* and the Royal Naval Museum have a chance to see a small portion of the fascinating world of the once mighty dockyard, mostly buildings dating from a great reconstruction in the late 18th century. Earlier buildings were either wooden or too small for later requirements; developments after 1805 were on reclaimed land, around basins specially built for the newly-arrived age of steam-power.

Such buildings as can be seen represent only a small part of the work-a-day life of Nelson's Navy. The dockyard had its own Academy, grand residences and terraced houses and still has its own church. There were great sailing warships on the stocks and all the workshops to build and prepare the equipment and stores needed by fleets all round the globe.

'HOW TO GET THERE'
From M27 continue down M275 into Portsmouth and follow signs to The Hard – turning right into Marketway, Alfred Road and Queen Street. Multi-storey car-park near Naval Dockyard gate. (Havant Street).

Centre:	Museum Interior
Top:	Old Engraving of Portsmouth
Bottom:	Lifesize display of modern warship operations room

Centre:	J.A. Hewes Southsea
Top:	Hampshire County Records Office
Bottom:	Royal Navy, Crown Copyright

Obvious enough to any eye is the porter's lodge sheltered behind the dockyard wall, both from the early years of the 18th century. For generations security was not tight; French spies slipped in and out, and visitors in the 19th century seem to have entered without difficulty to admire the newest industrial techniques of production. Moat and rampart defences added in 1770 were all removed one hundred years later.

Inside the main gate is a set of three large storehouse buildings built between 1763 and 1782. In these and many others were gathered the raw materials to make and mend, clothe and feed, power and light, anchor, rope and arm hundreds of ships and tens of thousands of men. Through the dockyard gates, or delivered to the quay, came wood for shipbuilding, hemp and tar for ropes, charcoal for furnaces, canvas for sails, iron for anchors and chains, shredded rope and pitch for caulking, glass for lanterns: the list is almost endless.

The oldest feature, left from the 17th century, is the mast pond, now used for boats. In it the masts were preserved under water before newly completed ship's hulls were brought to the harbour for fitting. Behind the pond is one of the yard's many innovations, an iron-framed building.

The biggest building, close to the dry dock of the *Victory*, is the great brickbuilt ropehouse on the site of an earlier ropery destroyed in 1776 by a saboteur sympathetic to the American cause. At 1,100 feet it was the longest building in the world of its day. The rope-makers could produce cables 306 fathoms long (1,836 feet) and eight inches in diameter. On the quayside by the rope-walk numerous piles of oak trunks were stored ready for the sawyers' attention until in 1795 excavation work began for the great ship-basin and the dry docks, in one of which the *Victory* lies today. The specially designed wooden lock at the entrance to the basin is still in use.

Out of sight to the north is the steam basin constructed in an extension in the 1840s. In the 1830s the Navy slowly and reluctantly adopted steamships, at first only to help the sailing ships to leave and enter port at will rather than having to wait for favourable tides and winds. Around the large new basin ships were constructed under cover, steam engines were built and there were iron foundries and smithies. With each passing decade ever greater battleships were produced, and in 1906 H.M.S. *Dreadnought* was built without cranes in four months! The dockyard's phenomenal growth came to an end after the First World War. Modern Portsmouth is still at the forefront of industrial and technological innovation but its economy is now less dependent on the Royal Navy.

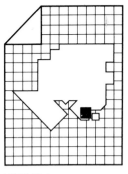

H.M.S. Victory
(Royal Navy)

H.M. Naval Base,
Portsmouth,
Hampshire,
PO1 3LR
Telephone
Portsmouth (0705) 822351
Ext. 23111

Price Guide-Free
(contributions accepted)

Car Park
Multi-storey car park outside
Visitors Gate of H.M. Naval
Base

Party Visits
By arrangement (Tel. as
above, Ext. 23347), only for
parties of British children

Publications etc.
Guidebook
Guided tours

Where to eat
Cafe, near H.M.S. Victory

Time to allow
1 hour

Open
All year (except Christmas
Day)
March - October: Monday -
Saturday, 10.30am-5.30pm
Sunday, 1-5pm
November - February:
Monday-Saturday, 10.30am-
4.30pm
Sunday, 1-4.30pm.

Public Transport
Bus Services -
Many inter-city coach
services run to Portsmouth
Hard outside H.M. Naval Base
Rail Services -
Portsmouth Harbour Station

Nearby Attractions
Royal Naval Museum Navy
Base
Portsmouth City Museum
Old Portsmouth
Southsea Esplanade and
Castle

Top. 1. Stern of *Victory*, with
Captain Hardy's cabin
above Nelson's Great
Cabin, and the Ward-
room below.

Left. 2. Bow with the
Hanoverian royal,
arms, and crown
supported by cherubs.

Right. Nelson on the decks
3. of *Victory*, painting by
Overend

1,2: J.A. Hewes, Southsea

3: Nelson Museum,
Monmouth

H.M.S. VICTORY

O n the fateful day of the 21st October 1805 the twenty-seven British ships off the Cape of Trafalgar include several which had been built in Portsmouth Dockyard and around the Hampshire shores, so it is especialy fitting that one can see here an example of the amazing carpentry which our ancestors performed on the beaches and riverbanks. As many as 2,500 mature oak trees alone were needed for this one ship, *Victory,* and it took six years to build her at Chatham in the early 1760s.

B y the time Nelson became Commander-in-Chief she was already an aged vessel with a long history. Although such "first rates" with more than 100 guns moved more slowly than smaller frigates, the *Victory* was renowned for being an unusually fast sailer for her size and her great height gave her an added advantage as a flag ship.

T oday, nearly two centuries later, the *Victory* is immensely impressive, whether viewed as a whole or in her every detail. She has been painstakingly restored to her appearance at the time of Trafalgar, her great masts towering more than 200 feet above the quayside. With full sail rigged the sight must have been breathtaking as the ship plunged through the waves with acres of heavy canvas billowing. Multiply this sight sixty times and you have some idea of Trafalgar before the roaring guns heralded an appalling inferno of smoke, fire, blood and splintering wood. The brilliant attack planned by Lord Nelson against the Spanish and French combined fleets was crucial because if the enemy had won, or even escaped, they would have sailed to join the heavy forces Napoleon had already gathered for the intended invasion of England.

B y the end of the battle Nelson was dead and his ship broken; the hull much damaged, the mizzen mast (at the aft) shot away, the main and foremasts shot through. Leaking badly she had to be towed to Gibraltar for repairs. Of the nineteen captured French vessels most were lost in the severe storms which followed. After temporary repairs *Victory* slowly returned to Portsmouth bearing the remains of Nelson preserved in a barrel of brandy. The ship returned to Chatham for a refit that took two years, yet *Victory* remained afloat for another 115, making a total of 157. Only one other British vessel has a record to compare, the *Foudroyant* (from the French for *Thunderer*), still moored in the harbour close by. Built as H.M.S. *Trincomalee* in India in 1816 her teak timbers have proved incredibly durable. Although she never fired her guns in anger, her story is nonetheless fascinating and is retold in an excellent booklet available locally.

F or more than a century, *Victory* also lay afloat in the harbour and visitors to Portsmouth who wanted to see over the historic battleship would go down to the beach and find a boatman to row them out for what amounted to a private viewing. A dry dock for the *Victory* was not found until the Society for Nautical Research launched an appeal after the First World War. Almost continuous restoration has been

'HOW TO GET THERE'
From M27 continue down
M275 into Portsmouth and
follow signs to H.M. Naval
Base, which is near The Hard -
turning right into Marketway,
Alfred Road and Queen Street.
Multi-storey car park in Havant
Street, reached by turning left
off The Hard.

undertaken since then to counter the ravages of the elements and the persistent boring of the Death Watch Beetle and other pests. Indeed, over the last 50 years a great part of the ship has been renewed. *Victory,* incidentally, was three times the tonnage and in appearance much less top-heavy than the *Mary Rose,* which had prominent "castles" fore and aft. By the 18th century two principal improvements had been made in Naval ships compared to Tudor vessels. They were able to sail better, because from 1700 they had the steering wheel, and could also operate far beyond the English Channel. The ships had reached a size which gave them the space to store the large quantities of food which could now be preserved. Such ships certainly played no small part in the growth of the British Empire.

T he most powerful impression left by the ship is of amazement that more than 800 men could have lived in such a small space and survived a regime which strikes us today as appalling. The cat-o'-nine tails gives one clue, but we have to remember that the Georgian world ashore was equally harsh. The *Victory* had briefly served as a hospital ship for the growing number of prison hulks on the Medway; such ships gave the Navy a ready supply of seamen. However, because of heavy losses from desertion, disease and death in wartime the hated pressmen frequently haunted not only the coastlands but also the surrounding waters. The risks taken by deserters show that many could not stand the life, and the official history of the Coastguards notes that a smuggler caught in disguise faced the penalty of being hanged 'without benefit of Clergy', a sentence which could perhaps be exchanged for service in the Navy! The sailor's life was made bearable, even filled with pride, by the devotion inspired by leaders such as Nelson.

E ach year nearly half a million people are shown round the cramped gun-decks, down into the Great Cabin where the admiral died and into the spacious cabin where Nelson entertained his officers. For such numbers to be guided over a ship which is only 200 feet long and 50 feet wide, visitors have to be conducted in controlled groups, which is skilfully accomplished by the young sailors and marines stationed at Portsmouth. A tour of the *Victory* is free but contributions to the Save the *Victory* Fund are warmly welcome, for the task of preservation must continue. The tour ends at a sales point on board the ship and a variety of guidebooks can be purchased here or in the H.M.S. *Victory* Shop nearby where a very wide range of souvenirs is available.

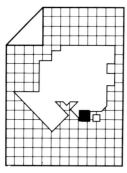

The Mary Rose
(The Mary Rose Trust)

(Office):
Old Bond Store,
48 Warblington Street,
Portsmouth,
PO1 2ET
Telephone
Portsmouth (0705)750521

Price Guide
Ship Hall - C
Exhibition - D

Car Parking
Multistorey car park nearby in
Havant Street

Handicapped
Exhibition and Ship Hall
both suitable

Party Visits
Parties welcomed. Visits c
be arranged at times to su.

Publications etc.
Booklets
Regular cinema show

Time to allow
Ship Hall: 20 minutes
Exhibition: 1-2 hours

Open
Every day except Christmas
Day. March-October,
10.30am-5.30pm.
November-February,
10.30am-5pm.

Public Transport
Bus Services
Numerous bus and coach
services run to Portsmouth
Hard Interchange just outside
the Dockyard gates.
Rail Services
Trains run from Southampton,
Eastleigh and London to
Portsmouth Harbour Station.

1. The hull of the *Mary Rose*, upright in the Ship Hall
2. Objects recovered and now on display
3. Bronze cannon recovered from the wreck in 1979
1.2.3. *Mary Rose Trust*

THE MARY ROSE

Just as the Tudor castle at southsea, which still stands on the seafront, marked the introduction of a new era of defence, so the *Mary Rose* was the forerunner of a new generation of sailing warships. Although not the largest ship of her day the *Mary Rose* was basically a new kind of vessel because she was perhaps the first ever built to use guns broadside against enemy ships, followed by the usual grappling and hand-to-hand fighting. Until the time of Henry VIII ordnance was confined to the upper deck and the high 'castles'.

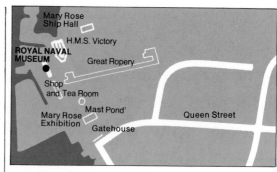

Portsmouth, she was about to use her guns for the first time in earnest when she keeled over and sank. Of the 700 on board only a handful

The *Mary Rose* was rebuilt in 1536 when the traditional overlapping clinker planking of her hull was replaced with a smooth skin of carvel planking. This made it possible to fashion watertight gunports in her sides, and these in turn allowed guns below decks, which could be bigger and much more numerous.

For some 34 years after being built in Portsmouth this flagship of the Tudor navy sailed uneventfully until a tragic day in July 1545 when, with a hostile French fleet facing

survived. The French claimed to have sunk the *Mary Rose* but luckily they departed after only diversionary raids on the Isle of Wight and a stalemate at sea. Their fleet included many galleys which had the considerable advantage of manoeuvrability but, as with the Armada four decades later, could not carry sufficient stores to support a lengthy amphibious operation.

The *Mary Rose* was called 'the flower of all ships that ever sailed'. It was perhaps ironic that she was named after Henry VIII's sister who

'HOW TO GET THERE'
From M27 continue down
M275 into Portsmouth and
follow signs to H.M.
Naval Base and The Hard-
turning right into Marketway,
Alfred Road and Queen Street.
Multi-storey car-park near
H.M. Naval Base gate.
(Havant Street).

was first married to a king of France, Louis XII, and then to the Duke of Suffolk, who was the commander of Henry's land forces at Portsmouth in 1545.

T he remaining starboard half of the hull of the *Mary Rose* can now been seen in the Ship Hall, a specially constructed enclosure built over an 18th century dry dock, where her timbers are continuously sprayed with cooled water. It was recovered from the bed of the Solent in 1982 after a highly publicised underwater archaeo- logical operation.

P ioneer divers in the 19th century recovered guns and much else, but then the site was forgotten until its rediscovery in 1967. Sinking

rapidly into mud 45 feet below the waves the *Mary Rose* had taken down every possession, weapon and tool. The objects lay preserved in an oxygen-free environment, which enabled many of them to survive - items made of wood, leather, fabric and bone. The divers have found archers at their stations with their bows, arrows and equip- ment and even the barber surgeon's chest has been found, complete with dressings and medica- tions. Such small finds in their thousands, many of them now on display, quite apart from the survival of so much of the vessel itself, clearly justify the claim that the warship is the most import- ant wreck yet discovered in European waters. The *Mary Rose* project has already drawn thousands of visitors to Hampshire including historical experts who have had their assump- tions overturned by the evidence of the ship, divers attracted to an operation that is setting standards for the future exploration of the deep, as well as technical problems involved. The most distinguished visitor, H.R.H. Prince Charles, the Prince of Wales, is President of the Mary Rose Trust and has himself dived on the ship many times.

T he long years of work culminated in the raising of the surviving starboard hull structure of the *Mary Rose* in October, 1982. In a complex underwater operation, the hull was lifted clear of the seabed, suspended beneath a 67-tonne lifting frame the size of a tennis court. The hull was then transferred - still underwater - into a cradle in which it was finally raised to the surface.

E ncased in steel, the hull was then taken by barge into Portsmouth Harbour. It was a true homecoming. The *Mary Rose* went back to the dockyard in which she was built - and in which she was prepared for her last, fateful voyage.

W ithin two months of the raising, the *Mary Rose* was resting safely in a dry dock. Henry VIII's revolutionary warship now lies immediately astern of Nelson's flagship H.M.S. *Victory*. Many of the objects recovered from this 'time capsule' of Tudor England are displayed in an extensive exhibition in one of the former dockyard boathouses. Some of the armaments recovered from the wreck are on show, including several superb bronze guns cast by continental gun- founders who were induced to settle in England. A section of the main and upper gun decks of the has also been reconstructed. Amongst the many objects on display is a cache of Tudor arrows: before the discovery of the *Mary Rose* only a single example was known.

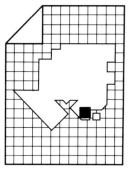

The Warrior Project
(The Maritime Trust)

The Maritime Trust, set up by
HRH The Duke of Edinburgh
in 1969, is the national organisation responsible for
preserving Britain's historic
ships. It now has some twenty
vessels in its care, on show to
the public or under restoration
berthed at St. Katharine's
Dock, London, with the
Trust's Historic Ship Collection, which also includes a top-
sail schooner, Thames sailing
barge, steam coaster and
steam herring drifter. They are
open daily and may be visited
all year round.

The Trust is a registered
charity and the very expensive
work of preserving old ships is
funded by the generosity of
the public - individuals,
companies and trusts. The
Maritime Trust is at 16 Ebury
Street, London S.W.1.
Donations for the *Warrior's*
restoration should be sent to
the Warrior Maritime Trust's
subsidiary, Warrior
Preservation Trust Ltd., The
Custom House, Victoria
Terrace, Hartlepool,
Cleveland.

**Expected date of berthing
at Portsmouth**

Spring 1987

Opening times

To conform with HMS *Victory*
and *Mary Rose*

H.M.S. WARRIOR

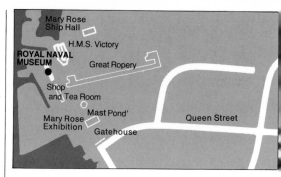

This special project is rather the odd-man
-out in this book. Indeed for the moment
the ship is far away in the North Country. Nevertheless it is appropriate to describe here the
exciting plans to bring back H.M.S. *Warrior* to
Portsmouth in the near future, for like the *Mary
Rose* she also was a revolutionary warship and
her return will give the city an historic collection of ships without rival anywhere in the world.
Her restoration, even though far away in the
north-east of England is a matter of great interest
to the people of Portsmouth, where so much hope
for the future is in tourism and the enjoyment
of the city's heritage.

battleships. Even so her cannon were heavy but
experimental: the very newest guns, breech
loading, rifled and able to fire shells weighing
110 pounds.

The *Warrior* was the first British armoured
battleship, built in 1860, a few years after
the Crimean War when the use of shells had
begun and iron-plating was adopted to produce
an invincible craft. The French *Gloire* was built
first with a wooden hull, and then within months
came the British riposte: the most revolutionary
ship ever built, constructed of iron, the fastest,
the longest, and the most powerful man-of-war
of her day. "The raven among the daws" she
spent her service days protecting the Channel
for this was the period of intense rivalry between
the recent allies, and the ring of forts around
Portsmouth represent a costly Victorian version of
an arms race in which the *Warrior* and her
sister ship *Black Prince* were trump cards.
Punch magazine quickly ridiculed the game as
"Beggar my neighbour" with Lord Palmerston out-
witting the French Emperor.

Many other battleships soon followed but
Warrior was one of the biggest and is still
today strikingly large, being over 400 feet long,
twice the length of *Victory*. She had a powerful
engine giving 1,250 horsepower, enough to steam
at 14 knots and with her sails unfurled she could
reach 17 knots. On her main deck were 40 cannon
mounted rather like those on *Victory* or even
those of the *Mary Rose*. In this she represented
the last of a long tradition for only five years
later came the first rotating turrets used on

What made *Warrior* even more powerful was
an immense box around her central section
constructed of four inches of wrought iron, backed
by 18 inches of teak, which ensured safety
from enemy artillery. She was practically unsink-
able but like all her contemporaries never went
into action. Relegated to port duties, laid up in
reserve and then sadly reduced to a hulk, she
spent many years in Portsmouth Harbour as a
classroom and workshop for H.M.S. *Vernon*, the
Torpedo School. Fortunately she continued to
remain afloat through the last half-century,
serving as an oil pipe-line pontoon at Pembroke
Dock fuel depot. Her wooden decks were covered
with inches of concrete to reduce fire risk so it is
easy to imagine the immense task of restoration.

At the moment *Warrior* can be seen at
Hartlepool in Cleveland where she is being
cleaned and refurbished by the *Warrior* Preservation Trust, a subsidiary of the Maritime Trust.
The project has created nearly 100 jobs and is
likely to cost between £4 and £8 million. In
Portsmouth work is in progress to construct a
special berth alongside the Hard, where the
restored *Warrior* will lay. In the thick of the work
of shipwrights and steel-workers in the North-
East the vessel has already proved a popular
tourist attraction. She will make a visit to
Portsmouth even more essential for those with an
interest in our great maritime past.

Painting: "Her Majesty's Iron
Cased Screw
Steam Frigate",
The Warrior

*Portsmouth City
Council*

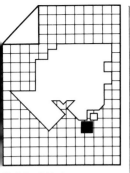

Spit Bank Fort
(S.P. Maguire)

c/o 15 Crofton Lane,
Hill Head,
Fareham, ·
Hampshire,
PO14 3LR
Telephone
(0329)665082 (evenings only)

Price Guide - E

Car Parking
Around ferry terminuses

Handicapped
Not suitable

Party Visits
By arrangement
Guided tours

Publications etc.
Leaflet
History and Guidebook
Video, Sea Fort

Where to eat
Cafe on the fort, pubs and
eating places around ferry
terminuses

Time to allow
2 hours, including the ferry
journey

Open
Easter - October during
hours to meet ferries

**Public Transport to Ferry
Terminuses**
Bus Services
To Gosport Hard and
Clarence Pier, Southsea, on
the mainland and to Sandown
Pier, Shanklin Pier and the
Esplanade, West Cowes, on
the Isle of Wight
Rail Services
Portsmouth Harbour Station,
with a bus to Clarence Pier,
Southsea, or a short ferry trip
to Gosport Hard. Stations at
Shanklin and Sandown for the
Piers.

Ferry Companies
Gosport Hard: Portsmouth
Harbour Ferry Co. Ltd.: (0705)
524551
Clarence Pier, Southsea: Blue
Funnel Cruises: (0705)
830665 or (0703) 23278
Sandown and Shanklin:
Mursell and Kemp (0983)
403155
The Esplanade, West Cowes:
Solent Cruises (0983) 64602

1.	Spit Bank Fort
2.	Central Stairway Spit Bank Fort
1.&2.	*Portsmouth & Sunderland Newspapers*

SPIT BANK FORT

The undoubted charms of this sea-girt fort - with its own artesian well, a maze of concentric passages and panoramic views of the Hampshire coast - are the unwitting legacy of military strategians. Senior officers 'playing war-games' with the Portsmouth area in the middle of the last century discovered that they were losing. Advances in the design of guns and the advent of steam-powered ships were the major factors which suddenly made the harbour and Spithead vulnerable to attack. Already worried by threats of French invasion following the emergence of the Second Empire, the Government of the day, led by Palmerston, set up a Royal Commission which in 1860 made detailed proposals for 'Fortress Portsmouth'.

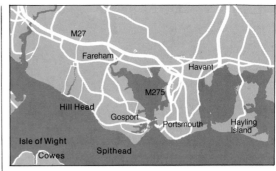

fort's gun positions are on the upper floor and shelter an attractive inner courtyard with a spiral iron stairway that leads down to the artesian well and basement stores. The whole structure was built by laying blocks of stone in position on the sea bed with the aid of divers, the method least preferred by the consulting engin-

Spit Bank Fort, which lies near the main deep-water channel into the harbour, was one of the many defence works on land and sea that were planned at this time. It was started in 1862 and finished 16 years later at the huge cost of £214,000. It was, however, one of the more lightly armed and therefore cheaper of the sea forts; the most expensive was No Mans Land Fort to the south, which had no less than 48 big guns and cost more than £700,000! By comparison, Spit Bank was originally armed with only 15 guns (7" and 10" rifled muzzle loaders, later 7" and 12.5"). Replicas of two of the guns, which weighed a total of 58 tons each and required 210 lbs of gunpowder for each shell, have been placed in the original positions on the fort. The winches for transporting powder and shells from the basement of the fort can be seen, and visitors are taken down to the dimly-lit, cork-floored passages where this formidable arsenal was stored. Safety was, of course, paramount and lighting was therefore indirect, a special lighting passage above the store enabling candles and oil lamps to be placed in thick-walled glass bowls.

Spit Bank Fort is a massive structure of granite and roach Portland stone about 50 yards in diameter which literally sits on a shingle bank: its walls at the waterline are 15 feet thick and to seaward it is protected by a teak/iron 'sandwich' which is 25 inches thick. The

eers engaged by the Government! Huts for the 70 workmen involved and a steam crane were sited on a wooden platform specially erected on the site.

The original war-time complement of the fort was an officer and 156 men, who slept on hammocks slung in any available space - the hooks are still in position. There were eight simple wash basins for the entire fort and two WCs, one for the officer and one for the men. Like the other defence works built at the time, Spit Bank never saw action, though it did once direct its guns (not the originals!) on a French ship, the *Courbet,* when she and other battleships were seized as they sheltered at Spithead after the uneasy Franco-German alliance of the last war. A Ministry of Information propaganda film of the time, *Sea Fort,* shows men scrambling for battle stations or relaxing with a book borrowed from 'the fort library'. Within the cramped confines of the fort the men even managed to stage theatricals, according to the film.

In the 1950s the Ministry of Defence formally recognised the complete obsolescence of Spithead's sea forts and put them up for sale. It was not until 1982, however, that Spit Bank Fort was eventually purchased, divested of a huge pigeon population and restored for public visits, an exercise which won its owners a British Tourist Authority Award. BS

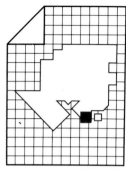

Portsmouth

Guided Tours of Old
Portsmouth throughout the
year (1½ hours)

Heritage Coach Tours
Around the City, including a
visit to Portsdown Hill

Trails
include Spice Island trail
(Point and Camber area)
Owen's Southsea and
Modern Architecture trail

Youth Hostel
Wymering Manor
Telephone
Portsmouth (0705) 375661

Tourist Information
Castle Buildings, Clarence
Esplanade, Southsea
Telephone Portsmouth (0705)
754358 and The Hard
(0705) 826722

City Museum and Art Gallery
(Portsmouth City Council)
Museum Road,
Portsmouth,
PO1 2LJ
Telephone
Portsmouth (0705) 827261

Price Guide - B

Car Parking
Free, nearby

Open
Every day except
December 25 and 26 and
other days around Christmas,
10.30am - 5.30pm

Nearby Attractions
Theatre Royal Portsmouth
Visitors welcome 10.30-5.30
Mon. to Sat.
Nationally important very
ornate Victorian Theatre being
restored.
Theatre tours
Restaurant/Bar
For further information
contact: Mr Graham Bishop
on Portsmouth (0705) 823729

OLD PORTSMOUTH

Like many cities, Portsmouth grew up as a
series of distinct parts which have since
joined together. The ideal starting point for any
visitor exploring the city would be on the Point
at Old Portsmouth where for many years
travellers and merchants have arrived at the
Camber, a small natural harbour. Between this
and the open sea of Spithead is a small tightly-
packed district of houses, inns, businesses and
fortifications, known in later times as "Spice
Island", which lay outside the nearby fortress
town across the Camber.

Old Portsmouth was originally a small fishing
village and landing place on a quiet inlet.
Then in 1194 Richard I created a new town,
with the High Street running through the middle.
The first royal dock development took place in
1212 when a timber dock on the side of an inlet
close to the town was made by King John. Little
of the old town is left except for some Tudor fortifications, small parts of the church (now a
cathedral) and a few well-built houses, for
mediaeval Portsmouth is thought to have had
few stone residences and even its walls were
mud-built until Tudor times. There is also the
Domus Dei, once a hospital like St. Cross in
Winchester, which was converted for use as an
armoury, then became the Governor's House
and later Portsmouth Garrison Church. Burnt out
in World War II it is now an ancient monument. Today the High Street is an attractive
mixture of Georgian and modern houses, the
latter replacing blitzed dwellings. Two fortunate
survivals give added interest: the Victorian
Barracks, now the Grammar School, and further
down the road the Cathedral.

From the narrow beach outside the sea walls,
which quickly becomes crowded on a sunny
summer day, countless unfortunate men caught by
the press gangs must have been rowed by wherry-
men to their grim new homes at anchor in
Spithead. Here the hardened sailors stepped
ashore again to celebrate their return for which
the Point was well prepared since its alehouses
were never closed. In wartime, however, the
women who crowded Point Beach were rowed out
to share a cramped life below decks with the
sailors who were confined to their ships. Today
the Point is well provided with bars that make
a lively atmsophere at the harbour-mouth.

A large millpond separated Old Portsmouth
from the Naval dockyard which grew from
the world's first dry dock, built in 1495. This mill-
pond was incorporated into an extended set of
18th century fortifications around the old town,
which was clearly separated from the newer
streets of Portsea built on the common land
surrounding the dockyard. Portsea and the docks
were given their own set of defences at the end
of the 18th century.

Outside the dockyard gates is the Hard where
the ferrymen with their rowing boats awaited
hire from passengers who wanted to cross the
waters to Gosport or more often to board ship.
The ferrymen had two levels of charging, peace-
time or wartime, and indeed, until the
Napoleonic wars the town was either frenzied

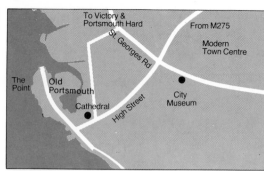

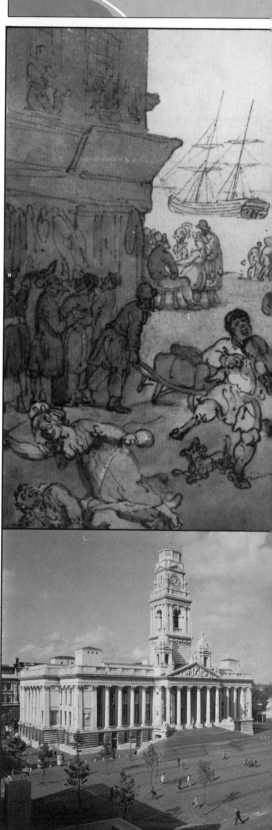

HOW TO GET THERE'

To Old Portsmouth from M27
continue down M275. Turn
right into Marketway and
Alfred Road, and then left
down Anglesea Road. Follow
one-way system, (signs for Old
Portsmouth) into Cambridge
Road. At next roundabout turn
left for City Museum, or straight
ahead up High Street, leading
to car parks in Broad Street.

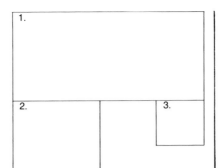

1. Point, in the late 18th century, sketched by Rowlandson
2. Guildhall and Square
3. City Museum & Art Gallery

Illus.: Portsmouth City Council

with activity in times of war, or stagnating in times of peace. Empire and its defence, and the need to replace the wooden warships with steam and iron kept up the momentum during the phenomenal growth of the 19th century.

The two new towns of Southsea and Landport then began to grow in the small fields outside the walls of Old Portsmouth and on the Common, beyond the Lion and Unicorn gates of Portsea. Portsmouth, once so poor in comparison with Southampton, now grew to several times the size of its 'civvy street' neighbour. The city centre of modern Portsmouth, with its great public buildings, grand facades and shopping streets, is in the Landport area. Much of the background and past history of the growing town and modern city is displayed in the galleries of the City Museum, housed in Victorian, chateau-style army barracks. These were built in 1880 on the site of the flattened ramparts and filled-in moats of Old Portsmouth. An excellent RIBA guide to the modern architecture of the city is available. Another published guide provides a key to the elegant terraces and villas built in Southsea by Thomas Ellis Owen in the 19th century.

Another leaflet helps visitors to discover the history of the Point and Old Portsmouth, where guided walks are also arranged for a few weeks each summer. A dramatised tour about the local history of the Point is given by Solent People's Theatre. Portsmouth can also be viewed in the summer by means of conducted bus tours, starting at Canoe Lake and including a stop on Portsdown. These are escorted by knowledgeable Portsmouth Tourists' Guides.

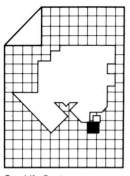

Sea Life Centre
(Group Manager,
David Mace)

Clarence Esplanade,
Southsea,
Hampshire,
PO5 3PB
Telephone
(0705) 734461

Price Guide - E

Car Parking
Ample metered parking
nearby

Handicapped
Suitable

Party Visits
Advance booking preferred

Publications etc.
Guidebook
Regular showings of audio-
visual production

Where to eat
Coffee shop and restaurant

Time to allow
1½ hours

Open
Daily

Public Transport
Bus Services
Frequent services from
Portsmouth. Hourly buses
from Southampton, and at
least every hour from
Fareham, Havant, Chichester
and Bognor Regis.

Rail Services
Nearest station Portsmouth
Town, two miles away

Nearby Attractions
D-Day Museum
Southsea Castle
Royal Marines Museum
Eastney Pumping Station
Old Portsmouth
Cumberland House Natural
History Museum

SEA LIFE CENTRE

Small boys on the pier, grown men on ships, ladies paddling - they all peer into the water for the marine life they know to be there. But few ever see a thing! Now for the first time visitors to Southsea seafront will be able without fail to see a wide variety of marine life in an authentic habitat at a fascinating new aquarium complex which is being opened in early summer 1986.

A major feature of the new attraction is that it will be possible to see the fish and other animals from angles that are normally only available to the sub-aqua diver. Overall, there will be seventy or more different species of native British creature 'in residence', depending on the season. There will be huge cod, which grow to five feet in length, together with massive conger eels, skate, rays and many smaller creatures such as pipefish, angler fish, octopus and a wide variety of crabs, lobsters and sea anemones. The tanks will contain hundreds of litres of sea water and will be so large that it will be possible to stock them with hundreds of shoaling fish such as herring and mackerel.

A new type of toughened glass laminate specially developed for the Sea Life Centre will enable visitors to look at fish from below as they weave amongst submerged anchors and shipwrecks. It will be just like standing on the

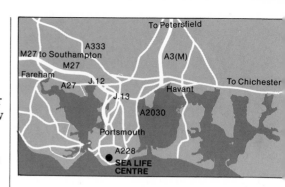

dwelling species of fish will be seen swimming in their natural habitat. This intriguing feature is being modelled on local cliff faces at nearby Portsdown Hill, where exhibition designers have been taking full-size latex mouldings.

Visitors to the Sea Life Centre, which is close to the main deep-water channel into Portsmouth Harbour, will be ideally placed to view Spithead and the comings and goings of large numbers of ships. The new building will incorporate on its seaward side an authentic replica of a ship's bridge so that would-be skippers can indulge their fancy to steer the cross-channel ferries and naval vessels which constantly ply these waters.

Outside the Sea Life Centre will be a play area for children, complete with a Seaside Touch Pool, where youngsters can examine all the inhabitants of a typical British rock pool - starfish, crabs, sea urchins and limpets. There will also be a

seabed more than twelve feet below the surface! There will also be a walkway to provide overhead views and places where the surface of the water will be only 'a few inches from the nose'. Some of the tanks will be frameless, made from side-bonded glass sheets to provide an all-round view of the marine life within.

One huge tank of 80,000 litres capacity will have its own artificial cliff where rock-

miniature railway and a relaxing water garden, close to one of the two cafeterias. The Sea Life Centre, in short, promises to provide what the normal trip to the seaside cannot offer - a sight of the fish! It is a unique blend of entertainment and education which will give pleasure in all weathers. BS

Photo: Sea Life Centre

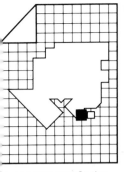

Eastney Pumping Station
(Portsmouth City Council)

Henderson Road,
Eastney,
Portsmouth,
Hampshire,
PO4 9PH
Telephone
Portsmouth (0705) 827261

Price Guide - B

Car Parking
Free, nearby

Handicapped
Unsuitable

Party Visits
By arrangement

Publications
Leaflet and guidebook

Where to eat
Suitable picnic area at
Eastney Beach

Time to allow
Half an hour

Open
April-Sept. 1.30-5.30pm
(In steam at weekends,
electric friction drive at other
times)
Oct.-March (Opened on the
first Sunday of each month, in
steam, 1.30-5.30pm)

Public Transport
Bus Services -
Portsmouth Corporation
buses from The Hard, Leigh
Park and Commercial Road.
Generally every Half-hour,
hourly on Sunday.
Rail Services -
Nearest Station, Fratton

Nearby Attractions
Cumberland House Natural
   Science Museum and
   Aquarium
Royal Marines Museum
D-Day Museum
Southsea Castle
Sea Life Centre

EASTNEY PUMPING STATION

There is one aspect of Victorian towns which we find difficult to understand – how strangely tolerant their society remained of the sight and smell of bad drainage and polluted water. A growing realisation of the connection between illness and tainted wells and water supplies came at the time of repeated, frightening epidemics of cholera. Yet the first Act of Parliament left the choice of action to Borough Councils, and the recommendations of an enquiry in 1848 were ignored for fifteen years before any drainage system was provided for Portsmouth. For such a flat island, nowhere more than twelve feet above high tide level, there could be no easy solution.

In 1864 a system of drains was laid to bring storm waters and waste from the large population flowing down to the open land at Eastney, where a large pumping house was built. The pumps then had to operate to lift the waste from the lowest pipe up to a higher level sewer which continued as a final large pipe into the tidal mouth of Langstone Harbour.

Unfortunately the system was far from adequate for the growth of population, and because the pumps had to stop during high tide the sewers became blocked. The beaches at Eastney

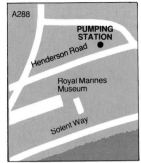

'HOW TO GET THERE'
From M275 follow signs to
Fratton and Milton. From A288
(Eastney Road) turn left into
Henderson Road.
From Southsea, South Parade,
continue along Southsea
Esplanade and Eastney
Esplanade, then turn left into
Henderson Road.

the tide rushed out.

The two magnificent engines were supplied by the firm of the celebrated James Watt of Birmingham and although found to be uneconomic after sixty-seven years' use have been preserved in meticulous condition. There are few experiences to equal the sight of such huge machines (150 h.p. each) to give a profound respect for Victorian engineers and an insight into how they combined their passion for engineering with their love for pomp and circumstance. The fascinating guide book by Dr. Edwin Course describes in detail the extraordinary occasion of the opening in 1887, when the dignitaries went on to watch the sluices opened and the discoloured water flow out to sea before their luncheon at the city lunatic asylum. The speeches they delivered made clear their belief in the connection between cleanliness and godliness.

were fouled with sewage which was released at low tide and the barracks of nearby Fort Cumberland had to be abandoned. Fortunately a solution was found in 1886 after a prize of £500 was offered: two much-more powerful engines were built in a new and elegant ecclesiastical-looking house. These engines were used continuously to fill enormous underground tanks in the outer defence works of the nearby fort. The sewage was then released and washed quickly into the channel as

Not everyone will feel immediately drawn to the idea of visiting a sewage pumping station. But it is, of course, a completely wholesome place today and even when in full swing the system of drains was always out of sight below floor level. The Eastney Pumping Station stands as a fascinating monument to the giants of power of a century ago and visitors to Portsmouth should not miss it, especially those who are interested in in engines of the Victorian period.

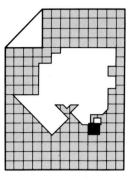

D-DAY MUSEUM
& SOUTHSEA CASTLE

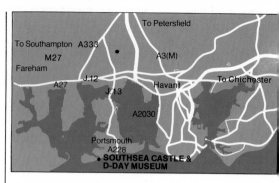

D-Day Museum
(Portsmouth City Council)

Clarence Esplanade,
Southsea,
Hampshire,
PO5 3PA
Telephone (0705) 827261

Price Guide - D
(Includes entrance to
Southsea Museum)

Car Parking
Nearby

Handicapped
Suitable

Party Visits
By arrangement. Booked
school parties, free.

Publications
Guidebook
Audio-visual show

Where to eat
Picnic areas and cafes on
Southsea Common

Time to allow
1 - 2 hours

Open
Daily 10.30-5.30pm (except
24, 25 and 26 December)

Southsea Castle
(Portsmouth City Council)

Clarence Esplanade,
Southsea,
Hampshire,
PO5 3PA
Telephone (0705) 827261

Price Guide - B
(Joint tickets with D-Day
Museum, D)

Car Parking
Nearby

Handicapped
Wheelchair access to two
ground-floor galleries only

Party Visits
By arrangement
Educational resources

Publications
Leaflet
Guidebook

Where to eat
Picnic areas and cafes on
Southsea Common

Time to allow
1 - 2 hours

Open
Daily 10.30-5.30 (except 24,
25 and 26 December)

Public Transport

Nearby Attractions
Royal Marines Museum
Eastney Pumping Station
Farlington Marshes
Old Portsmouth
H.M. Naval Base, Portsmouth
H.M.S. *Victory*
Mary Rose
Royal Navy Museum
Spitbank Fort
Royal Navy Submarine
  Museum
Naval Ordnance Museum
Sea Life Centre

If ever there was a turning point in the Second World War it was D-Day, 6th June 1944. To mark its fortieth anniversary, a brilliant 'Bayeux-like' embroidery and a mass of memories and records have recently been brought together in a purpose-built museum that stands beside Southsea Castle, itself a Tudor defence work.

Portsmouth and Southampton - and indeed the whole of Hampshire - are full of stories of the day that the liberation of Europe was started, for it was from the inlets and harbours of the Solent and Spithead that a great flotilla of men and ships emerged to rendezvous south of the Isle of Wight and make for the coasts of Normandy. Troops and armour had been amassing for some while under cover of the woods and forests of the county, masterminded by Supreme Commander General Dwight Eisenhower in his HQ at Southwick House, near Portsmouth. The operation board that was used to plot events in this real-life war-game is still there.

The planning and logistics that lay behind this huge operation, codenamed Overlord, are overwhelming, but fortunately the exhibits and an audiovisual production at the museum make it relatively easy for the visitor to absorb the details. The museum's centrepiece is the Overlord Embroidery, a work of art in itself, which tells the story from the Battle of Britain in 1940, through D-Day and the early months of liberation. There are short captions in English, French and German. This massive production, which is 272 feet long - 41 feet longer than the Bayeux tapestry - was designed by Sandra Lawrence and made by the Royal College of Needlework. Each of its 34 panels is an intricate collage of images based on contemporary photographs and expert military advice.

The painstaking work that went into the design of the Overlord Embroidery is well illustrated by Panel 17, which depicts a force of commandos reinforcing paratroops at a critical crossing of the Caen Canal. They are led by their CO's personal piper, Bill Millin, wearing the regiment's green beret. In an earlier design he was shown, not unreasonably, with a tin hat, but later research showed that in fact he wore a beret, even in the thick of the fighting!

The original idea of launching a full-scale assault on German forces in Europe can be traced back to 1940 and the leadership of war-time Prime Minister Winston Churchill. Planning this great enterprise eventually came into the hands of Lt-General Sir Frederick Morgan, who as Chief of Staff to the Supreme Allied Commander (COSSAC) devised a scheme with elaborate deceptions to keep the Germans guessing. Since most of the troops were to be from the USA, Churchill agreed with Roosevelt that overall command should be given to an American commander, and in December 1943 General Eisenhower was appointed. He chose General Sir Bernard Montgomery, universally known as 'Monty', to plan and implement the assault, but both men agreed that the COSSAC plan, which

involved three divisions of troops, was inadequate. It was therefore extended to five divisions.

The detailed planning that was needed to land 156,000 men on the beaches of Normandy within 24 hours and then to press ahead with the invasion was immense. Many of the details are

well known, but in the museum they come to life in a series of lively exhibits. To obtain information about the beaches the BBC launched a request for holiday snaps and postcards, without of course revealing why they were wanted. Ten million were received! Combined Operations parties travelled in midget subs to the beaches to measure gradients and take soil samples. Information on the French coast was collected at the Inter-Service Topographical Unit at Oxford and transferred to special maps, 170 million of which were subsequently printed in complete security. And plans were prepared for false landings that were so successful that the German High Command took a long time to realise that the Normandy assault was the real thing.

The nail-biting decision made by Eisenhower to postpone D-Day for 24 hours, after ideal

From M27 continue down
M275 into Commercial Road
and follow signs to Southsea.
The route is as follows: Turn
right into Market Way and
Alfred Road and continue
down Anglesea Road. Follow
one-way system and turn left
into Hampshire Terrace and
continue to the sea-front.
Turn left down Clarence
Esplanade. The D-Day
Museum and Southsea
Castle are on right-
hand side after half-a-mile.

1. Southsea Castle
2. Replica of Southwick House Overlord Invasion control room.
3. View inside Museum
4. Section of Overlord Tapestry with Lord Lovat's piper, Bill Millin.
5. Display of World War II artillery and vehicles.

Photos: D-Day Museum

conditions of tide and moon were confounded by poor weather, are illustrated by a mock-up of the map room at Southwick House. Few decisions can have had more impact on the course of European history! When finally the order was given, with those famous words 'OK, let's go', troops packed in landing craft or huddled in Horsa gliders sought their destinations. Overall the armada contained 4,200 troop vessels escorted by 1,200 warships, which travelled along ten corridors swept clear of mines by the Royal Navy.

Their target was the Atlantic Wall, a curtain of armed positions and minefields set up by the Germans. Throughout the operation, these defences were pounded by the Allied air forces, whose pilots flew more than 14,000 sorties on D-Day. The beaches were divided into sections: the Americans landed to the west, on Utah and Omaha beaches. The Utah attack went relatively smoothly, but the Omaha landing was difficult. Many landing craft and amphibious tanks sank and it was only after bitter fighting, at the cost of 3,000 casualties, that a slim beach-head was secured. To the east, on Gold, Juno and Sword beaches, British and Canadian troop fared better, but the horror of landing on foreign beaches under fire is almost impossible to imagine. Some of the types of vehicles involved in the landings are shown in the museum, notably the amphibious DUKW, 2,000 of which were involved in Overlord.

Of course, securing the beaches was only the first stage in the invasion. To speed up the landing of men and supplies artificial harbours called Mulberries were built. These enormous constructions of concrete and steel were made from huge components that were built at a number of locations around the Solent. Towed across the channel and sunk in position, they were an essential part of Overlord strategy, for the alternative approach - and one that the Germans thought would be taken - was to obtain 'quayage' by storming the Channel Ports, which military commanders reckoned to be impregnable.

Overall the D-Day Museum succeeds by telling a complex story in a lively way. Those who remember the war will recognise the war-time broadcasts and living rooms such as that of Portsmouth ARP Warden 'Mr White'. They will remember the air-raid shelter at the bottom of the garden. Ex-soldiers may recall the moment of landing, vividly portrayed in a mock-up, or even the view from a German bunker. But even those visitors who have no such memories should be impressed by that rare event, a war story with an unequivocally happy ending.

SOUTHSEA CASTLE

This fine example of a Tudor fortress was built in 1544 at a time when Henry VIII was strengthening the defences of the Solent and the South Coast in general. Positioned opposite the deep-water channel through which all large ships must enter Portsmouth Harbour, it was ideally placed and was soon at the centre of action. It was from here that the King is said to have seen the *Mary Rose* keel over and sink, during an attempted French invasion.

Today the rooms of the castle, including those of an extension dating from 1814, are used by Portsmouth City Museums to house a number of exhibits. One major display tells the complicated story of the defences of Old Portsmouth and the harbour, so-called Fortress Portsmouth, which was fortified in a succession of works, notably those of the Dutch engineer Sir Bernard de Gomme and 'Palmerston's follies'. There are also exhibits on the archaeology of the district and plans are advanced to open the Southsea Story, which will explain the growth and development of the seaside resort.   BS

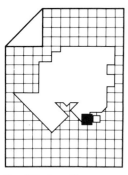

Royal Marines Museum
(Ministry of Defence)

Eastney,
Southsea,
Hampshire,
PO4 9PX
Telephone
Portsmouth (0705) 822351
ext. 6135

Price Guide - Free

Car Parking
Free

Handicapped
Suitable (warden assistant for lifting)

Party Visits
By arrangement

Publications
Guidebook

Where to eat
Tea garden, May-September

Time to allow
2 hours

Open
All year (except 24th Dec.-14th Jan.)
Daily, 10am-4.30pm

Public Transport
Bus Services -
Frequent daily Portsmouth Corporation buses from The Hard, Fratton and Southsea seafront. Half-hourly service from Cosham, hourly on Sunday.
Rail Service -
Fratton, Portsmouth and Southsea, or Portsmouth Harbour Station

Nearby Attractions
D-Day Museum
Southsea Castle
Sea Life Museum
Southsea Common
Eastney Pumping Station
Cumberland House Museum

ROYAL MARINES MUSEUM

Soldiers of the sea have always been an important part of the crew of warships, but not until the 1660s was the first proper maritime regiment of foot raised, the origin of the Royal Marines whose name is so well known today. This very special part of the Royal Navy has a distinguished and fascinating history, most recently in the Falklands Campaign. Their museum, which includes many audio-visual presentations, could claim to be one of the finest military museums in the country, having recently been voted European Museum of the Year. There are plans to install a 'talking head' in the form of an RM Sergeant-Major, who will brief visitors on their arrival. The setting is the imposing former Officers' Mess overlooking the great parade ground of the Marines barracks at Eastney, first occupied in 1864.

Few other branches of the Army or Navy have played such varied roles in the past, or such a specialised one as they do today. The Marines were the elite of unswervingly local detachments who served on board the old sailing ships. Up on the poop deck in battle, their fire-arms would be crucial as ship grappled with ship. They were used as a force of last resort if the other seamen came to mutiny and the First Lord of the Admiralty St. Vincent said of them "if the hour of real danger should come to England, they will be found the Country's sheet anchor". The marines took on the role of raiding units and there is much in the display about Gibraltar and the part played by the Marines in the capture and siege of the Peninsula in 1704.

As well as the gaining of the "Rock", the attack and capture of French Belle Isle, south of Brittany, in 1761, is also illustrated with old maps and engravings, and has ever since been commemorated by the inclusion of a laurel wreath in the corps' arms, for their gallantry. The Marines

'HOW TO GET THERE'
From M275 follow signs to Fratton and Milton then A28 towards Southsea. Entrance to Royal Marines Barracks on left.

have for most of this century provided the Navy's bands and their meticulously decorated instruments and proud music provide a colourful aspect of the museum.

The greatest excitement perhaps is to be found in the stories of the supreme gallantry which has brought the Royal Marines ten V.C.s, gathered together as the highlight of a large collection of medals and awards. The museum bears witness to the service marines have given at the furthest corners of the globe: during wars in China, in manning the out-posts of the Empire, in the territories of newly-discovered Africa and even on the Pacific shores of Canada, and most recently in the Falklands Campaign.

There is a reconstruction of a 1914 trench and a dramatic display about the 1918 raid on Zeebruge when the mole, heavily defended by Germans, was attacked. There is, of course, much to see about the combined operations so carefully planned to regain a foothold for the invasion forces of 1944. Twelve years later, as a fine model shows, the Marines made the first-ever helicopter assault at Port Said during the Suez War.

A recent addition to the display is a gallery on the present day forces, whose Captain General, the Duke of Edinburgh, has said "Nothing is impossible for the Royal Marines". Not only are they highly trained in special skills such as underwater swimming, but as the Navy's military spearhead have become specialists in all types of warfare: in the arctic, the desert, in jungles and even against urban guerillas.

Photo: Hampshire Recreation Department

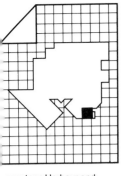

Langstone Harbour and Hayling Island

Farlington Marshes are freely open to the public. For information about the reserve, or about the Hampshire and Isle of Wight Naturalists Trust, contact them at 8 Market Place, Romsey SO5 8NB telephone (0794) 513786.

Solent Way
The route continues round Langstone Harbour on its western shore. A footpath from Henderson Road skirts Bransbury Park. Walk down Ironbridge Lane and turn right into Locksway Road, and then left into Furze Lane/Longshore Way. The seawall path then can be followed easily up to Farlington Marsh. Beyond the reserve the Solent Way joins the Wayfarers Walk around the coast at Langstone. A footpath from there crosses the fields to Warblington Church and then on to Emsworth, the eastern end of the walk.

Hayling Ferry For information about the ferry service telephone Portsmouth (0705) 732650.

Windsurfing Hayling Island Windsurfing Centre is at Northney Marina. Telephone Hayling Island (070 16) 67334

Tourist Information on Hayling Island is available from the T.I.C., The Smugglers Haunt, Seafront. Telephone (070 16) 67111 (summer only).

LANGSTONE HARBOUR
& FARLINGTON MARSHES

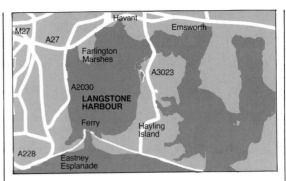

The enthusiastic explorer of Hampshire's coastline will be able to find many miles of paths around Langstone Harbour, although there is no one continuous path at present. The ferry between Portsea Island at Eastney and the Western tip of Hayling Island, which has recently been reinstated, crosses the rapidly-flowing channel mouth with beaches on either side. This is a rather dangerous place because the water is deep close in to the shore.

The Portsmouth shore of the harbour has a long wall popular with fishermen and a walk here is a good way to appreciate the rhythm of the daily ebb and flow of the tides.

In the north of the harbour a small car park is available for visitors to Farlington Marshes, a Hampshire and Isle of Wight Naturalists' Trust reserve, with a coastal walk well away from heavy road traffic. Most of the site is open grassland – rough-grazed meadows which were once saltmarsh reclaimed by the building of a seawall two hundred years' ago. There is a large lagoon of slightly brackish water, supplied also by freshwater ditches, and as a result the variety of reed-beds and scrub, marshes and meadows,

A large portion of the tidal mudflats and most of the small islands in the harbour are also a reserve, owned by the Royal Society for the Protection of Birds. From April to August the breeding communities of waders and Little Tern which nest on the islands especially need to be left in peace, so boaters are asked not to land there in summer.

An excellent information leaflet on Langstone Harbour has been produced by Langstone Harbour Board with information on its history, angling, ornithology and harbour facilities. This is available at the Portsmouth Tourist Information Centre.

By the causeway at Langstone is the wellknown landmark of a tidemill, and beside it the sail-less tower of a windmill, which could be worked

surrounded by the tidal harbour make this one of the best bird-watching reserves in Hampshire. The most important visitors to the harbour are certainly the Brent Geese who return each October from as far away as Northern Russia to stay for the winter until March.

Twelve species of bird reach internationally important numbers in Langstone Harbour. Farlington Marshes provides an important high-tide roost and feeding ground for many of these birds, including great numbers of Brent Geese, Black-tailed Godwit, Dunlin, Widgeon and Teal. The reserve supports over fifty species of breeding birds and is also very rich in plant-life. The Nature Conservancy Council have said that the protection of Farlington Marshes is the key to the conservation of the harbour as a whole. A booklet about the reserve is available from the Trust Office in Romsey (8 Market Place – 30p plus 20p p.& p.). Access is off the roundabout junction of the A27 and the A2030. The seawall and about a third of the reserve is open to the public. It is not an open space, but visitors seeking peace and quiet and the enjoyment of its wildlife are welcome. Dogs must be kept on a lead.

while the tide refilled the pond. Langstone was the mediaeval port for Havant and sailing ships called here until the nineteenth century. Local barges carried grain, coal, shingle and fertilizer. It was once a favourite haunt for smugglers who met at the mill or one of Langstone's two inns. Tradition has it that there is an underground passageway connecting all three. It is now a popular mooring place for boat-users seeking refreshment at the quayside public house. Not far away the one remaining ruined tower of Warblington Castle can be seen.

From Langstone, a coastal path can be followed across to Warblington Church and round to Emsworth. This is well signposted as it is the south-eastern start for the Wayfarer's Walk, a 72-mile long-distance route across Hampshire, ending near Newbury. Emsworth at the head of Chichester Harbour is another small port, an historic harbour-side town with an attractive square and elegant Georgian houses. It was once famous for a great oyster-fishing industry which tragically collapsed at the turn of this century after an unfortunate poisoning at a large dinner party in Winchester.

77

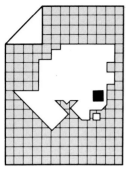

Queen Elizabeth Country Park
(H.C.C./Forestry Commission)

Queen Elizabeth Country Park
Centre,
Gravel Hill,
Horndean,
Portsmouth,
Hampshire,
PO8 0QE
Telephone
Portsmouth (0705) 595040

Price Guide - Free

Car Parking
Charge

Handicapped
Suitable. Some car park
passes available.

Party Visits
Tours and educational
assistance available

Publications
Guidebooks
Trail booklets
Displays
Films
Guided walks available

Where to eat
Cafe on site
Picnic areas

Time to allow
2 - 4 hours

Open
(Park Centre) March-October,
every day. November-
February, Sundays only
(Country Park) Open every day
of year

Public Transport
Bus Services -
Southdown buses every hour
from Petersfield and
Portsmouth, Monday-Saturday
Rail Services -
Petersfield Station (3-4 miles
away)

Nearby Attractions
Ashford Chase
Holly Combe
Uppark
Stansted Park
Sir George Staunton Country
Park
Denmead Pottery
Old Winchester Hill

Nearby Attractions
Dovecote, Manor Farm,
Langrish. Mrs Lambert
Open by appointment
Telephone
Petersfield (0703) 52726
**Manor Farmhouse
Hambledon**
(Mr S.B. Mason)
Visitors welcome by
appointment
Telephone or write
Hambledon (070 132) 433
Court House East Meon
(Mr Piers Whitley)
Restored 15th century house
surrounded by courtyard
gardens.
Visitors welcome by
appointment
Telephone
East Meon (073 087) 274

QUEEN ELIZABETH COUNTRY PARK

It is no exaggeration to claim that the "Queen Elizabeth" is one of the finest country parks in the British Isles, combining as it does dramatic scenery with superb facilities which help visitors enjoy and appreciate the downs. At its heart is a fine centre which provides a welcoming base for an outing as well as an exciting programme of events and activities to join in, while only a short walk away is the Butser Ancient Farm project.

The park extends for more than a thousand acres over the hills on both sides of the London to Portsmouth road. Butser Hill to the west is a massive open down with deep coombes, which is surmounted by a great radio tower and offers views in all directions over Southern England. It is both the western end and the highest point of the South Downs and sheep still graze everywhere though a few small areas of its steepest slopes are protected as nature reserves, for they contain many ancient yew trees.

Across the Portsmouth Road are two hills completely covered with a modern beech forest; the larger has been opened up to include a woodland drive to its highest point where there are picnic areas, long walks and even a work site where the forester's crafts can be seen. One can for instance see a reconstruction of an old saw-pit (the uncomfortable trench where the under-sawyer laboured in clouds of dust) and demonstrations of hurdle-making are put on each summer.

Until the 1930s the hills held a vast warren where for sport and money rabbits were encouraged to multiply, to be shot and sent to market in Portsmouth. There are still plenty of rabbits and other wild creatures on the hills and by following any of the multitude of paths through the forest the quiet walker may frequently encounter roe deer as they slip across one of the rides or firebreaks. On Holt Down, the smaller of the eastern hills, an elevated timber platform provides a look-out over a clearing where in the evening deer may be observed. The beech woods, though still young, have grown tall and walking through them is a pleasure; there is little under-growth and underfoot is the richly coloured carpet of fallen autumn leaves, while in spring there is the added delight of the radiant green leaves above.

At the entrance to the forest, with easy access from the A3, is the Park Centre which houses a large and informative display, an audio-visual theatre and the "Coach House Cafe", a reminder of the mail-coaches which once raced down the turnpike highway over the downs between Petersfield and Portsdown. Around a courtyard are facilities for schools as well as space for craftsmen to show their skills and sell their wares during weekends. Staff are on hand to answer questions and lead regular guided tours. Souvenirs and countryside publications for all the family are available in a small bookshop. Here, perhaps after watching a film show, one can buy a guide to one of various waymarked trails across the hills.

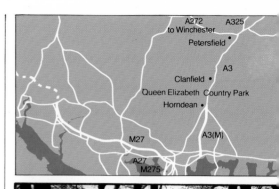

HOW TO GET THERE
from Portsmouth M275 to A27
eastbound, to join A3(M) to
Petersfield). From Winchester
A272 to Petersfield via
Bramdean then south on A.3.
Slip-road entrances to Park well
sign-posted. For Butser Hill
watch for signs to Clanfield, or
off A3 near the Hog's Lodge Inn.

1. View through the beech woods
2. Country Fair day on the slopes of Butser Hill
3. Near the Country Park Centre
4. Looking down into one of the valleys from Butser Hill
5. Grass ski-ing at speed
6. Early Purple Orchid

1-3: Hampshire County Recreation Department

An underpass beneath the main road leads to the open down, past the reconstructed Butser Ancient Farm. From this point it is possible to wander almost at will with just the occasional gate or stile to be crossed. Many a Butser shepherd has trod this land, and indeed an old wheeled hut is kept on the lower slopes with facilities for demonstrations of sheep handling. The most exciting day of each year's calendar is the 'Country Fair' in July, which includes an important competition for working sheep dogs, show ground events and stands for many countryside organisations.

The open hill sides are ideal for other activities, such as the modern sports of grass ski-ing and hang-gliding, while others fly kites or model planes. Other sports readily available in the park are wayfaring, (a gentle form of orienteering) and pony-trekking, for which horses can be hired.

The continuous grazing of sheep ensures that the downland turf is rich in wild flowers and these in turn encourage butterflies, including the common chalkhill blues. The intense competition between many species of plant for survival on the dry chalk results in different forms of leaf which shade the soil and keep it moist in sunlight, deep tuber roots to store food for long periods and, in the case of thyme, mats of vegetation to suppress other plants. The net result of this grim struggle for survival is a superb display of wildflowers displaying a range of glorious colours and delicate scents.

Adding to the interest of these chalk slopes are the subtle marks of ancient farmers: the banks built to mark off their lands or to defend their animals, the slopes of the terraces where they grew their crops, their curving tracks worn deep into the hill sides and on a peaceful ridge overlooking the Sussex Weald, their burial mounds.

Queen Elizabeth has almost everything that a country park can offer, whether one wishes to join in with popular activities, to watch others having fun or working, or to learn about the past and present of our countryside. At the same time anyone who seeks solitude and peace can easily find them by walking through the miles of beech-woods or on the paths around Butser. There can surely be no other park to compare with it!

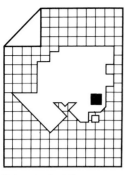

Butser Ancient Farm Demonstration Area
(Managed by Butser Ancient Farm Project Trust)

Queen Elizabeth Country Park,
Gravel Hill,
Horndean,
Hampshire,
PO8 0QE
Telephone
Portsmouth (0705) 595040

Trust Office
Nexus House,
Gravel Hill,
Horndean,
Hampshire
Telephone (24 hours)
(0705) 598838

Price Guide - C

Car Parking
Nearby

Handicapped
Suitable

Party Visits
By arrangement
Educational resources

Publications etc.
Leaflet and guidebook
Displays
Museum shop

Where to eat
Cafe in Q.E.C.P. Centre

Time to allow
1 hour

Open
Easter - End of October
Weekdays - afternoons
Sundays - all day

Public Transport
Bus Services -
Southdown buses every hour
from Petersfield and
Portsmouth, Monday -
Saturday
Rail Services -
Petersfield Station (3-4 miles
away)

Nearby Attractions
Sir George Staunton Estate
Havant Museum

BUTSER ANCIENT FARM

Set in the Queen Elizabeth Country Park is one of the most exciting archaeological research projects ever undertaken, which has been described as unique in world archaeology: the re-creation of a working prehistoric farm from the middle of the pre-Roman Iron Age, about 2400 years ago. It is the first full scale open-air research laboratory of its kind, scientifically testing the ideas which have been developed from discoveries in many archaeological excavations. The most important research has studied food production, storage of the crops, and animal husbandry. The basic prehistoric cereals, Einkorn, Emmer and Spelt wheats are grown, in addition to a multitude of very rare and unusual plants in a terraced hillside herb garden. A number of rare breeds of livestock are kept including the Soay sheep, direct

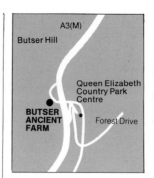

'HOW TO GET THERE'
In Queen Elizabeth Country Park, ¼ mile walk from Park Centre. On west side of Portsmouth Road. From Winchester, A272 to Petersfield, via Bramdean, then south on A3. From Portsmouth M275 to A27 eastbound then join A3(M).

demonstration area is a round-house, over 13 metres (42 feet) in diameter, the largest prehistoric building ever reconstructed. It is named the Pimperne House for it was based on a remarkable set of post holes discovered at an excavated farmland site at Pimperne in Dorset which was probably the equivalent of a manor-house. To build it over 200 trees were used and eight tons of wheat straw for thatch. The walls were made with ten tons of daub plastered onto wattle hurdle walls. Designing the roof proved an

descendants of the prehistoric domestic sheep of Southern England, and Shetland sheep, as well as Highland and Dexter cattle which have been trained to the yoke and are used to plough the fields. The Iron Age method of construction was based upon circular forms, and the reconstruction of buildings has given the project its best-known feature, the gigantic round-house, but there are a variety of other farm buildings.

The main farm or 'laboratory' is situated on Little Butser, a spur to the north of Butser Hill. This began in 1972 but in 1976 a second site, near to the Country Park Centre, was developed as a living museum area. Here the public are welcomed to see the crops and animals and to learn about the research. At the centre of the

engineering feat, for the archaeologists at Pimperne found no sign of a central post, and so none was used here to support the six main rafters which hold the great weight of thatch.

There are frequent displays each summer of the crafts and small-scale industries of the Iron Age people, including weaving, pot making and iron smelting. The whole project is so remarkable that not only has it attracted great public attention, but it has achieved an international reputation with scholars and students coming from all over the world, many to help with the work. Already the research has clearly shown that Iron Age men, far from scratching a subsistence from the soil were, with little doubt, successful and accomplished farmers.

Photo: Butser Ancient Farm Project

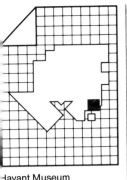

THE HAVANT MUSEUM

L ike the museum at Andover, Havant Museum is a young and developing one which also houses an art gallery for touring contemporary exhibitions and local history rooms which are often changed as new items are donated to the collection. Among the curious pieces on display are some of the instruments for cutting leather for gloves, one of the traditional industries of the town having been 'fellmongering', the working of leather as well as the making of parchment.

T he pride of Havant Museum though is a splendid collection of firearms which are securely displayed in three rooms of the building, originally a private house. One of them is arranged as a period private gun room.

T he collection belonged to a successful engineer Cecil Vokes who died in 1961. He invented the automatic windscreen wiper as well as filters for cars and later tanks and aeroplanes in World War II. Some of the earliest guns, using matchlock (burning cord), wheel-locks and flintlocks are included, from the 17th century. As an engineer Vokes obviously collected examples to show the development of firearm mechanisms: percussion caps, cartridge guns, muzzle loaders, breech loaders and all manner of extraordinary inventions to help make the guns fire more quickly. These include some with as many as four, six or even eighteen revolving barrels. The pride of the collection is a 'Winchester' of the 1860s, a specially engraved and gilt decorated one believed to have belonged to 'Buffalo Bill' Cody.

T here are also numerous unusual guns, disguised as walking sticks, knives and purses, or even built into a knuckle duster. There are also a pistol crossbow, air guns and an elastic gun!

T he story of wildfowling is told here, which is appropriate, because the coast nearby was an ideal area for the sport, with sailors and fishermen

Havant Museum
(Hampshire County Museum Service)

East Street,
Havant,
Telephone
Havant (0705) 451155

Price Guide
Free

Car Parking
Free

Handicapped
Assistance available, wheelchair access ground floor only

Party Visits & Tours
By arrangements
School holiday activities

Publications
Leaflet

Where to eat
Cafe etc, in town nearby

Time to allow
½-1 hour

Open
All year Tuesday-Saturday
10am-5pm

Public Transport
Bus and rail stations nearby
Frequent Southdown buses from Portsmouth and Southsea daily. Hourly services every day from Chichester and Bognor Regis.

Nearby Attractions
Sir George Staunton Estate
Queen Elizabeth Country Park
Solent Way (Emsworth)
Stansted Park

'HOW TO GET THERE'
From Southampton or Portsmouth, take M27 or A27 in direction of Chichester. Do not take A3(M) turn or Park Road South opposite Langstone Road. Continue on bypass to Warblington roundabout and turn left into Emsworth Road. Museum on left, beyond Lymbourn Road.

as well as experts on gunnery and a ready market for fresh game in Portsmouth. Canoe-like craft and heavy guns were used for patient stalking before firing a single, devastating shot. Immense skill was needed because with no cover at all in the channels and mudflats the hunters were in full view of the quarry, and weather and tides made it possible only two or three days a month. "There is something magical about it. The dawns, the calling tides, the winter gales and the great skeins of shouting birds riding the wild wind. They get you utterly bewitched as do the roar of the great guns and the smoke".

Photos: Hampshire County
            Museum Service

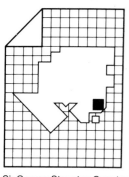

Sir George Staunton Country Park
(Portsmouth City Council,
Department of Leisure)

Middle Park Way,
Off Petersfield Road,
Havant,
Hampshire,
Telephone
Havant (0705) 451540

Price Guide - B

Car Parking
Free

Handicapped
Suitable (although no special
toilets available)

Party Visits
Welcomed

Publications
Leaflet and guidebook

Special Project
The Estate will become part
of a 100,000-acre informal
country park involving the
local woodlands of the Havant
Thicket and agricultural land
of the Havant Gap.

Where to eat
Cafe and tea-room on site
Picnic tables on site

Time to allow
2 - 3 hours

Open
Farm Trail & gardens
Good Friday-September,
open every day
Out of Season-Wholly closed
but arrangements can be
made for parties.

Public Transport
Bus Servies -
From Havant (½ hourly)
From Commercial Road,
Portsmouth (½ hourly)
Rail Services -
Havant Station

Nearby Attractions
Queen Elizabeth Country Park
Havant Museum
Fort Widley
Stansted Park

Stansted Park
Rowlands Castle
(Earl and Countess of
Bessborough)

Neo-Wren House and Theatre
museum set in forest. Sunday
cricket matches.
Open May to end Sept.
Sunday to Tuesday,
afternoons only.

SIR GEORGE STAUNTON COUNTRY PARK

Sir George Staunton was one of Portsmouth's 19th century M.P.s and he purchased the estate of Leigh, near Havant, in 1819. He was a botanical collector of note, who as a boy and a young man travelled much in the Far East. In 1792 at the age of 12 he accompanied our first ambassador to China and was the only member of the Embassy able to converse in Chinese. He served the East India Company until returning to England in 1817 and by this time he had sent back many unknown plants from China. In his memoirs he recorded that during thirty years in the House of Commons he never spoke a word, even during the bitter passage of the Reform Bill.

Around his house he created an important landscape park which included a variety of gardens, an attractive artificial lake with three islands and a selection of rustic follies. The house was pulled down in the 1860s, and its successor also has gone. Of the 1000-acre estate less than a fifth remains as a public open space, for after the last war the property was bought as an area for resettlement for the bombed-out population of Portsmouth. It is a miracle that the beautiful gardens have been conserved.

The park, with its pleasure grounds, some of the woodland walks and the home farm have been gradually restored by Portsmouth City Council. Where the gardens had fallen into neglect replanting with rhododendrons has been made in tune with the original layouts. A wide range of trees and shrubs have also been established including all of the plants introduced from China by Staunton.

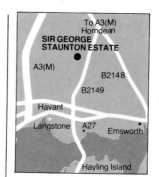

'HOW TO GET THERE'
From M27 continue east onto A27. At roundabout junction with A3023 from Hayling Island turn left into Havant, take the B2149, (sign-posted to Rowlands Castle). Car-parking signed to left, off Middle Park Way.
From Petersfield, turn off A3(M) at Horndean and follow B2149 to Emsworth.

Sir George Staunton Country Park is almost unique in one respect for it is one of the very few landscape parks in Britain to be protected as a conservation area. It contains more than a dozen listed buildings which include all the elements at the heart of a country estate, apart from the house. The walled gardens, the home farm built in 1821 together with the coach house and stables and part of the original farmland have all survived and are now used for rare breeds of farm animals and poultry. The collection is considered one of the best in the country, covering cattle, sheep, pigs goats and waterfowl, the aim being to save the different species as well as give pleasure and education. The park has a farm trail and a nature trail.

One of the special pleasures of visiting the Country Park is to discover several follies built as part of the landscaping between 1828 and 1832. The earliest was a memorial constructed out of ornamental flint work which contains stone plaques commemorating Sir George Staunton, his wife and friends. Soon followed a small Ionic temple, and an octagonal library in Gothic style both designed by Lewis Vulliamy. Unfortunately a 50-foot obelisk built in 1832 in memory of George Canning no longer stands. The library now houses a photographic display of Staunton's life and the gardens he created.

Photo: The Gothic Library
(*Portsmouth City Council*)

WINCHESTER AND CENTRAL HAMPSHIRE

The Water Meadows,
St. Cross, Winchester
Photo: Terry Southwell

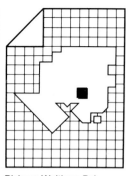

Bishops Waltham Palace
(Mr. A. Martineau)

Managed by English Heritage, Historic Buildings and Monuments Commission for England,
Spur 17,
Government Buildings,
Hawkenbury,
Tunbridge Wells,
TN2 5AQ
Telephone
(0892) 48166
Telephone (Monument)
Bishops Waltham
(0489) 32460

Price Guide - B

Car Parking
Free

Handicapped
Mostly grassed area - Suitable for wheelchairs

Party Visits
No special arrangements needed

Publications
Leaflet

Where to eat
Cafes in Bishops Waltham town

Time to allow
Half an hour

Open
All year (except Mondays)
Tuesday-Sunday
afternoons only

Special Projects
Display planned for The Dower House, building on site.

Public Transport
Bus Services -
Every hour from Winchester and Fareham on Monday-Saturday (every 2 hours on Sunday). Buses every 2 hours from Southampton and also limited service from Petersfield Monday-Saturday

Nearby Attractions
West Walk
Marwell Zoo
St Catherines Hill
Carron Row Farm and Country Park
Titchfield Abbey

BISHOP'S WALTHAM RUINS

Even today it is not difficult to imagine the grandeur of the hall and other apartments of the palace belonging to the Bishops of Winchester that was sadly destroyed in 1644, after a short siege in the Civil War, shortly after the Battle of Cheriton. The unfortunate bishop of the day was apparently there and only escaped by disguising himself as a farm labourer and riding out on a dung-cart! Around the ruins the ditch which was once a moat is clearly visible. The palace-cum-castle was one of several belonging to Winchester and was first built by King Stephen's brother, Bishop Henry de Blois, but his fortress was completely detroyed when Matilda's son, Henry II, ascended the throne.

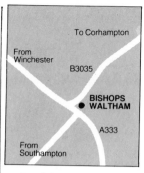

'HOW TO GET THERE'
From Southampton, A334 over Northam Bridge to Botley, then B3035 to Bishop's Waltham.
From Portsmouth M275 and M27 to Junction 10 (Fareham east), A32 to Wickham, then A333 to Bishop's Waltham.
From Winchester A333 off Winchester by-pass, fork left at Fishers Pond.

gained from the gift of a bed of gold and damask, and arras hangings, left by Cardinal Beaufort (Henry V's uncle) to Queen Margaret of Anjou.

Walking round the ruins today one can visualise the gatehouses and walls now gone which would have enclosed the work-a-day outer

In the years that followed a palatial group of buildings was erected where the nobles of the land met Henry II in 1182 and granted money for England's first Crusade. King Richard is said to have feasted here on his one brief appearance in England.

Two centuries later, and twice again during the next century, there was further rebuilding. Bishop William of Wykeham retired to Waltham, which he made his final home, dying there at the age of 80. In 1415 Henry V stayed here shortly before sailing from Southampton to France with the army which triumphed at Agincourt. Some idea of the lavish furnishings of the palace can be

court, with its servants' offices, stables and pilgrims' quarters. Beyond that was the private inner court, surrounded by the wings of the house and towers whose foundations may yet one day be revealed by archaeologists.

The name of Waltham came to be known far and wide centuries later when the untamed heathland park of the Palace, the Chase, became the haunt of a notorious gang of vagabonds who terrorised the countryside, disguised with blackened faces, until a draconion law was passed to deal with the 'Waltham Blacks'.

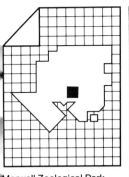

Marwell Zoological Park
(Marwell Preservation Trust Ltd.)

Colden Common,
Near Winchester,
Hampshire,
SO21 1JH
Telephone
Winchester (0962) 74406

Price Guide - E

Car Parking
Free

Handicapped
Fully equipped

Party Visits
Tours welcome and educational resources

Publications
Leaflet and guidebook
Guided tours available
Displays

Where to eat
Cafe and licensed restaurant/bar on site
Refreshments and ice-cream kiosks
Picnic tables on site

Time to allow
3 hours minimum

Open
Every day of the year
(except Christmas Day), from 10am

Public Transport
Bus Services -
Every 2 hours from Winchester and Fareham daily. Buses from Southampton on Sundays, and from Southsea on summer Sundays.
Rail Service -
Winchester or Eastleigh stations

Upper left, 1	Eastern Grey Kangaroo
Upper right, 2	Scimitar Horned Oryx
Below, 3	Siberian Tiger
1:	*Nick Skinner*
2,3:	*Marwell Preservation Trust*

MARWELL ZOOLOGICAL PARK

Marwell is not only one of the most important zoos in Britain, it is also one of the most attractive. Set in more than a hundred acres of Hampshire countryside, it is of special interest to animal lovers, naturalists, photographers and all those with an interest in wildlife.

Opened to the public in 1972, it has become well known as a centre where several endangered species can be seen. Overall, there are 1000 animals in paddocks and enclosures which adjoin the road system round the zoo. This road is two miles long and visitors can either walk round or, for an extra charge, drive round. There is a self-service restaurant, shop and kiosks, as well as ample picnic sites, and a children's play

'HOW TO GET THERE'
Marwell is within easy reach of the M3 and M27, on the B2177 between Colden Common and Bishop's Waltham.

Leopards. Of particular interest are the Asian Lions, the only ones in Britain.

Birds are not ignored at Marwell which has a good collection of flightless birds; there are ostrich and rheas, as well as several species of crane and pheasant. Amongst other zoo favourites

area with swings, radio controlled boats, climbing frames and other amusements.

The zoo has a fine collection of hoofed animals such as deer, zebra, antelope, wild cattle and wild horses, several of which have never been kept in Britain before, and two species are of particular interest. The Scimitar Horned Oryx is on the verge of extinction in Africa but the Marwell Herd is the biggest in the world and plans have been made for Oryx calves bred at Marwell and some other zoos to be returned to reserves in the wild. The Przewalski Horse is the only truly wild horse alive today; it is already extinct in the wild and the herd at Marwell produces more foals than at any other zoo. There are about 400 animals alive today.

Marwell also specialises in Big Cats such as Asian Lions, Siberian Tigers, Leopards, Jaguars, Cheetahs, Lynxes, Servals and Snow

are giraffe, camels, llamas, kangaroos, monkeys, red pandas and owls.

If you are coming to Marwell Zoo you should allow at least three hours to see all the animals, and many families now bring a picnic or eat in the restaurant and stay all day.

The newest attraction at Marwell is a 'farm-yard' area where children can make contact with a variety of animals. There is also a special exhibit on wildlife conservation, in the historic house overlooking the many paddocks. The house has its own ghost story about a newly-wed bride who disappeared during a game of hide-and-seek and whose remains were supposedly discovered much later in an attic chest. It was at Marwell Hall that Henry VIII courted, and tradition has it, secretly married his third wife Jane Seymour, after receiving news of Anne Boleyn's execution.

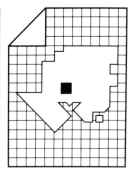

St Catherine's Hill
(Winchester College)

Managed by The Hampshire
and Isle of Wight Naturalists'
Trust
Market Place,
Romsey,
Hampshire,
SO5 8NB
Telephone
Romsey (0794) 513780

Price Guide - Free

Car Parking
Free, nearby

Handicapped
Unsuitable

Time to allow
1 - 2 hours

Open
At all times

Public Transport
Bus Services -
Frequent services from
Winchester and Southampton
to St. Cross (nearest bus stop)
Monday-Saturday and every
hour on Sunday.
Rail Services *
Winchester and Shawford

Nearby Attractions
St. Cross, Winchester
Wolvesey Castle
Winchester College
Winchester Cathedral
Museums

ST. CATHERINE'S HILL
& THE ITCHEN NAVIGATION

O ne of the greatest assets enjoyed by the
citizens of Winchester and their visitors is the
way the countryside begins only a few minutes'
walk from the town centre. Within half-an-hour
one can be climbing up the steep slopes of St.
Catherine's Hill, one of the finest examples of a
downland Iron Age fort.

T he ditches and banks around the rim were the
defences of the Iron Age predecessor of the
new Roman city laid out down below. On the
summit is a clump of beech trees which seem to
add a sense of antiquity but are in fact a
comparatively recent feature of the landscape; the
seedlings of this clump were planted in 1762 to
mark the site of a chapel which had stood there
for many centuries, until the reign of Henry VIII.
Close by is a genuine curiosity, the mizmaze. It is
not only children who enjoy trying to follow the
course of the maze, which is formed by a path cut
into the turf! No one can say how old it is of what
strange ritual purpose it may have served, but it
has certainly been used by boys for centuries
because Winchester College owns the hill and once
used it as 'the school playground'.

T o-day the hillsides are managed by the
Hampshire and Isle of Wight Naturalists'
Trust as a nature reserve and are grazed by cattle.
Countless feet tramping up and down St.
Catherine's have worn deep paths on the steep
slopes, which need repair. Flowers must be
protected and the grassland cleared of spreading
prickly hawthorn, a task which is undertaken by
volunteers. In summer there are many different
kinds of wildflowers to be seen on the hill. Among
these for instance is the horseshoe vetch, the food
plant of the chalkhill blue and of the much rarer
Adonis blue butterfly.

O n the North side of the hill is a lovely tranquil
valley where victims of the plague from
Winchester were taken for burial. From the higher
slopes of the fort can be seen shadowy traces of a
vast network of drainage channels through the
meadows. These were created by farmers to
enable them to flood their fields in winter with the
relatively warm stream waters. This system
enriched the farmers' fields with silt and
allowed their flocks to fatten up on the rich grass
which could be grown. The hay mown from the
meadows was carted to farms in the surrounding
countryside and the sheep were penned on the
nearby downs at night so that their dung would
fertilise the turf.

R eaching St. Catherine's from the small lay-by
beside the heavy traffic of the Winchester by-
pass is not recommended. A much more attractive
approach is from the Itchen Navigation, separated
from the busy road by the embankment of a dis-
used railway line. There is a small car-park by the
bridge in Garnier Road and the same point can be
reached from the city via footpaths through the
meadows. Certainly the most enjoyable way to
visit the hill is by way of the banks of the Itchen
Navigation, which has its own fascinating story.

O ne of Winchester's bishops gained the right to
levy tolls after making the river navigable at
the close of the 12th century and it is probable
that much of the stone for the Cathedral arrived

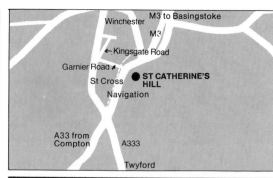

'HOW TO GET THERE'

From north Hampshire, A34 or
M3 to A33 Winchester by-
pass where there is limited
parking in lay-by.
From Southampton or
Portsmouth, A33 or A333 to
Winchester, and after St. Cross
turn right into Kingsgate
Street, and then right again
into Garnier Road. Car-park
beside Itchen Navigation.

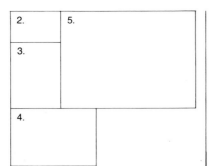

1. Plan of mizmaze, as
   drawn in 1710

2. St. Catherine's Hill and
   College boys, 19th
   Century

3. Bathing in the
   Navigation at Tonbridge

4. Barges, near the quay at
   Winchester, early 19th
   century

5. St. Catherine's from
   the water meadows

1,2: *The Warden and
Fellows of Winchester
College*

4: *Winchester City Council*

5: *Tony Nutley*

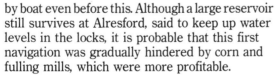

by boat even before this. Although a large reservoir still survives at Alresford, said to keep up water levels in the locks, it is probable that this first navigation was gradually hindered by corn and fulling mills, which were more profitable.

After the Restoration new plans were made for the Itchen Navigation and artificial cuts dug to avoid the mills. The river carried goods again for nearly two centuries until the 1860s, by which time the railways had captured all the trade. The contractors had built locks and a proper towpath, and for many decades all goods (of which the main cargo was always coal) were transported in their barges.

The ten-and-a-half miles of navigation are still in existence and dedicated walkers can follow the path, with a few deviations in places. It is fair to say, however, that the most pleasant section is between Winchester and Brambridge, near Otterbourne. Further south the meadows near the Itchen have been used for the railway works and airport between Eastleigh and Southampton.

The first stretch of the navigation out of Winchester can be found by Domum Road, Wharf Hill. It offers an ideal walk to St. Catherine's Hill, with ready access through the railway tunnel south of the elegant Mansbridge.

Walkers have to leave the towpath later to cross the Winchester bypass at Hockley traffic lights. The way then crosses the water-meadows to Shawford where there is an attractive open space beside the water, and car parking nearby. The pleasant walk along the towpath continues for another few miles to Brambridge, a large house where Maria Smythe grew up, better known after her first marriage, as Mrs Fitzherbert and remembered for her second marriage to the Prince of Wales, George IV.

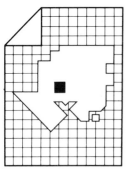

St Giles's Hill
(Winchester City Council)

(Office)
Colebrook Street,
Winchester,
Hampshire,
Telephone
Winchester (0962) 65406

Price Guide
Free

Car Parking
Nearby in Chesil Street

Handicapped
Unsuitable

Where to eat
Picnic areas or cafes in City
centre

Time to allow
Half an hour

Open
At all times

Public Transport
Bus Services -
Winchester bus station
nearby
Hampshire Bus service every
30 minutes from Southampton
(hourly on Sunday). Buses
every hour from Guildford,
Alton and Farnham (every 2
hours on Sunday). Buses
every hour from Romsey on
Monday-Saturday and every
every 2 hours from Andover
on Monday-Saturday (limited
service on Sunday). Additional
buses run from Oxford and
Newbury (daily) and from
Petersfield on Monday-
Saturday (limited service).

Rail Services-
Winchester Station 1 mile
away

Nearby Attractions
Winchester City Mill
Winchester College
Winchester Cathedral
Wolvesey Castle
St John's Rooms

ST. GILES'S HILL

Looking at the steep wooded hillside rising so beautifully above Winchester's High Street and the statue of Alfred in the Broadway, it is difficult to realise that the top of this hill was once one of the great centres of European trade, a Common Market of the mediaeval world. Today, although its face has been quite changed with quarrying and tree planting, St. Giles's Hill is the ideal place for any visitor to the city to begin, for there is no more spectacular viewpoint in Hampshire; the town lies at one's feet with its cathedral, college, churches and streets all looking like models.

We know that on the hill the last of the Saxon earls was executed for conspiracy, betrayed by his Norman wife. The fair on the plateau began some years later in 1094 when Rufus allowed Bishop Walkelin the right to hold court each autumn over the market. The market drew traders from as far away as Spain and spread over as many as twenty-four days, during which time all other business for miles around had to cease, including trade in Southampton and even legal business in London! The city gates below the hill were locked and its economic life moved up to the stalls, which were left to stand from one year to another.

'HOW TO GET THERE'
From Winchester by-pass enter at turn-off for Bar End and Morestead. Large car park in Chesil Street. St. Giles's Hill sign-posted (footpath behind Art Gallery, or near the Old Chesil Rectory past the 'Rising Sun').

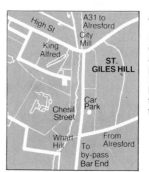

The Bishops of Winchester grew rich and the Cathedral was abundantly endowed with the tolls levied on all the goods and imports brought to market. The city's speciality, cloth, was exchanged for iron from Spain, wine from Gascony, spices from the East, woad from Toulouse, as well as textiles, madder and brass-ware from the Low Countries and the Rhineland. Anyone with a fancy for outlandish creatures could find apes, bears and all kinds of strange beasts.

The Bishop's rule was, however, severe and although the period of the fair was reduced to sixteen days its closure was still greeted with relief by local people. The city minstrels accompanied the authorities at the fair's end as they went to reclaim the city's weighing machine from the hill. The market virtually died with the calamitous Hundred Years War when overseas traders no longer came and there were few goods to bring the merchants from distant cities and towns.

Below the hill a large car park has been created on the site of an abandoned railway line which cut sharply into the side of the down, while another large section of the hill has been removed by chalk quarriers. At the foot of St Giles's is 'The Old Chesil Rectory', one of Winchester's best half-timbered buildings, and a public house called "The Rising Sun" whose cellars derive from the lock-up for those committed by the Bishop during the fair. His court was named "Pie Powder" (French for 'dusty feet') for it dealt mostly with travellers.

*Top: View of High
            Street from
            St. Giles's*

*Bottom: Amidst the hill's
            beautiful trees*

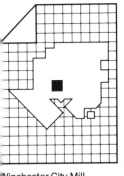

Winchester City Mill
(National Trust - Leased to Y.H.A.)

1 Water Lane,
Winchester,
Hampshire,
SO23 8EJ
Telephone YHA Warden
Winchester (0962) 3723

Price Guide - A

Car Parking
Nearby, Chesil Street

Handicapped
Unsuitable

Publications
Leaflet

Where to eat
Suitable picnic areas and cafes in City

Time to allow
¼ - ½ hour

Open
April to end Oct. -Tues to Saturday and Bank Holiday Monday (afternoons)
Nov. to end Mar. -By previous arrangement with resident Warden between 10 and 5 on Wed., Thurs., or Friday only.

Public Transport
Bus Services -
Winchester Bus Station nearby.
Every 30 minutes from Southampton (hourly on Sunday). Buses every hour from Guildford, Alton, Romsey and Fareham (every 2 hours on Sunday). Every 2 hours from Andover on Monday-Saturday (limited service on Sunday). Additional buses run from Oxford and Newbury (daily) and from Petersfield Monday - Saturday (limited service).
Rail Service -
Winchester station 1 mile away

Nearby Attractions
Winchester College
Winchester Cathedral
Wolvesey Castle
City Museum
Riverside Walks
Heritage Centre

Chesil Theatre
Chesil Street, Winchester (Winchester Dramatic Society)
Former medieval church
Open by appointment
Telephone
Winchester (0962) 67086

WINCHESTER CITY MILL

Just outside the former Eastgate of the city, at the foot of St. Giles's Hill, is the City Mill, an 18th century building on an ancient site. It stands beside City Bridge, a low arched crossing with a particularly fine balustrade. The date on the outside is 1744 and for almost 200 years corn was milled in this building. The National Trust took it over in 1929 to ensure its preservation and, shortly afterwards, leased it to the Youth Hostels Association, allowing open access by the public during the season.

Well before the Norman Conquest there was a mill here belonging to the nunnery at Wherwell, for the abbesses had much property in the town. The Black Death severely affected Winchester and the building seems to have been left derelict for three centuries until the 1740s. This was one of many mills in Winchester, which in mediaeval times - and possibly earlier - was an important European centre for woollen cloth. Another mill can be seen in the Abbey Gardens, a small park off the Broadway, and a further one is in the Weirs, a riverside park to the south.

The City Mill is an attractive building and in summer vistors can go inside to sense the full force of the river rushing below. But unfortunately the old wheels are derelict. The large timbered hall upstairs, used by the hostellers as a common room, can also be visited, as well as a small island garden.

The River Itchen splits into several streams above the city and the lower and middle brooks, mentioned in street names, can be heard in many parts of the town, sometimes flowing below pavements and streets, sometimes rushing through gardens and parks.

The City Mill is a good starting point for walks from Winchester along the Itchen Valley. Water Lane, a small street alongside leads to a footpath to the Worthys and the Pilgrims Way, while to the south a riverside path leads through the water meadows to St. Cross and Shawford.

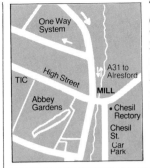

'HOW TO GET THERE'
(See St Giles's Hill) From other directions follow Winchester one-way system down North Walls and follow signs to Petersfield by King Alfred's statue and across City bridge. Turn right into Chesil Street for large car park. Mill by bridge.

Top: National Trust

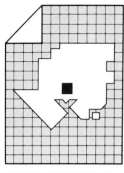

HISTORIC WINCHESTER

To follow the walk - From the City Bridge (by the Riverside Inn) head south through the waterside gardens, until reaching large mill. Bear right along the medieval walls and into College Street for several hundred yards. Turn right under Kingsgate and immediately right again through a second medieval gate into the Cathedral Close. Aim for the western end of the Cathedral, where a doorway leads through to the Cathedral green and West Front. The path beside the avenue of young trees comes out by the City museum and close to the High Street. The walk can be made in less than half an hour at a leisurely pace.

Tourist Information The T.I.C. in the Guildhall is the starting point for guided walks of the City (Two or three times daily in Summer, Saturday mornings only in Winter). Walks leaflets, an events programme and accommodation booking service.
Telephone Winchester (0962) 68166, 65406 (weekends only).

Youth Hostel City Mill, Telephone Winchester (0962) 53723

Winchester Heritage Centre

52-54 Upper Brook Street, Winchester
Telephone (0962)51664
Permanent displays of the city's heritage, its history, buildings and environment.
Open Wednesdays 12-4pm, Thursday - Saturday, 10am-12.30pm. 2-4pm, Sundays 2-4pm.

Nearby Attractions
St. Johns Rooms Winchester (Leading Leisure)
Old medieval hospital, and historic social centre of Winchester. Old Assembly rooms magnificently restored. Open during normal licensing hours.
For further information contact Southampton (0703)592512

HISTORIC WINCHESTER

Winchester is in many ways an exceptional city, little spoilt by the powerful forces of change which have so dramatically 'modernised' other towns. Perhaps the greatest difference is that only hundreds now live where thousands of people were once crowded inside the old city walls, working at industries which have long disappeared. The High Street shops may be as large and busy as in any other city, but, with traffic diverted away from the centre, walking in Winchester can be a pleasure.

Visitors are advised to park in Chesil Street, below the city's wooded hillside park called St. Giles's Hill. A tour can begin on the hill at the City Mill nearby, which straddles the River Itchen. The bridge by the City Mill is a good starting point for a delightful walk around the town, eventually arriving in the most pleasant part of the High Street. Visitors may find it useful, however, to call in at the Tourist Information Centre in the Guildhall where a variety of tourist publications can be bought, including a trail leaflet for this walk.

The recommended route, taking about three-quarters of an hour, starts beside the Itchen, through a park called the Weirs. Along this garden runs a substantial section of the wall which once surrounded the city and the castle of the Bishops of Winchester. The Itchen disappears beneath a great corn-mill converted into luxury flats, but the path runs on beside the high flint wall into College Street, where there is a view of the 17th century Palace built beside the ruined castle of Wolvesey, one of the homes of the Bishops of Winchester. Before the Norman Conquest the Saxon kings had ordered the Welsh to pay tribute of 300 wolves' heads each year to be delivered here in Winchester, and so came about the name 'Wolvesey'.

Nearby is the start of a path across the water meadows to St. Cross. (continue walking south, and the track starts at the end of the gravelled path on the right.) In College Street is the entrance to Winchester College (see page 93), the Headmaster's house, and also the house where Jane Austen was nursed before her death. Kingsgate Street to the left is one of the most attractive in the town, but the trail turns right under Kingsgate, one of the City's two mediaeval entrances which still stands, the other is the Westgate. Within Kingsgate is the Hampshire Bookshop, and a small church, St. Swithun-upon-Kingsgate, above the gate's archway.

From here turn right through the gate of the Cathedral Close to Cheyney Court, a fantastic rambling half-timbered building, and the barn-like stables of the Priory which now form part of the Pilgrims School, where the boys of the Cathedral and College choirs are educated. Only the hall of the Pilgrims School is open to the public. This is part of a much longer hall which has the earliest hammer-beam roof in the country (dated about 1295). Contrary to the comparatively recent tradition it is unlikely that the building was erected to shelter pilgrims. Entrance to the hall is obtained

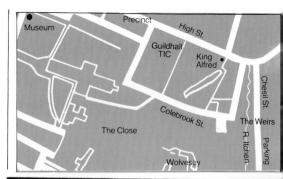

at the left of the main school building.

Opposite the hall are the Judges' Lodging and the only late 'intrusion' in the Close, a street which was built in the late 17th century and named Dome Alley. Among many other buildings the Deanery is of particular interest. Here lived the Priors before the Dissolution, when the cloisters and many other buildings were destroyed. There remains a splendid 13th century arched porch where pilgrims waited for alms of meat left over from the Prior's table.

From the Close, a footway leads to the west front of the Cathedral and the church yard. Alternatively, a way out to the east leads through

HOW TO GET THERE'

Follow direction as for City
Mill and St. Giles's Hill to large
car park in Chesil Street. Street
car parking in City Centre
easier on Sundays.
To get to Winchester from
Portsmouth, A333 via
Bishop's Waltham or via M27
to north Southampton interchange with A33. From New
Forest follow M27 to A33.

Top left: College Street
            where Jane
            Austen died.

Below left: Cheyney Court at
            the entrance to the
            Cathedral Close

Top right: The entrance
            gateway to the
            Close.

Bottom   The Weirs, river-
left: side walk between
            the City Mill and
            College Street.

Bottom   The shopping
right: precinct, The
            Buttercross and
            the Pentice in the
            High Street.

Engraving   Victorian view of
left: the High Street.

Top, left, Mike Goddard
below left,
top right:

the "Slype", beneath the Cathedral library, coming
out through Water Close where a beautiful small
water garden seems to have a magical quality.
Each night the three ways into the Close are
locked at ten o'clock and residents must carry a
great key to let themselves in after that time.

War memorials stand on the Cathedral green,
as well as a much-photographed gravestone
in memory of Thomas Thetcher, a soldier who died
from drinking too much small beer on a hot day.

'A good soldier never is forgot,
whether he die by musket or by pot'.

Beside a newly-planted avenue of limes a
path leads to the Square, the City Museum
and the picturesque Eclipse Inn. The richly-varied
shop fronts and the crowded, covered passageway through to the precinct in the High Street
make this one of Winchester's most delightful
corners. Recent restoration in Gilbert's Bookshop
has reopened a mediaeval hall, and the Church of
St. Lawrence next door has been beautifully
restored after a tragic fire. The Butter Cross,
through the passage, was erected early in the 15th
century but was largely restored in the 1860s.
The covered Pentice, an arcade, dates from
Elizabethan times, but the lavish, fascinating
front to Boots, with its carvings of former bishops,
went up in this century. Over the street, W.H.
Smith's shop also has a 'mediaeval' hall but this too
is entirely modern and was once used as a tea-
room by the firm. Godbegot House, the old Guildhall (Lloyds Bank) and the Royal Oak are a few
among many ancient well-preserved buildings in
this area.

Turning back towards St. Giles's down the
High Street, the Victorian Guildhall of 1873
stands like a fantasy castle. The Tourist Information Centre is located here. Just beyond is the
Abbey Garden, the site of St. Mary's, a Saxon
nunnery which was destroyed in the 15th century.
Until ninety years ago the gardens were the
private grounds of Abbey House, built in 1748,
which strangely enough looks like a gothic castle
on one side and a classical Regency house on the
other! The stream through the park disappears
into a mill disguised as a small temple.

Evening is perhaps the best time for this
walk around Winchester, for the running
water can be heard as the daily traffic dies, as
well as the bells of the College, the chimes of
the Cathedral and the old Guildhall clocks. Each
night in Winchester the curfew is still rung, a
signal to extinguish fires (the word curfew comes
from the old French 'to cover fire'). To enjoy, or to
escape, a surfeit of bells visitors should note
that Wednesday evening is always a practice night
for the Cathedral ringers!

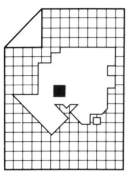

Wolvesey Palace
(Church Commissioners)

Managed by English Heritage,
Historic Buildings & Monuments Commission for England,
Spur 17,
Government Buildings,
Hawkenbury,
Tunbridge Wells,
Kent,
TN2 5AQ
Telephone (0892) 48166

Price Guide - C/D

Car Parking
Street parking nearby

Handicapped
Suitable

Party Visits
No special arrangements needed
Educational visits free if prior arrangements made

Publications
Leaflet
Briefing notes

Where to eat
Wide choice in Winchester

Time to allow
Half an hour

Open
29th March - 31st October
Monday - Saturday,
9.30am - 4.30pm
Sunday, 2 - 6.30pm

Public Transport
Bus Services
Regular services from Southampton, Romsey, Eastleigh, Salisbury and Petersfield. Bus station 10 minutes walk.
Rail Services
Winchester Station,
15 minutes walk.

Nearby Attractions
Winchester College
Winchester Cathedral
City Museum, Winchester
Winchester Heritage Centre
St. Catherine's Hill
Itchen Navigation

WOLVESEY CASTLE

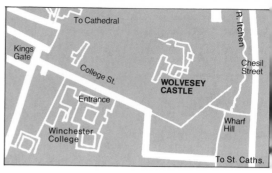

A demand by a Saxon king for 300 wolves' heads to be brought yearly to Winchester by a Welsh prince is said to account for the name of this traditional site of the principal palace of the Bishop of Winchester, close by the Cathedral. The bishop still lives in this quarter of the city, in a remaining wing of a palace attributed to Christopher Wren, though for many years the prelate's main residence was Farnham Castle, Surrey. The creation in 1927 of the diocese of Guildford brought back the bishop to Winchester. Visitors to Wolvesey are asked to remember that the 'modern' palace is therefore now a private home.

The ruins of Wolvesey Castle have only recently been opened to the public following centuries of antiquarian curiosity. The gaunt flint ruins are the remains of a huge castle started by Bishop William Gifford about 40 years after the Norman Conquest and completed by one of the most powerful of Winchester's bishops, Henry de Blois,

Blois's brother and sister. The bishop sided first with one then the other in a bitter war for succession that saw Flemish mercenaries at Wolvesey flinging fire-balls at Matilda and her troops in the Castle to the north-west. Stephen eventually triumphed and de Blois lived on at Wolvesey and elsewhere for 20 years.

The East Hall of the castle was its main public room and was entered to the south. To the east were three kitchens, loftily built to disperse the intense heat from huge open fires. Many have mistaken them for a keep. Opposite was the West Hall where the bishop had his private

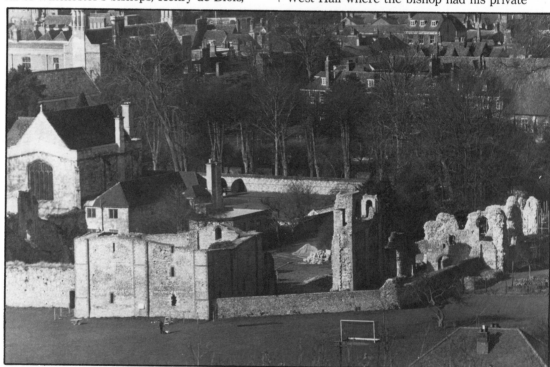

grandson of William the Conqueror. The site had long held the palace of the Saxon bishops and its great enclosing flint walls, which still stand, were once at the request of King Alfred hung with the bodies of Danes who travelled up the River Itchen nearby and attacked the city. De Blois, too, as well as being a man of God was much interested in defending himself, which explains why Wolvesey's walls were so massive. It was by far the grandest of six castles he built in the region and consisted of a great central courtyard with a chapel and two halls. It was a palace to match de Blois's ambitions - unsuccessful as it turned out - to make Winchester an archbishopric.

Parts of Wolvesey were built with the rubble of the palace that William had built after the Conquest. This stood near the present Butter Cross in High Street and was destroyed in the midst of the pitched batles that the city saw in the troubled time of 'Stephen and Matilda', de

apartments. These were later used by the succession of royal visitors to Winchester, the last to do so being Mary Tudor on the occasion of her wedding to Philip of Spain in the Cathedral in 1554. Hereafter the bishops stayed mainly at Farnham Castle, Surrey, which was centrally placed in a diocese that at the time stretched from the South Coast to Southwark in London.

Wolvesey Castle was largely demolished in the 1680s to provide building materials for a new palace being raised alongside. This was at a time when Charles II was planning his own palace to the west of the city and the new mansion was presumably built to provide the bishop with seemly accommodation, but in the event the King's House was never completed and Wolvesey Palace fell into disrepair. The present palace incorporates at its north end a 15th century private chapel that was once a part of the medieval building.   BS

Photo: Hampshire Chronicle

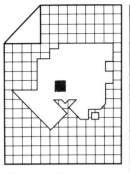

Winchester College
(The Warden and Fellows)

College Street,
Winchester,
Hampshire.
SO23 9NA
Telephone
Winchester (0962) 64242

Price Guide - B

Car Parking
City Centre and Chesil Street
car parks

Party Visits
By arrangement with Bursary

Handicapped
Suitable for wheelchairs

Publications etc.
Leaflet
Tours available
(see below)

Time to allow
¼ hour, or one hour for guided
tour

Open
All year with the exception of
Christmas Day and Boxing
Day
Tours - April - September,
11am, 2pm and 3pm.
May - August, 11am, 2pm,
3.15pm and 4.30pm

Exhibitions
College Treasury: May -
September, Thursday,
Saturday and Sunday, 2-4pm
October - April, Saturday
and Sunday, 2 - 4pm
Occasional exhibitions in the
Moberly Library.

Public Transport
Bus Services -
Winchester bus station
10-minute walk
Rail Service -
Winchester railway station
1 mile away, buses to town

Nearby Attractions
Wolvesey Castle
Water Meadows
Itchen Navigation
St. Catherine's Hill
Cathedral
City Museum

Top: The Trusty Servant

Below: Chamber Court,
the centre of
College Life

WINCHESTER COLLEGE

Winchester College recently marked its 600th anniversary in 1982 for in 1382 William Long, better known as William of Wykeham, founded the College. It was not the first school in Winchester for William, born in 1324, had himself been a student in the grammar school run by the Cathedral Priory's monks in the years shortly before the Hundred Years War between France and England. When the terrible Black Death appeared this young man had already begun a successful career as an architect for King Edward III, but it was a bad time to be an architect with the population ravaged by disease and the economy collapsing. William became ordained and after only six years was appointed Bishop of Winchester; he was ideally suited to complete the delayed rebuilding of the cathedral, and later funded Winchester College as well as another, 'New College' in Oxford.

For such troubled times the College gatehouse was made strong enough to serve in defence of the boys, their teachers and the college staff inside. Beyond the porter's room is the first or Outer Court where, just as in the abbeys, the brewhouse and other domestic offices (the granary, stables and slaughterhouse) were sited. Today the brewhouse contains a library. A second gateway leads into the Chamber Court around which are rooms for the seventy scholars, the chapel, "Seventh Chamber" (which was the original schoolroom) and, above it, the Hall where the scholars still dine.

The chapel has not only excellent carved wood misericords (small tip-up seats) but also fine stained glass, fan tracery timber vaulting and early XVIth century tapestries. The celebrated Trusty Servant portrait can be seen nearby; an ancient satirical cartoon on the traits of a man servant, with the head of a pig, ears of an ass and the feet of a stag.

'HOW TO GET THERE'

Follow directions as for City Mill and St. Giles's. Very limited street parking during week-days in College Street. From Chesil Street turn down Wharf Hill and follow road over bridge into College Walk.

Beyond the chapel the present-day school has spread across the meadows and occupies much of the south of central Winchester. However, to this day the scholars, marked out from their fellow-students by the customary gowns, live, eat and worship in and around the Chamber Court. Conducted tours also include the 15th century Chantry and Cloisters where teaching used to take place in summer time. "School", a late 17th century building large enough for several classes in the one room, can be seen from the outside but is not open to visitors.

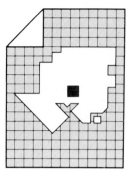

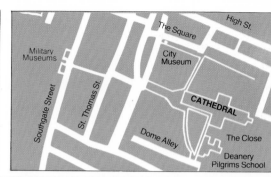

WINCHESTER CATHEDRAL

It is more difficult to do justice to this one building, what it is and what it means, than to all the other places described in this book, for this is no mere tourist attraction but a place of pilgrimage where, in the words of a poet, "God offers the Water of Life from a wellspring 900 years deep". It is also a focal point where people can sense English history before the arrival of the Norman overlords and their powerful churchmen.

Here are traces of Canute and Queen Emma, St Swithun and King Alfred. Here the Norman masons raised their massive columns and arches, which their descendants clad with beautiful columns which spring to the ceiling of the ribbed roof of what seems an endless nave. Here were laid to rest, in their own rich tomb-chapels, bishops of incomparable power and wealth. During the Reformation, the tomb of St. Swithun was destroyed. In this Cathedral the kingdoms of Spain and England were briefly joined together when the Catholic Bishop Gardiner married Mary Tudor to Philip of Spain in 1554. During the Civil War soldiers marched in and destroyed the effigies and relics, riches and monuments so despised by the Puritans. After 1660 the Deanery nearby was restored and the life of the Cathedral and the wealth of its properties returned. In due course the Library was repaired and refurnished with books, a generous legacy of Bishop Morley.

There are memorials to the reflective angler, Izaac Walton, "a man of peace in a country torn by civil war", and in the calm of the north aisle of the nave is the resting place of Jane Austen. Beneath the cathedral is the crypt, on which the massive weight of the choir is supported. The story of how William Walker, the diver, saved the cathedral must surely be the most extraordinary in any church history. During the years 1906-11 he worked in flooded pits dug beneath the foundations, inserting concrete where the Norman timber balks were sinking into the mud below.

This story and many others of inspiring events in the life of the Cathedral are told in numerous booklets which are on sale, while guides are ready to answer questions and show visitors round. There is the opportunity to visit the library, where precious volumes were once kept chained. The most prized possession here is the Bible produced by the 12th century Winchester School of Artists, whose work reached its peak in the brilliantly painted images of the great initial letters. These make the book one of the masterpieces of western civilisation, for the artists illustrated Old and New Testament scenes which reflected the life and events of their own times. During the summer months when the waters recede the crypt is open to visitors, and a special exhibition of the church's treasures of plate is on view.

The Cathedral is central to the religious life of Winchester and Hampshire. Its music is joyous and rich, and every three years there is a music festival. Annually there are Services of Thanksgiving and Remembrance, Celebrations and Blessings which bring splendid sights of

Winchester Cathedral

Cathedral Office
5 The Close,
Winchester,
Hampshire,
SO23 9LS
Telephone
Winchester (0962) 53137

Price Guide
Contribution of 75p per head suggested

Car Parking
City Centre car parks and Chesil Street

Handicapped
Suitable (wheelchairs availble and ramp is present for easy access)

Party Visits
By arrangement
Tours and educational resources

Publications etc.
Leaflet and Guidebook
Displays
Trails

Where to eat
Grounds suitable for picnics and cafes nearby in High Street

Time to allow
1 - 2 hours

Open
Every day of the year
(7.30am - 6.30pm)
Library - Winter - open Wednesday and Saturday
Summer - open except for Sunday and Monday mornings

Public Transport
Bus Services -
Winchester Bus Station
10 minutes walk
Rail Services -
Winchester Station ¾ mile

Nearby Attractions
Wolvesey Castle
Winchester College
City Museum
Hampshire Regiment Museum
Royal Hussars Museum
Great Hall and Round Table

Pilgrims Hall
(The Dean and Chapter, Winchester Cathedral)
Pre reformation lodging for pilgrims. Remarkable 14th century hammerbeam roof.
Open all year daily (except when booked for private functions etc.)
Parties must give advance notice.
Telephone Winchester
(0962) 53137

11 The Close
(Dean and Chapter of Winchester Cathedral)
Late 17th century house
Visitors welcome by appointment
Telephone Winchester 68580

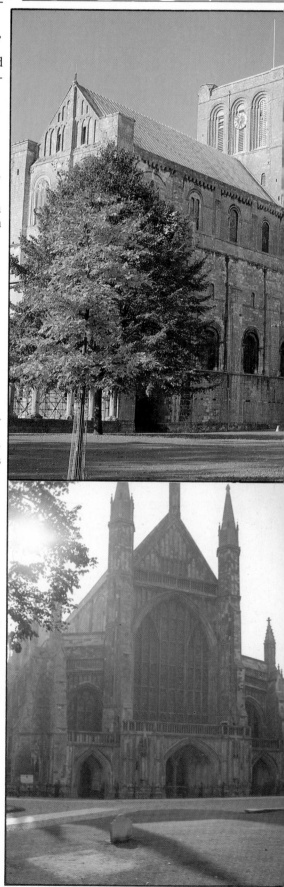

HOW TO GET THERE'

Weekdays - follow suggested directions to Chesil Street (see City Mill/St Giles's Hill). Sunday parking available in local streets - High Street, The Square etc. From A333 Southgate Street turn right at 'Green Man' into St. Swithun's Street Cathedral on right. Alternative: from King Alfred's statue and Broadway turn left into Colebrook St. (Public car-park).

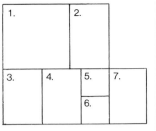

1.	From the Close	6.	Bishop William of Wykeham
2.	Water Garden at Colebrook Street entrance to Cathedral Close	7.	Wood Carving of a beggar on a choir stall
3.	West Front		
4.	St. Swithun's Shrine	2.	Tony Nutley
5.	Illumination from the Winchester Bible	3.	Mike Goddard
		4-7.	Murray Davison

pageantry, processions, pomp and circumstance. But most important of all, the Daily Services are said or sung as they have been for hundreds of years.

Each year, for one day only at the end of July, there is an opportunity to ascend to the top of the tower, treading the worn steps up the narrow spiral stairs. Above the ringing chamber the stone turret rises higher and higher to emerge in the open air 160 ft. up, with the views in every direction - ample reward for the exertion.

There is too much to see and to sense in one visit: a treasure house of the arts; a sanctuary from the bustle of modern life; a memorial to our long history; a centre for excellence; a building raised to the Glory of God.

In 1979, the ninth centenary year, visitors to the Cathedral were each given a poem with the lines:

> Cup your hands
> Like a bowl
> Let me overflow ...
> Bend down and drink
> I am the Water of the Well
> That makes Men whole
> I am the cold Water
> That restores your Soul.

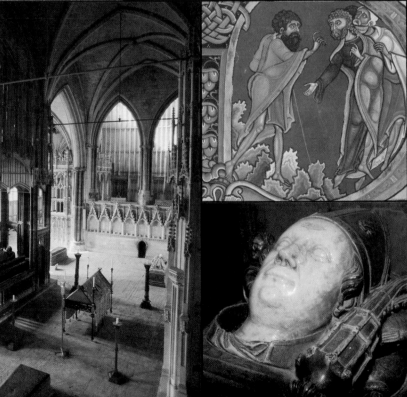

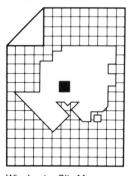

Winchester City Museum

(Winchester City Council)

The Square,
Winchester.
Telephone
Winchester (0962) 68166
Ext. 269

Price Guide - Free
Adults 20p Children Free

Open
April 1 to end of Sept. - every day
October to March - closed Mondays

Royal Hussars Regimental Museum,
Lower Barracks
(Ministry of Defence)

Southgate Street,
Winchester.
Telephone
Winchester (0962) 61781
Ext. 239

Royal Hampshire Regimental Museum

(Ministry of Defence)
Serles House,
Southgate Street,
Winchester,
Telephone
Winchester (0962) 61781
Ext. 261

Price Guide - Free

Open
All year except weekends and Bank Holidays

West Gate
(Winchester City Council)

High Street,
Winchester.
Telephone
Winchester (0962) 68166
Ext. 269

Price guide - A

Open
Main season - open every day
Out of season - closed Mondays

Royal Green Jackets Museums

Peninsula Barracks,
Romsey Road,
Winchester.
Telephone
Winchester (0962) 61781
Ext. 288

Price Guide - Free

Open
April - end September,
Monday-Friday, 10am-12.30pm, 2-4pm
Saturday, 2.30-4.30pm
October - End of March,
Monday - Friday, 10.30am-12.30pm, 2-4pm

Museums unsuitable for handicapped except ground floor of City Museum.
Allow ½ - 1 hour for each museum.
Party visits by arrangement

WINCHESTER MUSEUMS

Winchester citizens have always taken pride in their rich history and Hampshire's first museum was built in the city close to the Cathedral, in 1903. It is a three-storey building with an elegant flint-decorated front which has a splendid variety of relics from the past. Few cities have been subjected to such thorough archaeological investigation and painstaking historical research, particularly in recent years. A large mosaic floor from a nearby Roman villa, discovered with its geometrical design in near perfect condition, is on show; Saxon pottery and mediaeval jewellery can be seen, and the moot horn used for calling city meetings in the early 13th century is also on display. From the early 18th century there is a wooden ceiling beam rescued from the city's first hospital with a painted inscription addressed to its patients: 'Despise not Thou the Chastening of the Almighty'! The forerunner of the ambulance, a Sedan chair, can also be seen.

The most outstanding attractions of the museum are two recently installed shops from the High Street. The chemists, 'Hunts', closed their old shop after a century of business, (the firm still continues elsewhere), and the generous gift of much of the antique equipment and furniture has been used to recreate a Victorian shop which would have seemed quite modern to the founders of the museum. The second shop is a tobacconists which is by no means an antiquity but it will hopefully be valued as such by coming generations.

A short distance to the west, in Southgate Street, are two more museums. The Georgian building, Serle's House, lies back from the busy street, set in a fine garden that is a memorial to the fallen through three centuries of battles in which the Royal Hampshire Regiment has fought. Not only does their small museum have old Colours, uniforms and weapons of the 18th century Militia, but also mementos from the Western Front of 1915, the landings at Gallipoli, from North Africa, Normandy and Northern Ireland.

The newest museum in Winchester is the Royal Hussars Regimental Museum. The Hussars (the 11th) took part in the Light Brigade charge at Balaclava, and Hussars also fought in the Boer War and served for generations in India. After the First World War their chargers were gradually exchanged for light tanks and armoured cars, examples of which stand outside. The story of the Cavalry is shown with fitting panache using dashing costumed figures, gleaming trophies, excellent models and intriguing photographs from the days of Imperial India.

At the top of Winchester High Street stands the Westgate through which all citizens had to pass on their way to Romsey, or to enter the Castle whose entrance was outside the city wall. The doors of the gate were, of course, always closed during emergencies and for hundreds of years they were shut each night. A small porter's lodge was lost when a foot passage was cut through in the 19th century, but until 1959 traffic still passed through the arch.

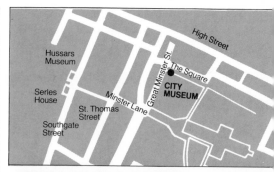

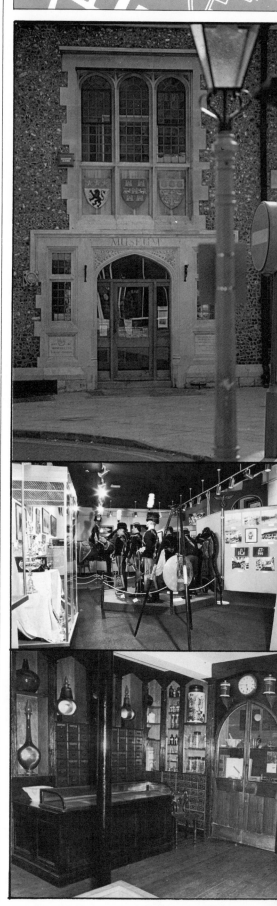

'HOW TO GET THERE'

From the Cathedral the City Museum is easily found at the corner of the Green. To Serles House on foot, follow Great Minster Street round to Minster Lane. Turn left in St. Thomas's Passage to Southgate Street, opposite Serles Co. Turn right towards town centre for Hussars museum, 5 yards on left. Westgate and Royal Green Jackets Museums near Great Hall.

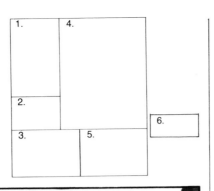

1. Entrance to the City Museum
2. Royal Hussars Regimental Museum display
3. 'Hunt's' Chemist shop in Winchester City Museum
4. Winchester Westgate
5. Serles House, home of the Royal Hampshire Regimental Museum
6. The Ancient Castle

1: Mike Goddard
2,3,4,6: Winchester City Council
2: E.A. Sollars

I n a large room over the arched gate is a small museum. In the one room can be seen, carved on the walls, the names and even the drawings of prisoners held captive here in the 16th and 17th centuries, including pictures of a three-masted ship and a windmill. The museum has a fine decorated panelled ceiling, installed at Winchester college for the warden in 1554, when Mary and Philip were married in the city. The site of the Gate possibly goes back to Roman times, but the present structure was built over the three centuries after 1100 and it may once have had a drawbridge and portcullis, as well as primitive cannon. There is a fine view of the High Street from the roof of the Westgate, which is accessible to visitors.

N earby in Romsey Road is the entrance to Peninsula Barracks, so named because the three former regiments which were amalgamated to form the Royal Green Jackets all fought against Napoleon's armies in the Spanish Peninsula. Their fine Regimental Museum traces the regiments' histories in peace and war from 1741 to the present day. There are hundreds of trophies and mementos of the battlefields, the barracks and the messes, from campaigns and colonies all over the world. To name only a few from a hall full of fascinating exhibits, the remarkable collection of uniforms includes the court dress-coat worn by the first Duke of Wellington as Colonel-in-Chief of the Rifle Brigade; a special display illustrates the long connection between the Royal Family and the King's Royal Rifle Corps; a painting and diorama commemorate the capture of the bridges over the Caen Canal and the River Orne by glider-borne troops of the 52nd Light Infantry early on the 6th June 1944, D-Day.

T he Royal Green Jackets have recently moved from the Peninsula Barracks after an association that dates back to 1858, though the museum is remaining in situ. The barracks stand on the site of the Norman Castle demolished by order of Oliver Cromwell after the Civil War. They derive from the ambitious plans of Charles II to build a palace in the city. Designs were drawn up by Sir Christopher Wren and building commenced, but the grand scheme was incomplete at the time of Charles' death in 1685. Never occupied as a palace it was subsequently used to house prisoners of war and later, French refugees, until becoming a barracks in 1796. Destroyed by fire in 1894 the barracks were rebuilt, incorporating some of the features of Wren's design for the King's House. The Museum contains a small display covering the history of the castle site.

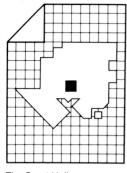

The Great Hall
(Hampshire County Council)

The Castle,
High Street,
Winchester,
Hampshire.
Telephone
Winchester (0962) 54411

Price Guide - Free

Car Parking
City Car Parks

Handicapped
Suitable

Party Visits
The Great Hall is included on
city guided tours

Publications etc.
Leaflet and guidebook

Time to allow
½ hour

Open
April - September - Every
day (Sundays, afternoon only)
Winter - Every day (Saturday
and Sundays, afternoon only)
Closed Good Friday and
Christmas Day

Public Transport
Bus and rail stations within
walking distance

Domesday Exhibition
To mark the 900th anniversary
of the Domesday Book, written
in Winchester, an exhibition
will be held in the Great Hall,
close to the site where the
monks and barons carried out
the work.
27th March - 1st November,
1986, every day 10am-6pm,
with 8pm closing during June,
July and August.

Price Guide - C

Nearby Attractions
Royal Green Jackets
Museum
Westgate Museum

THE ROUND TABLE & GREAT HALL

There is no other part of Hampshire which the visitor is likely to find as confusing as the Winchester Castle site, for although this is one of the most richly historic places in England it is also surrounded by feint and pretence. Next to the Great Hall are Victorian offices designed to look like an extraordinary castle in finely-worked flint, while recent extensions to these offices and the adjoining new Law Courts have created a dramatic and completely new landscape. The original castle above the hill-side was built by William I, destroyed by Cromwell, redesigned by Wren and rebuilt again at the turn of the last century; even this last rebuilding was faithful to the 17th century style. The Hall itself was built between 1222-1236, a century-and-a-half after the Normans established the castle, and even this one remaining building was apparently later reduced in size.

Inside on the east wall is a mock-mediaeval Victorian painting recording the names of all the Hampshire Knights who had served in Parliament. Facing this is 'King Arthur's' Round Table, whose origin is still uncertain. It was probably built in the reign of Edward III, who in 1344 founded his own romantic brotherhood of chivalrous knights based on the Dark Age mythology. Even then, it seems that the painting on the table top was made two centuries later, at the wish of Henry VIII, to impress Charles V, Holy Roman Emperor, when he visited Southampton and Winchester in 1522. So the 'King Arthur' of the table top is a portrait of Henry VIII. A further twist to the story is that Arthur, Henry's elder brother, born in the very castle of Winchester, would have inherited the throne if he had not died in 1502, leaving the younger prince to succeed both to his throne and his wife.

The table is 18ft in diameter, and was originally built to stand on legs. Its weight is a massive one-and-a-quarter tons and it has places for twenty-four knights. It is known to have been hanging on the walls of the Hall certainly since 1378. Exhaustive research was undertaken recently and showed that the legend that the table was used by King Arthur must be false. Indeed it was built nearly 1,000 years after the period when Arthur and his knights are conjectured to have lived.

For centuries courts were held here; Sir Walter Raleigh was twice tried as a traitor in this room and eventually executed, as was Alice Lisle, who gave sanctuary in her home at Ringwood to fugitives from the unsuccessful rebellion against James II in 1685. The unfortunate lady was tried by the odious Judge Jefferies who wished her burnt at the stake. Cleared now of its cells, bench and other court fittings, the hall remains as the 'finest mediaeval hall in England after Westminster'. A finely wrought set of stainless steel gates separate the Great Hall from the modern Law Courts. They were installed to commemorate the wedding in 1981 of the Prince and Princess of Wales and incorporate the initials of the royal couple.

'HOW TO GET THERE'

ituated at top of Winchester
igh Street. Follow signs for
omsey (A3090) and by
nedieval Westgate turn into
ower Street for public car-
ark. On foot from High Street,
hort cut through Law Courts
recinct'.

1.	2.
	3.

1. Hall and table
2. Detail of the Round Table painting
3. Domesday Exhibition - Norman Warrior

1,2: Hampshire County Council

3: Domesday Office

99

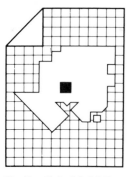

The Hospital of Saint Cross and Almshouse of Noble Poverty
(The Trustees of Saint Cross)

The Hospital of Saint Cross,
St. Cross Road,
Winchester,
Hampshire.
SO23 9SD
Telephone
Winchester (0962) 51375

Price Guide - B

Car Parking
Free (local streets)

Handicapped
Suitable - ramp provides easy access to Chapel

Party Visits
By arrangement

Publications etc.
Guidebook, and leaflet in different languages
Guided walks available

Where to eat
Suitable picnic area in the water meadows

Time to allow
1 - 2 hours

Open
All year except Sundays, Christmas Day and Boxing Day
Main Season - 9-12.30,2-5pm
Out of Season - 10.30-12.30, 2-3.30pm

Public Transport
Bus Services -
Hampshire Bus services every 30 minutes from Southapton and Winchester City Centre to St. Cross on Monday - Saturday (hourly on Sunday).
Buses every hour from Eastleigh and Fareham on Monday - Saturday (every 2 hours from Fareham on Sunday)
Additional buses run from Andover and Guildford on Monday - Saturday and from Newbury and Oxford (daily).
Rail Services -
Winchester Station

Nearby Attractions
Winchester
St. Catherine's Hill

ST. CROSS HOSPITAL

The Hospital of St. Cross is acknowledged by many to be the oldest charitable institution in the country. It is certainly one of the most beautiful collections of mediaeval buildings still in use today. It was founded in 1136 when this country was going through one of the blackest periods of its history. It was a time of Civil War and severe famine and it was against this background that the Bishop of Winchester, who was also the King's brother and grandson of William the Conqueror, conceived the idea of providing a secure home for thirteen poor, enfeebled old men and a Chapel where the "poor in Christ might humbly and devoutly serve God"; to this he added that the "home" should provide a daily meal for an additional hundred poor men.

The history of St. Cross during the past 850 years is a fascinating one and has been excellently retold in the present Guide Book. There have been times when corruption, controversy and maladministration have nearly closed it. Frequently the Bishops of Winchester installed as Master relatives or friends, who took advantage of every means to enrich themselves. Because of constant arguments with the Knights of St. John, who gained control of St. Cross in 1151, the church and many other buildings were without proper roofs, unfinished or in ruins for the first two hundred years. Later there were Masters who thought nothing of selling the hospital properties, keeping revenues, even pulling down buildings and turning out the Brethren.

There have also been times of prosperity and expansion, especially in the 15th century when Cardinal Beaufort added the Almshouse of Noble Poverty for those "who once had everything handsome about them, but had suffered losses". Fortunately the Hospital has always survived and continues today to implement the aims of its founders and provide a safe haven for elderly gentlemen. The Hospital is situated alongside the water meadows, just off the St. Cross Road. One of the loveliest ways to approach the Hospital is to walk along the river bank from Winchester.

Between the two gates is the Outer Court which contains the kitchen and the site of the hall where the hundred poor men were fed. At the Porter's Lodge, inside the 15th century Beaufort Tower, travellers can still ask to receive

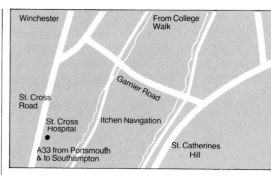

HOW TO GET THERE'

From Southampton, A33 and then bear left at beginning of Winchester by-pass (signposted St. Cross and Compton). From Portsmouth, A333. Cross Winchester by-pass at Hockley and turn right at next junction. St. Cross ¼ mile. Parking in nearby streets.

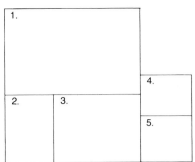

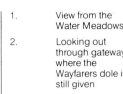

1.   View from the Water Meadows
2.   Looking out through gateway where the Wayfarers dole is still given
3.   Alms houses seen across quadrangle
4.   St. Cross Church
5.   The outer court-yard

2,4:   *Mike Goddard*

the traditional Wayfarers' Dole - a small glass of beer and a little bread. Ancient records were kept in the Master's room above the gate and next door is the Brethrens' Hall where resident Brothers used to feed together; smoke from the open fireplace escaped through a hole in the high roof.

On one side of the main quadrangle is a row of tall chimneys which mark the quarters of the twenty-five Brothers, who still wear their distinctive gowns and hats. On the other side is the attractive 16th century Ambulatory, a cloister-like passage over which there may have been an infirmary to accommodate sick Brothers.

The greatest glory of St. Cross is the Chapel which is late Norman. It contains excellent stone carvings round many of the windows, beautiful mediaeval glass and an early English lectern which has an eagle's body and a parrot's head. Visitors can walk in the Master's Garden where there is a large pond, or through the water-meadows and parkland which surround the Hospital. Books, walk-around guide books, and postcards can be obtained from the Porter's Lodge.

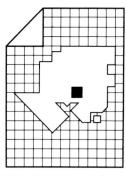

Farley Mount Country Park
(Hampshire County Council
County Recreation
Department)

and West Wood
(Forestry Commission)

Sarum Road,
Winchester,
Hampshire.
Telephone
Park - (0962) 60948
Office - (0962) 64221

Price Guide - Free

Car Parking
Free

Handicapped
Suitable, disabled toilets and
tracks

Publications etc.
Leaflet

Where to eat
Picnic tables on site
Barbecue shelter and grill,
booked parties only

Time to allow
1-2 hours

Open
At all times

Nearby Attractions
Hillier's Arboretum
Danebury Hill
West Down and Test Valley

FARLEY MOUNT
COUNTRY PARK & WEST WOOD

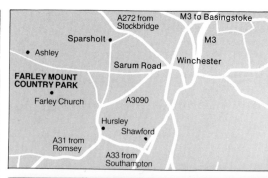

The present road from Winchester to Salisbury passes through Stockbridge, though the Romans, as might be expected, followed a direct line to Old Sarum across country, fording the Test at a place called Horsebridge. This first section of their road climbs steeply out of Winchester to 'Sarum Road' and can be followed for several miles over the Downs through beautiful Hampshire countryside. It passes through Farley Mount Country Park, more than a thousand acres of open downland, ancient woodland and Forestry Commission plantations.

Here there is ample car parking, acres of richly varied woodland and miles of way-marked paths to explore and endless places to picnic. Each summer very large numbers of people enjoy the park yet it remains one of the most valuable natural history sites in Hampshire, protected for its Special Scientific Interest, with orchid-rich turf and even a successful and rather surprising oak wood, which is unusual for downland. In nearby West Wood only a short distance from the ancient main road, a Roman villa has been discovered. Its excavation revealed the almost complete mosaic on show in Winchester Museum. A small but very attractive stand of beech trees nearby shelters prehistoric burial mounds, while some of the steep hill slopes to the west are covered with the "Hampshire weed", the yew.

It is at this western end that one can find the strangest feature of the country park, a monument in the shape of a pyramid built on top of a large prehistoric burial mound. A typical 18th century eye-catcher, it was raised as an eccentric tombstone on the grave of a horse by its proud owner; having saved its master from a dangerous fall into a quarry the horse had been renamed "Beware Chalk Pit", and soon after won a trophy in races near Winchester.

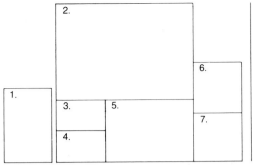

HOW TO GET THERE'

From Winchester, take Romsey road past Hospital turn right into Sarum Road. Follow lane for about three miles, car-parks sign-posted after crossroad.
Park also sign-posted off A3090 Winchester to Romsey Road near Hursley.
Approaching from north, access through Sparsholt village, (road to Hursley).

1. Excavators at work at Sparsholt Roman Villa
2. Farley Mount Monument
3. Barbecue Centre
4. Kite flying
5. Walking over Beacon Hill
6. Ashley, cottage with built-in-well
7. Ashley Church

1: *Hampshire Recreation Department*

The impressive slope here is known as Beacon Hill and certainly played its part in one of the mediaeval 'telegraphs' which passed by way of Popham and Beacon Hill near Burghclere, into the Midlands. The actual basket in which the fire was lit on top of a pole still exists in the church at Farley Chamberlayne. There is a most attractive walk to this church, which is not far from the park. All trace of the great house which once stood here has gone. Nearby there is, however, the ruin of an old semaphore station intended to relay messages between London and Plymouth. This was in view of Cheesefoot Head where the next one up the line stood. Another delightful walk on local paths over farmland and through bluebell woods is to the unspoiled hamlet of Ashley, whose tiny Norman chapel was within the boundary of a castle which has disappeared.

There are facilities at Farley Mount for group barbecues, and even a large barbecue shelter which can be hired by parties who book well in advance.

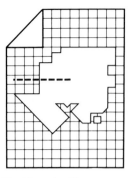

The Clarendon Way
(Hampshire Recreation
Department)

Price Guide - Free

Car Parking
There are many car parks in
Salisbury and Winchester and
limited spaces at places in
between, notably Pitton,
Winterslow, Broughton and
King's Somborne. Farley
Mount Country Park on the
outskirts of Winchester has
extensive car parks and picnic
sites.

Publications
Leaflet
Guidebook

Public Transport
The bus and rail stations in
Salisbury and Winchester are
close to the respective ends of
the walk.

Attractions En Route
Salisbury
    The Cathedral
    Salisbury and South
    Wiltshire Museum
    Mompesson House
Broughton Dovecote
Farley Mount Country Park
Winchester
    St. Cross Hospital
    Wolvesey Palace
    Winchester City Mill
    Winchester Cathedral
    City Museum
    The Westgate Museum
    The Great Hall
    Royal Hampshire Regiment
    Museum
    Royal Hussars Regimental
    Museum

THE CLARENDON WAY

This new long-distance footpath runs between two famous cathedral cities, the capital cities of Wiltshire and Hampshire. A road between the two places has always been well trodden, though its exact route has varied, particularly in response to the changing location of 'Salisbury'. The Saxons favoured Wilton as their capital (hence the county name), the Normans Old Sarum to the north, while the site of the modern city dates from the early 13th century. Even Clarendon Palace to the south-east, a little-known site that has been chosen to give the walk its name, must have influenced the way that people made their way to Winchester.

Salisbury cathedral, around which the modern city grew, stands on five rivers, notably the Avon. In a bold move it was purposely moved to this valley site from Old Sarum nearby for a variety of reasons. The former Norman cathedral was on a cramped hill-top site that was shared with military men. It was also very exposed, so that the choir had to compete with the wind! But perhaps the most important influence was trade, which could more easily be carried out in the large, accessible market place which was built close by the cathedral. Whatever the exact reasons for the move, the cathedral that resulted is generally regarded as one of the finest in the country.

For much of its route the Clarendon Way runs across open downland or skirts remnants of forests where Norman kings once hunted - for the larder and sport. Its general direction is against the grain of the land, which makes it rise and fall with the rivers and their valleys, notably the Test but also several other much smaller streams that drain to the south. En route it passes through Pitton, formerly a 'forest village' where woodmen lived and worked and more recently the home of the writer Ralph Whitlock.

Follow the Country Code

Guard against all risk of fire.

It also passes through Winterslow, well known as the country home of William Hazlitt, and the place where the truffle hunter Eli Collins and his dogs lived.

After a long stretch along the route of the Roman road that ran between Old Sarum and Winchester, the Clarendon Way reaches Broughton, a pretty village with an interesting dovecote alongside its parish church. This contains 500 nesting boxes and was a vital source of meat during the winter months. Pigeons were induced to lay egg after egg on a six-week cycle to rear 'squabs', young birds weighing about a pound. The wooden mechanism or 'potence' which enabled the keeper to kill the birds and maintain the dovecote has recently been restored and opened to view.

Beyond the valley of the Test the path enters King's Somborne, another village where the crafts of the woodman are a recent memory. It was here also that John of Gaunt's deer park was situated, though this celebrated son of Edward III is thought never to have visited it. The river at King's Somborne is a winterbourne, an intermittent stream, though its source has fallen in response to changes in the water table.

The final section of the Clarendon Way winds its way into the St. Cross district of Winchester via Farley Mount, a fine viewpoint and local beauty spot which is crowned with a monument - to a horse!

BS

The Clarenden Way Country
Photo: David Molden

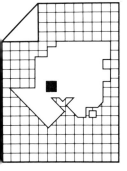

The Hillier Arboretum
(Hampshire County Council)

County Estates Department
Jermyns Lane,
Ampfield,
Near Romsey,
Hampshire.
SO5 0QA
Telephone
Romsey (0794) 68787

Price Guide - C

Car Parking
Free

Handicapped
Suitable

Party Visits
By arrangement

Publications etc.
Guidebook
Colour Guide
Camellia Booklet
Seasonal Leaflets

Where to eat
Suitable picnic area including
picnic tables on site

Time to allow
2 - 4 hours

Open
All year Monday - Friday,
10am-5pm
March - 2nd Sunday in
November: Weekends and
Bank Holidays, 1-6pm

Public Transport
Bus Services -
Every hour from Winchester
and Romsey on Monday -
Saturday.
B.S. Ampfield, Jermyns Lane,
10 minutes walk. Connections
available at Romsey to and
from Southampton and
Salisbury.

Nearby Attractions
Broadlands, Romsey
Farley Mount Country Park
The Clarendon Way
The Test Way
Danebury Hill Fort

Photos: The Hillier Arboretum

THE HILLIER ARBORETUM

Hampshire is fortunate to have near Romsey one of the greatest collections of trees and woody plants in the temperate world. Since 1977 this has been open to the public as a result of a trust now administered by Hampshire County Council. The founder of the arboretum was Sir Harold Hillier, whose private house and garden provided a starting point to the venture in 1953. By the late 1970s the arboretum had grown in area to well over 100 acres. It contains an amazing 10,000 species and varieties of woody plants, the largest collection of its kind in the British Isles, as well as bulbs, herbaceous plants and many others.

The objectives of the trust are to maintain and improve the collection, giving particular attention to the conservation of endangered species. A number of the plants in the arboretum are very rare in their native habitats, largely due to man's activities such as clearing land for agriculture, excessive grazing etc. The arboretum also has a role to play in education and the interpretation of our enormous resources of woody plant material, as well as providing a very attract-

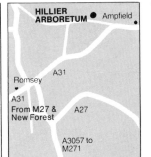

'HOW TO GET THERE'
From Southampton - A27 to Romsey, and then take A31 in direction of Winchester, turning left into Jermyns Lane Car-park on right.
From Winchester follow Romsey Road (A3090) turning right after Ampfield.

The site lies on two very different soil types. To the south is an outcrop of Bagshot sand; a very light, sandy heath which warms up quickly in spring but dries out in summer. To the north is an area of heavy London clay. These two differing soils dictate the order of the planting. The arboretum stands at the top of one of the highest points for several miles, which means that it can be windy but has excellent views, particularly to the north across the Hampshire downland. It always has features of interest to offer and the miles of paths meandering through the collections allow easy access. The Arboretum guide, which is available for sale, gives information about some of these trails and a choice of walk of either one or two hours.

ive setting in which to see many very rare plants.

The total British flora contains only some 35 species of tree, whereas the arboretum contains nearly a hundred times this number, with trees from many parts of the world, from Tierra del Fuego to the slopes of Mount Everest.

Visitors will find the collection at its most colourful during April and May when a succession of rhododendrons, magnolias, cherries and azaleas provide a blaze of different colours. These are followed in high summer by more subtle colour effects from many shrubs and trees, whilst the air is filled with the rich fragrance of Mock Orange and other plants. Autumn follows summer with its blend of spectacular tints and hues as the leaves of deciduous plants prepare to fall; in many ways this is the best season of all. Winter does not provide many flowers but there are still some to be found. Evergreen trees, and the winter silhouettes and bark of deciduous trees provide the greatest feature until late winter when witch hazels and camellias commence flowering, bringing us back into the rich glory of spring.

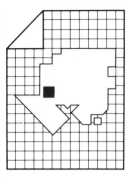

Romsey Abbey

Romsey,
Hampshire,
SO5 8EN
Telephone
Romsey (0794) 513125

Price Guide
Contribution suggested

Car Parking
Town car parks nearby

Handicapped
Suitable

Party Visits
By arrangement

Publications etc.
Leaflet and guidebook
Tours available

Where to eat
Suitable picnic area in the
churchyard
Cafes in town

Time to allow
1 - 2 hours

Open
Every day of the year
9.30am-5.30pm

Public Transport
Bus Services -
Every 30 minutes from
Southampton Monday -
Saturday (every 2 hours on
Sunday). Buses every hour
from Salisbury Monday -
Saturday. (B.S. Romsey Bus
Station, short walk).
Rail Services -
Romsey Station

Nearby Attractions
Broadlands
King John's House
Hillier Arboretum
Mottisfont Abbey
Paultons Country Park, Ower
The Test Way

*Photo: Hampshire County
Planning
Department*

ROMSEY ABBEY

The sad turn of events in recent years has made Romsey Abbey one of the most heavily visited churches in Hampshire, for here is buried Lord Louis, Earl Mountbatten of Burma, close to the family pew. However, visitors who come on from Broadlands to pay their final respects will discover that this is a remarkable building well worth exploring in its own right. The story of its origin is also of great interest stretching back 150 years before the Normans arrived. The first timber framed church for the Saxon nuns did not last long, destroyed with the rest of the town by raiding Danes coming by long-ship up the river Test. The small church that replaced it a thousand years ago could have stood comfortably inside the nave transepts of the present church which was built after about 1120.

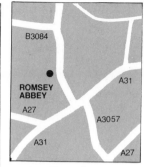

'HOW TO GET THERE'

From Southampton, take A36 and M271 out of town to join A3057 up to Romsey. Turn left onto A31 and opposite entrance to Broadlands turn right into town. Follow one-way system. Car-parks at back of shopping centre by bus station, or carry on, turning right into Market Square. Very limited parking near entrance to Abbey.

many other places, swept away in the 1540s. Just the refectory survives for it was converted into a house and recently discovered under a later facade. Unfortunately some of the last abbesses to serve gained a bad reputation for laxity, expecially eating, drinking, gossiping, bad language and spending the night in the town. The suppressed abbey was sold for £100 to the towns people, who had been allowed an extension to the northern aisle to use as their church.

The nuns of the original foundation were great teachers and attracted distinguished pupils. Two daughters of the Scots king Malcolm were entrusted to their aunt at the abbey. Later, after the death of Rufus, one of the nuns, Eadgyth, was plucked from Romsey by his successor Henry I, who was given a special dispensation to marry her. Soon after her death the Abbey was again rebuilt, but it took 130 years to complete. This gave it a harmony of styles which makes it one of the finest Norman buildings in Europe, second only to Durham Cathedral. "Different styles there are, but so fitted to each other that they seem but parts of a concerted whole that makes by orderly progress, for perfection. It is music in stone."

To the south side of the church lay the cloister and monastic complex which was, as in so

There are numerous points of interest inside the Abbey including mediaeval wall paintings, a Saxon rood, modern tapestries, 14th century tiles, and 16th century wooden reredos. On Lord Mountbatten's grave are the simple words "In honour bound". Nearby is the attractive monument to the St. Barbe family of John and his wife Grissel, who died in 1658. It shows their sons praying at their feet. The family owned the Broadlands site before the Palmerston family, and in the Civil War fought against the king.

During the past decade £300,000 has been spent on the fabric of the Abbey. Receiving no financial support from the State, and having been stripped of all its endowments and property by Henry VIII, the Abbey is dependent on the donations of parishioners and visitors who can show their appreciation by their generosity.

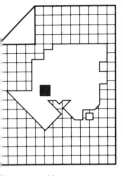

King John's House
(Trustees of King John's House)

Church Street,
Romsey,
Hampshire.
Telephone
Romsey (0794) 512200

Price Guide – A.

Car Parking
Nearby Town car parks

Handicapped
Not suitable for wheelchairs

Party Visits
By arrangement

Publications etc.
Guidebook
Displays
Tours available
Town trails around Romsey

Where to eat
Cafe/tea-room and Licensed
restaurant/bar in town
Suitable picnic area at Abbey

Time to allow
Up to half an hour

Open
Spring Bank Holiday – End of
September
Closed Sundays and Monday
mornings.
10.30am - 12.30pm, 2 - 4pm

Public Transport
Bus Services -
Every 30 minutes from
Southampton Monday -
Saturday (every 2 hours on
Sunday). Buses every hour
from Salisbury Monday -
Saturday. (B.S. Romsey Bus
Station, short walk)
Rail Services -
Romsey Station

Nearby Attractions
Romsey Abbey
Broadlands
Romsey Town
Mottisfont Abbey

Mead Mill Museum
Mill Lane Romsey

(Mr D.G. Baker)
Farming bygones museum
and watergarden by the river
Test.

Left: View of hall upstairs
Top right: Exterior of King
John's House as it
may have looked in
the fourteenth
Century
Below right: The hall as it might
have appeared then
Drawings: Trustees of King
John's House

KING JOHN'S HOUSE

Visitors to the Romsey Abbey should not miss a call at the town's oldest house which stands nearby to the east. It has close historical connections and is now used as a cultural centre and museum.

As with so many other "King John's Houses" the building was erected later, in about 1240, as a merchant's house. By the sixteenth century it was owned by the abbey but this was no ordinary house as it was used by the nobility passing through the town. On one occasion, King Edward I stayed here, as can be seen by the graffiti on the walls! The building has a later Tudor cottage extension which obscures the original porch and staircase which led up to the first floor. The ground floor was a store room. For safety the cooking was done in a detached building and the food carried to the house and upstairs to the hall which was used for dining and living. Downstairs a unique cobbled surface made from cattle bones can be viewed through a trap door in the modern boarded floor, and there is also a 'Samson' post which once held up the large hearth stone for the open fire which was in the centre of the hall above.

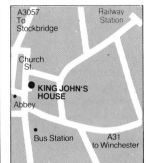

'HOW TO GET THERE'
From Southampton, take A36 and M271 out of town to join A3057 up to Romsey. Turn left onto A31 and opposite entrance to Broadlands turn right into town. Follow one-way system. Car-parks at back of shopping centre by bus station, or carry on, turning right into Market Square. Very limited parking near entrance to Abbey.

Perhaps of most interest in the local history display are several items on the Reverend Berthon, the vicar of Romsey who invented a successful design for folding lifeboats and a boat which could be dismantled and carried on horseback. The craft were much used by the Victorian army and his name is still kept alive in a Lymington Boat Yard. He also re-roofed part of the Abbey with moulded laminated timber trusses, a unique use of the skills of the Victorian shipwrights.

On sale at King John's House is an excellent town trail booklet to help visitors explore Romsey. The walk begins nearby in the attractive town market place.

A modern inserted staircase leads to this hall where the plasterwork still has scratched pictures and coats of arms from the 13th century. The fireplace is much later but it is the roof which is most impressive, being nearly seven-and-a-half centuries old. An exciting piece of historical detective work on its carpentry has shown how the great timbers have had to be strengthened every hundred years or so to prevent the roof from toppling like a set of dominoes, or pushing the thick walls outwards.

The building, with two others round a courtyard, served as the workhouse for Romsey. Later partitions created numerous squalid tenements and perhaps as many as sixty people lived in the present building. The Tudor cottage upstairs is used for exhibitions, and the hall for live performances, concerts etc.

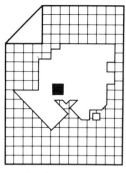

Broadlands
(Lord Romsey)

Romsey,
Hampshire,
SO5 9ZD
Telephone
Romsey (0794) 516878

Price Guide - D

Car Parking
Free

Handicapped
Access to the house and
exhibition, ground floors only.
Access to riverside lawn.

Party Visits
Available (booking preferred)
Mountbatten Exhibition open
in winter for booked groups.

Publications etc.
Guidebook

Where to eat
Cafe on site
Picnic tables on site

Time to allow
2½ hours

Open
27th March - 30th September.
Closed Mondays except in
August and September and
on Bank Holidays.

Public Transport
Bus Services -
Every 30 minutes from
Southampton, Monday -
Saturday, every two hours on
Sunday. Buses hourly from
Salisbury, Monday - Saturday.
(B.S. Romsey Bus Station,
short walk)
Rail Service -
Romsey Station, 15 mins.
walk

Nearby Attractions
Romsey Abbey
King John's House
New Forest
Mottisfont Abbey
Paultons Country Park, Ower
The Test Way

BROADLANDS

Opened to the public in 1979, only months before the tragedy of the senseless murder of Lord Mountbatten, Broadlands has now become a place of pilgrimage. This combined with the classical beauty of the perfectly proportioned house, idyllically set beside the silent River Test, and the wealth of art treasures and decorations inside will ensure that as long as it is open this will be one of Britain's most popular houses.

As a tribute and a memorial to his grandparents, Lord and Lady Mountbatten, the present owner Lord Romsey has planned a large exhibition to illustrate their lives and their achievements. In 1981 the Mountbatten Exhibition was opened in a converted stable block near to the house. The official opening was performed by Prince Charles, who returned with the new Princess of Wales later that summer at the start of their honeymon, following in the footsteps of his mother, Her Majesty the Queen, and Prince Phillip in 1947.

The only trace of how Broadlands has evolved as a building is apparent as one enters the house, for the domed entrance hall fills part of a central courtyard which was once quite open to the east but is now enclosed by the east portico. The panelling in the Oak room and the spiral oak staircase are evidence of the original sixteenth century house.

From the 1760s the house was transformed by the father of the 3rd Lord Palmerston who became the great Victorian Prime Minister and who was to be remembered nationally for his gun-boat diplomacy and locally for the Palmerston "follies", as the Portsmouth fortifications were called. In 1801 at the age of 17 Lord Palmerston inherited the elegant Palladian mansion which had been transformed by 'Capability' Brown and his son-in-law Henry Holland. Visitors can see in the house a portrait of Lord Palmerston by the Houses of Parliament, appropriately mounted on a horse, for he often rode from Romsey to London until the Southampton railway was built in 1840.

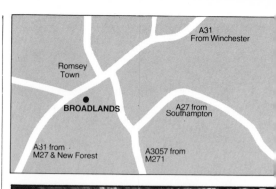

'HOW TO GET THERE' ·

From Southampton, take A36
and M271 out of town to join
A3057 to Romsey. Turn left onto
Romsey by-pass (A31). House
sign-posted on left.
From New Forest – M27 to Ower
(junction 2) then A31 to
Romsey. House sign-posted to
right.

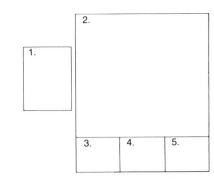

1. Lord Mountbatten on the
    bridge of H.M.S. *Kelly*
2. West Front of the House
    viewed across the Test
3. The stricken Kelly limps
    home
4. The Wedgewood room
5. Part of the Mountbatten
    Exhibition

1-5: *Broadlands Romsey Ltd.*

Throughout the house there is a classical elegance, with fine decorative mouldings on the walls and beautiful mirrors, as well as personal mementos of Lord Mountbatten, his life of service and his family. There is an unusually warm and charming atmosphere and room attendants are on hand to answer questions and to point out features of interest. In the Oak room, for instance, three massive Russian coronation books highlight Lord Mountbatten's family associations with the Russian Czars. There are paintings of may other European and royal ancestors, including Queen Victoria, who held the baby Lord Louis, one of her many great-grandchildren, at his christening.

Four of the bedrooms can be seen. First is the Portico room decorated with flowered chintz, its design disguising profiles of Victoria and Albert, together with its dressing room decorated with exquisite Chinese wallpaper. The Green room was Lady Palmerston's bedroom, and what is now the Hesse room was once Lord Palmerston's room. He had the house extended greatly with an extra 28 rooms, but this rather ugly Victorian wing was demolished in 1954 when Lady Mountbatten restored the house to its eighteenth century proportions. The most recently opened is the Wolfsgarten room which has a great feeling of warmth imparted by the floral pink patterning of the furniture.

Visitors to the house will find the exhibition extremely well planned. There is a sophisticated audio-visual show which traces the eventful lives of Lord and Lady Mountbatten. There are displays about Lord Mountbatten's father, who was First Sea Lord until 1914, his childhood and schooling; panels abouth his friendship and world cruise with the Prince of Wales in the 1920s are followed by more about his marriage, and the life of his wife, Edwina Ashley, who died in 1960. Mountbatten's technical expertise in electronics, his naval commands and many other aspects of his full life are illustrated with an amazing collection of personal possessions and photographs and even, at one point, part of a battle-ship.

The exhibition contains a gift shop with souvenirs and also publications of local interest for visitors who may wish to go on to explore Romsey and its neighbourhood. There is a second gift shop in the charming eighteenth century "dairy" building which also houses the visitor reception centre.

For grandeur and beauty Broadlands is certainly the finest house in Hampshire. Despite the death of Lord Mountbatten it will remain a family home since his eldest grandson, the film and television producer Lord Romsey and his wife will continue to live there.

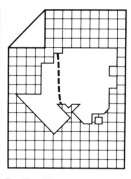

THE TEST WAY

The Test Way

Price Guide - Free

Car Parking
Totton - Limited space on roads

Inkpen Beacon - Free at Walbury Hill nearby

There are numerous places to park along the route, some of them with only limited space, including: Nursling, Romsey, Mottisfont, Horsebridge, Stockbridge, Leckford, Chilbolton, Wherwell, Longparish, St. Mary Bourne, Hurstbourne Tarrant and Linkenholt.

Publications
Leaflet
Guidebook

Public Transport
Totton:
Bus Services -
Southampton - Totton
Rail Service -
Totton Station, ½ mile away

Inkpen Beacon
No public transport

Attractions En Route
Romsey Abbey
King John's House
Broadlands
Mottisfont Abbey

One of Hampshire's hallmarks is its chalk streams. None is more famous than the Test, known the world over by fishermen and celebrated for its sheer picturesqueness. The Test Way has been signposted to enable the walker to explore this great river and its valley. Starting at Totton, near Southampton, it runs for 60 miles to the Hampshire - Berkshire borders, where it ends on a breathtaking scarp above Inkpen. The walk literally crosses the breadth of Hampshire and offers a sort of 'cross-section' of the county, from marshy estuary to high bleak downland.

Follow the Country Code

Fasten all gates.

thatched cottages and epitomise the rural idyll. Although most of the houses are not now lived in by villagers, they retain a charm which is well suited to the pace of the walker.

The first leg weaves across the Lower Test Nature Reserve on its way to Romsey. This is traditionally a part of the river known for its salmon fishing, though in recent years catches have declined. Romsey itself is an attractive country town with a fine abbey church and is renowned for its connections with Palmerston and Mountbatten. On the way to Stockbridge the Test Way passed through Mottisfont, also well known for its 'abbey', which is in fact a monastery-cum-country house.

Beyond Mottisfont the path follows the former route to the Test Valley Railway and the Andover Canal which it superseded. This is now a rich area for birds, though traces of the old railway and canal exist, particularly at Horsebridge, where they were crossed by the line of the former Roman road. Elsewhere on the walk there are signs of other now-defunct communications, such as the canal that joined (or nearly joined!) Salisbury and Southampton and the curious railway link between Hurstbourne Priors and Fullerton. Some of the prettiest parts of the valley are hereabouts, above Stockbridge, a small town that thrives on trout fishing and other country pursuits. The path passes through Leckford, Chilbolton, Wherwell and Longparish, villages that contain many

Above Longparish the walk leaves the main river and takes to the valley of the Bourne Rivulet, a small tributary whose waters are unbelievably clear. It is an intermittent stream that 'comes up' in the early months of the year, when its waters run in a bed lined with long flowing blades of grass. This is a part of Hampshire that is still relatively unknown; the route of the Test Way makes good use of the terrain, keeping to high lands that make the entrances to St. Mary Bourne and Hurtbourne Tarrant particularly dramatic. The path climbs progressively into what have been called the 'Hampshire Highlands', bleak chalk hills containing small villages and ample evidence of others that have been deserted.

After passing briefly into Wiltshire the Test Way climbs to its end: below is the valley of the Kennet and the western edge of the London Basin: it is one of the finest vantage points in the South.

With the exception of the lowest stretches, the Test Way offers firm ground underfoot at most times of the year. It is probably at its best in the spring, when the dead edges of the river burst into life, though the greatest challenges come in the depths of winter, when the Hampshire Highlands live up to their name. BS

Photo: Adrian Harvey

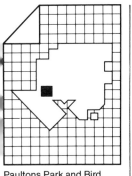

Paultons Park and Bird Gardens
(The Mancey Family)

Ower,
Romsey,
Hampshire,
SO5 0AL
Telephone
(0703) 814442

Price Guide - D

Car Parking
Free on site

Handicapped
Suitable in most areas

Party Visits
Welcome

Publications
Leaflet
Guidebook for park
'Romany Life and Customs'

Where to eat
Cafe/restaurant
Picnic sites
Pub nearby

Time to allow
At least 3 hours

Open
Daily, 10am-7pm (April -
August),
10am-6pm (September and
March),
10am-4.30pm (October -
February)

Public Transport
Excursions and summer
services operated by local bus
companies from
Southampton, Bournemouth
and elsewhere.
Park is a mile from the routes of
hourly services from
Southampton, Romsey and
Salisbury, Monday - Saturday.

1.   At the lakeside

2.   Reading Wagon,
       1915

1:   Anne Ruffell

PAULTONS PARK

S tanding at the end of a long lane close to the M27, Paultons is an ideal place for a family 'day out'. It offers the beautiful parkland of a former country house, a large collection of rare birds and other animals, museums of country life and a wide range of fun activities.

J ust wandering amongst the aviaries of the bird gardens can take hours, for this is one of the finest collections in England. There are exotic pheasants, squawking parrots and parakeets, glossy ravens, sullen-looking vultures and many others - stern owls (notably the huge European Eagle Owl), long-beaked storks and their showy cousins, the ibises.

'HOW TO GET THERE'
From M27, exit at Junction 2
and take A36 to Salisbury,
turning left to Paultons almost
immediately. From
Southampton, take A36 and
turn left after crossing over
M27.

O ne intriguing exhibit shows how 'patrin' signs, made by arrangements of twigs or chalked up, enable gipsies to leave messages for their kin. These include such phrases as 'Nothing to be had', 'Friendly people', 'Gypsies not liked' or 'Beware fierce dog'!

M uch of the 140 acres of the park is given over to the animal paddocks, where there is a wide variety of unusual breeds, such as Barbary Sheep, Pygmy Goats and Zebu Cattle. There are also more familiar animals such as the miniature Shetland Pony, Red Deer and Llama.

T he park includes several easy walks, including a narrow bankside path which runs around a large lake formed from the Cadnam River. This provides a chance to view 'the largest privately owned collection of wildfowl in the South of England', nearly 100 species, half of which live freely on the water. The path leads past an enclosure of flamingoes to a huge undershot waterwheel, once used to drive a timber saw and recently restored. Elsewhere is an attractive boardwalk which passes through a rhododendron 'tunnel' and allows easy access to marshy copses of willow and alder that stand beside the river.

O ne of the most recent additions to Paultons is a virtually unique Romany Museum and display of caravans and wagons. There are beautifully restored examples of such sought-after relics as the Bradford Flat and the Reading Wagon, said to have cost almost three times the price of a house at the time it was built in 1915.

T here are also displays of 'bender' tents - erected by inserting sticks taken from the hedge - and the traditional gypsy occupations of making pegs and artificial flowers. The migration of the Romany peoples from their roots in Northern India, nearly a thousand years ago, is demonstrated, together with fascinationg traces of linguistic links. For example, the gypsy words 'eck, din, trin', meaning 'one, two, three', are close to 'ek, du, tin' from Hindu.

N earby is a Village Life Museum, with displays of the workshops and tools of such craftsmen as the wheelwright, farrier and bootmaker. All these, and many other tradesmen, would have served the original Paultons Estate, which covered 3,000 acres. It takes its name from John de Palton, who acquired the land in 1323. During the 18th century the gardens were landscaped by Capability Brown and the lake was created by damming the river. Cadland Bridge, which gives access to the modern car park, dates from 1868 and is said to take its name from the Derby winner which enabled it to be built.

T he original house, dating from the 17th century, was burned down more than twenty years ago. The modern park is the creation of the Mancey family, who acquired the land and spent three years clearing the 'jungle of scrub, brambles and heaps of brick rubble before opening to the public in 1984.   BS

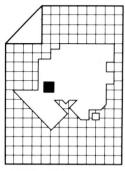

MOTTISFONT ABBEY

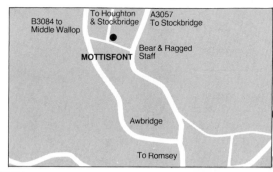

Set deep in the peace of the Test Valley stands the National Trust house of Mottisfont Abbey, surrounded by a glorious garden bordered by an almost magical stream running past towering ornamental trees. Here in a walled garden is a newly established, but already famous rose garden which is at its peak in late June and July.

Mottisfont Abbey
(The National Trust)

Mottisfont,
Nr. Romsey,
Hampshire,
SO5 0LP
Telephone
Romsey (0794) 40757

Price Guide
House and Grounds - D
Grounds only - C

Car Parking
Free

Handicapped
Grounds - Suitable
House - Cellarium only

Publications etc.
Guidebook

Where to eat
Teas are available at the local Post Office

Time to allow
1 - 2 hours

Open
April - end of September only.
Grounds - Sunday - Thursday, 2.30-6pm
House - Wednesday and Sunday 2.30-5pm
(Cellarium and Whistler Room only)
Visitors should obtain time-stamped tickets from the entrance kiosk, since immediate access to the house may not be possible at peak times.

Public Transport
Bus Service -
Limited service Monday - Saturday from Romsey to B.S. 'Bear and Ragged Staff' connections available at Romsey to/from Southampton, Winchester and Salisbury.
Rail Service -
Dunbridge Station ¾ mile away.

Nearby Attractions
Romsey Abbey
Broadlands
Danebury Hill
Hillier Arboretum
Test Valley

Although most visitors to Mottisfont come first and foremost to enjoy the grounds, the house, open two afternoons each week, is of great interest for two principal and amazingly different rooms visited on a conducted tour, the one above the other. Below is a cellarium with powerful vaulting which was once the canons' estate business office and storeroom. The masterpiece of Mottisfont Abbey, however, is on the floor above and is no more than fifty years old; a large sitting

'HOW TO GET THERE'
From Romsey take A3057 (to Kings Somborne and Stockbridge). After "The Bear and Ragged Staff" turn left at sign for village.

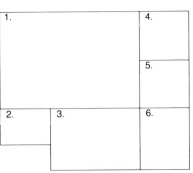

1. North Front of the Abbey
2. The Cellarium
3. The Drawing Room decorated by Whistler
4. View of Walled Garden
5. Pond in the centre of the garden
6. Terrace near the Abbey

2-6: *The National Trust*
2: *Kit Constable Maxwell*
3: *A.F. Kersting*

room created in the late 1930s and decorated by Rex Whistler, the English painter and designer of stage sets. Sadly, he was killed soon after in the war which had already begun as he left his finishing touches, the images of a match-box and paint-pot high up on a painted cornice. The room is indeed a theatrical trompe l'oeil, as if prepared for an 18th century play, with pretend alcoves and clever trickery to produce gorgeously draped curtains. This was the last of only five such rooms created by the artist.

The building is especially interesting when compared with Titchfield Abbey, for in both the nave was converted for private use. Mottisfont Priory (for technically such it was) was sold to Lord Sandys of The Vyne, and he converted the small monastery into a private house of which little trace survives. The house was modernised in the 1740s to give the strange symmetrical front to the south side, while the north still clearly shows the outline of the original church. The priory was founded in 1201 by William Briwere from whom the former owner, Mr. Gilbert Russell, could trace his ancestory via 26 generations. The Hampshire Record Office in Winchester holds a beautifully illuminated manuscript, the Mottisfont Rental, which gives a detailed view of the priory in the 14th century.

In in the park-like garden is a beautiful spring from which flows a crystal-clear stream to join the Test. Massive trees, London Planes and Cedars of Lebanon and many other fine specimens, give great dignity to the grounds where most years there are special entertainments, open-air plays and, even, Fêtes Champêtre. The grounds also contain a large icehouse, one of only a few that can be seen in Hampshire. Ice was imported from the Baltic, Norway and even America and bought from warehouses in Southampton Docks in the days before refrigerators were known.

There are several reminders that the house was once owned by the Mill family whose crest, a muzzled and chained bear, surmounts the gate piers at the end of the drives. A fine stable block to the north of the house was built in 1836 by Sir John Barker-Mill, a cleric-hunter who led a notable pack of hounds.

Each year more and more people come to visit the rose garden laid out in 1972-3 by Graham Thomas as a show place for the National Trust's collection of historic roses gathered through his long career as their Garden Adviser. Most of the roses bear French names, for the great period for the cultivation of roses was in early 19th century France. Garden paths meet at a delightful pool and fountain, and fine herbaceous borders add greatly to the beauty and interest of the different walks.

113

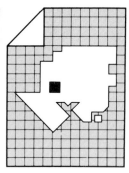

Danebury Iron Age Hill Fort
(Hampshire County Council, County Recreation Department)

Near Stockbridge, Hampshire.
Telephone (Office)
Winchester (0962) 64221

Price Guide - Free

Car Parking
Free

Handicapped
Not suitable. (Locked gates can be opened by prior arrangement).

Publications etc.
Guidebook available from:
County Recreation Department,
North Hill Close,
Andover Road,
Winchester SO22 6AQ
Price 60p (plus p. & p.)
Trails on site

Where to eat
Site suitable for picnicking

Time to allow
1 - 2 hours

Open
At all times

Public Transport
Bus Service -
Limited service from Winchester and Andover to Stockbridge Monday - Saturday
Rail Service -
Winchester or Andover stations

Nearby Attractions
River Test
West Down, Chilbolton
Stockbridge Down

Marsh Court, Nr. Stockbridge
(Marsh Court School)
Spectacular Lutyens House built of hewn chalk. Gardens overlooking the Test valley by Gertrude Jekyll.
Visitors welcome by appointment
Telephone Andover
(0264) 810503

Houghton Lodge
near Stockbridge
Gardens by the River Test,
(Capt. & Mrs M.W. Busk)
Cottage Ornee, lawns down to the Test, walled garden, woodland walks and grotto.
Open March to August (incl) Weds and Thurs afternoons and East Sunday and Monday and Bank Holidays in May.
Also open by appointment
Telephone Andover
(0264) 810502

Danebury Hill Fort

Danebury Hill Fort is the finest of the Iron Age camps in Hampshire. Not only is it the largest and most thoroughly investigated prehistoric site in Britain, but it also offers pleasant walking and attractive views across the beautiful surrounding countryside.

When compared with Old Winchester Hill above the Meon, or St. Catherine's Hill overlooking the Itchen, Danebury Hill is not by any means impressive, with no more than a gentle slope down to the River Test. Its strength and impressive grandeur, even after 2,000 years, depends on massive earthworks, deep ditches and huge banks constructed in a great ring around the flattish hill-top, enclosing altogether some 13 acres. Nevertheless, from between the trees which cover the hilltop walkers will discover distant views in all directions across rich farmland. Today nearly all the fields are arable, but during the Iron Age and until this century they would have been filled with sheep and smaller numbers of cattle.

The trees which crowned Danebury were planted in the last century and are sadly dying. Some have been blown down in storms but many others have had to be felled because of a dangerous condition caused by the fatal beech bark disease. They are being replaced gradually with a hardier variety of young tree. As the trees have come down archaeologists have been able to excavate each year, to the extent that over the last seventeen summer seasons an area of the camp covering seven acres has been examined in great detail. Some of the most dramatic archaeological digs have been right through the ramparts and ditches, and there has been a complete opening up of the elaborate entrance gate area on the Test Valley side of the fort. This superb defence formed a death trap for any attackers, who were forced into a deep walled road beneath the guards. The way continued as a heavily-used road crossing right through the fort to a second gate on the far side.

Removing the shallow soil above the chalk of the interior has revealed an extraordinary "lunar" landscape made up of a multitude of deep pits. These were used for storing grain and also made convenient rubbish tips. Danebury has also been found to have traces of the oldest man-made cobbled roads in Britain, as well as streets, buildings and workshop areas. It is clear that many of the buildings were supported with insubstantial stakes which only very careful digging can reveal. Traces have also been discovered of bizarre ritualistic customs, including cannibalism. There is evidence also of a well-organised trade in salt, iron and pottery. The fort may have been attacked on occasions but was successfully reoccupied again and again. For some 500 years before the first Roman invasion the hill seems to have been a successful community which came to be a shopping or trading centre for the residents of all the smaller rural settlements of the district.

Further digging has revealed signs of buildings, which archaeologists believe may have been a form of temple. The researchers are examining carefully the surrounding landscape with aerial

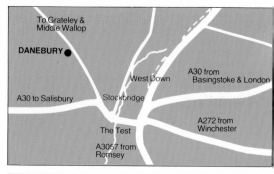

'HOW TO GET THERE'

From Stockbridge follow A30 (to Salisbury) up hill. After 200 yards turn right across the dual carriageway. Danebury is approx. 2 miles on the left. From Andover follow A343, Salisbury road and turn left, where road signed to Stockbridge. Danebury 3 miles on right.

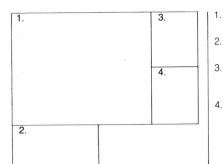

1. View of Danebury Hill from the east

2. Excavation party at work in the woods

3. Unexcavated part of the ramparts with beech trees

4. Learning about the archaeology: section cut through the ramparts

2-4: *County Recreation Department*

photographs and the results of the dig are being analysed in great detail with the aid of computers which should provide a thorough understanding of the way the hill fort developed and how its residents lived from day to day. Analysis of bones discovered has already suggested that horses were used for draught and for meat, and that stallions were probably rounded up from wild herds which roamed the countryside. The sheep, although small compared to modern animals, provided most of the meat as well as the wool which was important.

In 2,000 years since the settlement ended little else has happened at Danebury. Shepherds have sheltered their sheep now and then, and warreners have bred rabbits. For some years an annual market was held in the Ring. In the last century crowds certainly came up to the fort to stand and watch the once-famous Stockbridge races in the fields nearby, until they too ceased in 1898. The grandstand, now in a poor state, can still be seen in the adjacent field to the south.

Excavations progress each August and there is a trail around the site. A booklet about the archaeology is also available from staff on site or from the County Recreation Department in Winchester and the director of the dig, Professor Barry Cunliffe, has published a full-length book, *Danebury: Anatomy of an Iron-Age Fort.*

Much of the Danebury material is being used in new displays created in the Andover Museum.

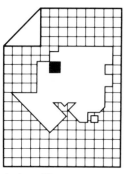

ANDOVER MUSEUM
& THE MUSEUM OF THE IRON AGE

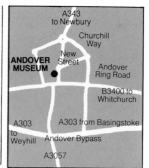

'HOW TO GET THERE'

From BullingtonCross A303/A34, follow A303 west to junction for Andover ringroad signposted Newbury. Follow ringroad to Churchill Way and at junction with A343 turn left into New Street. At first roundabout bear right into Church Close.

Andover Museum
(Hampshire County Museum Service)

Church Close,
Andover,
Telephone
Andover (0264) 66283

Price Guide
Main Museum - Free
Iron Age Galleries - C
(Prebooked school parties - Free)

Car Parking
Free

Handicapped
Very limited access for wheelchairs

Party Visits
By arrangement
School holiday activities

Publications
Leaflet

Where to eat
Cafes and restaurants in Town centre nearby

Time to allow
3/4 - 1 hour

Open
All year Tuesday-Saturday
10am-5pm

Public Transport
Bus Services
Frequent buses to town centre from most parts of Andover, Monday-Saturday. Half-hourly service from Salisbury, hourly on Sunday. Buses every two hours from Winchester, three journeys on Sunday. (B.S. West Street, East Street or Bridge Street, short walk).

Rail Services
Andover Station

Nearby Attractions
The Hawk Conservancy
Harewood Forest
Danebury Hill Fort
Museum of the Iron Age due to open in September 1986

C lose to the Town's church is the new Andover Museum and Art Gallery opened in 1981. This occupies the old grammar school and the former Headmaster's house next door. The museum contains a rich variety of aspects of life of the neighbourhood and the natural history of the Test

Valley. In particular, it will shortly become the first museum in the country with a special emphasis on the Iron Age, based largely on the findings of extensive excavations at the Danebury Hill Fort, near Stockbridge.

T he new Iron Age galleries are planned to give a comprehensive view of Iron Age society and culture in Southern England. There will be a reconstructed round house - in fact several, showing how archaeological evidence can be interpreted in various ways. There will be displays of domestic life and agriculture, including full-size replicas of grain storage pits. The place of Danebury within the ancient settlements of the Upper Test Valley will be shown in a detailed model, and there will be many other displays - on the crafts, curious burial customs and the transition from late Iron Age to Roman Britain.

A nother prime attraction of the Museum is the story of a local firm, Taskers of Andover, who made a wide variety of agricultural machinery and implements. Its origins go back to 1809 and the village of Abbots Ann, a few miles outside the

town. Here the family produced anything from ploughs to gates, and door knockers to mile plates. Their business grew to occupy a large foundry known as the Waterloo Iron Works. By 1869, they had built the Country's first traction engine, beginning a line of steam tractors and lorries that did well until 1919, and even until 1926 steam rollers were still being built.

A large gallery is used to show temporary exhibitions of local artists and various other subjects. There are also galleries on the local history of Andover, and the natural history of the downs, including a small aquarium containing trout, pike, crayfish and other native species. An attractive geology gallery shows many examples of the flints and fossils that can be picked up on the downs.

The 'Hero', 1st tractor engine built by Taskers

Photo. *Hampshire County Museum Service*

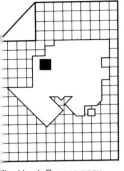

THE HAWK CONSERVANCY WEYHILL

The Hawk Conservancy
(R.D. and H. Smith)

Weyhill,
Near Andover,
Hampshire.
SP11 8DY
Telephone
Weyhill (0264) 772252

Price Guide - E

Car Parking
Free

Handicapped
Suitable in dry weather

Party Visits
By arrangement
Educational resources

Publications
Leaflet
Displays

Where to eat
Large grassy car park
provides suitable picnic area

Time to allow
2 - 3 hours

Open
March-October - Every day
Spring and Autumn -
10.30am-4pm
Summer - 10.30am-5.00pm

Public Transport
Bus Services -
Services to Weyhill from
Andover and Salisbury, half-
hourly Monday-Saturday,
every hour on Sunday.
Rail Services -
Andover Station

Nearby Attractions
Andover Museum
Museum of Army Flying
Danebury Hill Fort
Finkley Down Farm and
Country Park

There are few members of the animal kingdom with whom man has had a closer or more respectful relationship than the birds of prey. They have been the passion of noble sportsmen down the centuries, have provided some of the most spectacular sights of the world of nature and have given warning of the dangers of polluting or destroying our environment. Hawks, at the peak of their own pyramid of food chains, quickly reflected the adverse side-effects of chemical pesticides added to the land, and they nearly disappeared from much of England because of persecution by game-keepers protecting their pheasants. A serious decline also began in the last war, when shooting was encouraged to safeguard carrier-pigeons released by airmen who had to 'ditch' out at sea. Another threat to these endangered aristocrats comes from ruthless falconers, often from overseas, who are willing to pay great prices for the illegally taken young birds or eggs of such rare beauties as the Peregrine, the 'wandering' falcon, renowned for spectacular aerobatics at high speed.

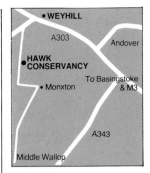

'HOW TO GET THERE'
From Winchester take Andover Road B3420, crossing A30 and past Wherwell turn right onto A3057. Soon turn onto A303 Andover by-pass in direction of West Country. Shortly after A343 turning turn left into lane to Monxton. Conservancy is nearby on right.

It is fortunate that in Hampshire we have a very fine collection of birds of prey, many of them in breeding pairs. These include not just the smaller and faster flying falcons but also hawks, eagles and owls, vultures and kites. The large collection at Weyhill provides a marvellous opportunity to view these beautiful birds close up, many of them perched in the open air. Each day, weather permitting, there are regular demonstrations of the birds in flight. A visit is invaluable for the enthusiast ornithologist, but equally it shows what a rich part of our heritage the Hawks are. The Conservancy is constantly receiving injured raptors or providing immediate alerts for ecological or pesticide problems. Recovered birds are returned to the wild while the breeding of new generations allows Tawny and Barn Owls, and Kestrels to be released into suitable areas.

The Conservancy is set in downland which was once known far and wide as the meeting place for the ancient, and enormous Weyhill fair, where up to half a million sheep are said to have been sold as well as horses and hops, cheeses and quills. The fair took place at Michaelmas but is said to date back to pre-Christian times.

Top Photo: The Hawk Conservancy

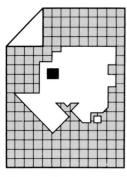

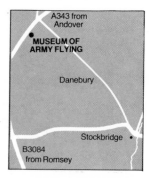

MUSEUM OF ARMY FLYING

Almost thirty years ago the present Army Air Corps (AAC) took over the airfield at Middle Wallop. Today it is the largest and busiest grass airfield in the country, with more than 120,000 aircraft movements per annum. Here the Army trains its pilots, first on fixed wing aircraft - currently Chipmunks - and then helicopters, the Gazelle and the larger Lynx.

Completed in 1940, Middle Wallop airfield served as one of the front-line RAF fighter stations during the last war. Men such as Wing-Commander 'Cats Eyes' Cunningham, who commanded 604 Squadron, were responsible for destroying many Luftwaffe aircraft during and after the Battle of Britain. Later in the war the base was used by the United States Air Force and the RAF, and also had a spell as a Royal Naval Air Station, *HMS Flycatcher.*

Army flying itself has had almost as varied a career as its major base. The full story - from balloons and man-carrying kites to modern, hedge-hopping helicopters - is now told for the first time in the Museum of Army Flying, where historic aircraft and displays have recently been housed in superb new premises.

The Army first took to the air in balloons in Bechuanaland. Technical developments of the day meant that the range of artillery extended beyond the view of the gunners themselves. It therefore became necessary to set up forward observation posts to relay information about 'hits and misses', a task that could be done more effectively from the air. Later, in South Africa, 'balloon sections' played an important part during the Boer War.

When manned flight became a possibility, the Army was involved in the very earliest British experiments. In 1906 man-lifting kites designed at Farnborough by S.F. Cody were were attached to balloon sections and two years later this American pioneer made the first sustained flight in the UK in a machine that was later designated Army Aeroplane No.1. Although the Army later withdrew from these experiments, on grounds of cost, by the outbreak of the First World War it had become involved in the Royal Flying Corps, albeit with a motley collection of aircraft.

As the war progressed, the RFC grew dramatically, eventually employing some 24,000 aircraft. Pilots showed convincingly that in addition to the earlier task of directing gunfire, they could carry out a variety of other tasks, including bombing, general reconnaissance and air warfare, better known as 'dogfighting'. The museum shows a reconstruction of the trenches of Flanders, where the legendary 'Red Baron', Manfred von Richtovan, dressed in the very leather coat he once wore, is seen chatting to an RFC pilot who has been brought down. Another scene shows British pilots working from a tent at a forward base on French soil: nonchalantly tossed into one corner is a wicker seat, typical of those used on early aircraft. Army pilots gained no less than thirteen Victoria Crosses during the First World War.

Museum of Army Flying
(Ministry of Defence)

Army Air Corps Centre,
Middle Wallop,
Stockbridge,
Hampshire.
SO20 8DY
Telephone
(0264) 62121 x 421/428

Price Guide - C

Car Parking
Free

Handicapped
Suitable

Party Visits
By arrangement preferred

Publications
Leaflet
Guidebook

Where to eat
Cafe on site. Eating places in Stockbridge, Andover and Salisbury

Time to allow
1 - 2 hours

Open
Daily 10-4.30

Public Transport
Bus Services -
Buses every hour for most of the day, from Andover and Salisbury, Monday-Saturday.

Nearby Attractions
Danebury Hill Fort
Mottisfont Abbey
Andover Museum
Hawk Conservancy
Finkley Down Farm and
Country Park

Between the wars, Army flying declined an was eclipsed by the RAF, formed in 1918. T

needs of the Army were met by so-called Army Co-operation Squadrons, flying biplanes and communicating with field commanders via one-way Morse code transmission. In the early 1930s some Army officers realised that artillery fire could be directed much more effectively by using small aircraft equipped with two-way radio.

AOP squadrons were kept busy for the rest o the war, using a succession of Auster variants, some of which are shown in the museum. The much-loved Auster remained in service until the mid-1960s and was flown in many parts of the world, including Malaya where in the 1950s it was used against guerilla forces camped in the jungle. 'Bandit' hideouts could be pinpointed from the air and then rooted out by assault forces. This often involved jungle marches lasting several days and the Auster became an invaluable aid to navigation.

One of the most intriguing aspects of Army flying is the use of gliders during the last war. These 'throw-away' machines, made almost entirely of wood, were piloted by the men of the Glider Pilot Regiment (GPR). The notion of using gliders in warfare developed from a Churchillian directive to build up airborne forces, following

'...W TO GET THERE'

...m Romsey, take A3057
...l immediately outside town
... left onto B3084 through
...bridge. Cross A30
...ckbridge-Salisbury) and
...n right on A343. Museum
...-park short distance on
...t.

...m Winchester take A272 to
...ckbridge, continuing on
...D Salisbury road to
...ssing of B3084. Turn right,
...d continue as above.

Photograph of experimental autogyro fitted to army jeep in preparation for D-Day invasion.

German successes with paratroopers in the Low Countries. There were three types of operational craft, the Horsa, a rare example of which is on view in the museum (incidentally, recovered from Abingdon gaol), the Hamilcar and the American-built Hadrian. The Horsa could take 28 fully-equipped men and a crew of two, while the Hamilcar was designed to carry a light tank and a self-propelled gun. Using the skills of furniture makers, more the 3500 Horsas were turned out during the war.

The GPR suffered more casualties than almost any other Army unit. Pilots on its first major operation in 1943, a landing in Sicily, discovered that they had to fly an unfamiliar American glider in darkness - and first they had to assemble their craft from crated parts! Not surprisingly, more than half of the 137 gliders used in the attack landed in the sea and only a dozen reached their target. In the following year, however, the GPR had its first great success, when 220 Horsa and 30 Hamilcars were engaged in the D-Day invasion: almost all of them reached their targets. Moreover, in the opening minutes of D-Day, shortly after midnight, two separate Horsa forces landed beside key French bridges, and within minutes had captured them. One of the bridges, that over the Caen Canal, was later named Pegasus Bridge.

Three months later the GPR were involved in the well-known battle to capture Arnhem on the lower Rhine, an ill-fated operation that claimed the lives of 157 men and left 469 either missing or prisoners-of-war. The regiment lost so many pilots that 1500 RAF aircrew had to be transferred as a matter of urgency to take part in the last major glider assault of the war, the crossing of the Rhine.

Since the last war Army flying has changed dramatically; almost all operations are now carried out with helicopters. 'Give one hundred men helicopters and they will do the job of a thousand', one senior officer has remarked. Between the wars Army Cooperation squadrons carried out early experiments with autogyros, though the first tentative trials with military helicopters date from 1944. For several years a Joint Experimental Helicopter Unit was based at Middle Wallop, where the Sycamore and Whirlwind were evaluated for battlefield use. When the AAC was formed in 1957, the Skeeter, a light two-man helicopter had just entered service, later replaced with the Scout, the first Army helicopter to carry missiles.

The needs of the Army are today met by the Gazelle, which carries a pilot and four passengers, and the heavier Lynx, which carries two crew and eight passengers and is equipped with anti-tank, wire-controlled missiles. Finding what cover he can, the pilot emerges briefly to fix a tank in his sights and then 'flies' the deadly missile to its target.

But the backbone of Army flying is still reconnaissance and direction. As one officer remarked a few years ago: 'I command my brigade with a Scout helicopter. I cannot do it any other way.

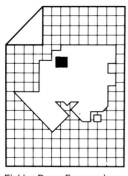

Finkley Down Farm and Country Park
(H. Waters)

Picket Piece,
Andover,
Hampshire.
SP11 6NF
Telephone
(0264) 52195

Price Guide - D

Car Parking
Free

Handicapped
Suitable

Party Visits
Preferably by arrangement

Publications
Leaflet
Spotter Pack

Where to eat
Cafe, picnic sites
Eating places in Andover

Time to allow
2 - 3 hours

Open
10-6, from Easter or 1st April,
whichever is the earliest, until
30th September

Public Transport
Bus Services -
Andover - Nos. 290,291,296,
297
Rail Services -
Andover Station, 3 miles away

Nearby Attractions
Andover Museum
Hawk Conservancy
Whitchurch Silkmill

FINKLEY DOWN FARM AND COUNTRY PARK

Fun and a touch of nostalgia are the trademarks of Finkley Down. Here is a place where children can safely 'muck around' on old tractors or play on swings, slides and other conventional apparatus. Here, too, the whole family can see a wide variety of animals, both traditional and exotic, and look at displays that capture the flavour of 'old times' on the farm.

Various farm tools and implements are set out in a 'Barn of Bygones'. These include such items as a wimble for winding straw ropes, a humbeller for knocking the 'bristles' off barley before winnowing and many other once-familiar sights around the farm. There are also some interesting local shop signs on display, such as that of H.W. Burden of Andover, 'Contractors to H.M. Government', who were 'rabbit salesmen' and 'ice merchants', in addition to being fishmongers, poulterers and fruiterers.

Finkley Down has a small collection of caged birds, including some unusual species of peacock and pheasant and old breeds of poultry. These include Polands, which came from Eastern

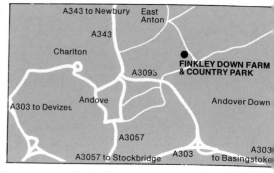

bees enter through a hole in the wall, so there i no danger of being stung!).

Also at Finkley Down is an interesting collectio of Romany caravans, including a Reading o 1905, a Burton and an example of a bow-top wago As a small display explains, gypsies and their 'faithful lurcher dogs' lived from the countrysid and made a living from making such things as peg and artificial flowers, picking fruit and trading horses. The farm also has a typical shepherd's hut made of corrugated iron sheeting and lined with wood. Inside is a simple bed, a candle lanterr a small iron stove and the tools of the trade - crook, bell and brander.

Finkley Down Farm, which has been in the same family for almost a century, originally covered an area of 200 acres. Sheep and breedin

Europe in the middle of the last century, Marans, which have a distinctive speckled plumage and take their name from a French town, and Sumatra Game, which have a long tail feather like a pheasant and are prolific egg-layers.

Nearby are kept traditional farm animals such as Hereford bull calves in deep straw litter, pigs and turkeys, as well as unusual residents like flop-eared Anglo-Nubian goats. A stable block is home for several horses, while outside may be seen Shires, the work-horse of yesteryear. A variety of small animals are also kept, such as baby chicks, rabbits and goats, while for those interested in beekeeping there is an observation hive (the

Shire horses were its main concerns until after the last war, when arable farming became more important. When Andover was developed as a London overspill town in the mid-1960s, 70 acres of the farm was purchased compulsorily for the nearby Walworth Industrial Estate. This marked the break-up of the old farm, which now only covers 32 acres, including the 14 acres of the country park.

In a district that has become highly industrialised, Finkley Down looks back to a way of life that has now gone, and young children feed the animals that farm labourers once tended.

BS

Photo: Finkley Down Farm & Country Park

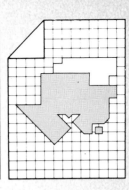

Highclere Castle
from Beacon Hill, Burghclere
Photo: John Holder

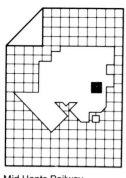

Mid-Hants Railway
(Mid-Hants Railway plc)

Alresford Station,
Alresford,
Hampshire.
SO24 9JG
Telephone
Alresford (096273) 4200 or
3810

Price Guide - E

Car Parking
Free at Alresford.
B.R. car park at Alton.

Handicapped
Suitable. Toilet at
Ropley

Party Visits
By arrangement (party
discounts)
Educational resources
available

Publications etc.
Leaflets, timetables and
guidebook
Displays

Where to eat
Buffet facilities on most trains

Time to allow
1 - 2 hours

Open
Hourly service 8th March-
26th October: Saturdays,
Sundays and Bank Holidays,
plus: End of May-last week of
July: Wednesdays and
Thursdays. Last week July-
31st August: Daily running.
Santa Specials operate at the
weekend throughout
December.

Public Transport
Bus Services to Alresford:
Alder Valley buses weekdays
every hour from Guildford,
Alton and Farnham, every half-
hour from Winchester. Every
two hours on Sundays.
Additional buses from
Southampton.

Rail Services -
Alton Station direct
connection and Winchester
Station (connects with bus)

Nearby Attractions
Avington Park
Alresford Town
Beresford House Museum
Alresford House
The Grange
Curtis Museum, Alton

THE WATERCRESS LINE

When the first railway in Hampshire started running from London to Winchester and Southampton in 1840, people flocked to see the unbelievable sight of locomotion. By the time that the Mid-Hampshire Railway, better known as the Watercress Line, was promoted 21 years later any town without its own station feared for its future. Portsmouth, Andover and Alton were all on a line by then and it was hoped that the new connection from Alton to Winchester might usefully link the great new Army camp of Aldershot with other barracks, as well as the rising hospital at Netley. The engineer for the line, apparently a Cuban, settled a route which despite deep cuttings and long embankments had one of the steepest gradients in southern England with rises of one in sixty: so steep that the engine of a long train was several feet higher than the last coaches.

The line was never a real success. Even in the peak of the railway age, in the 1920s, such an agricultural area could not generate much business. It did, however, become celebrated for its special traffic in watercress, which could be delivered swiftly nationwide, and so the line certainly helped the local economy. Today, we can barely imagine the many other advantages to a community of having a railway: the arrival of news, the saving of long walks to the nearby city or market, the luxury of evenings out in town and the cheap deliveries of coal.

The railway did prove of use to the military with many trains bringing troops to embark for South Africa and the widespread battle fronts in two world wars. Alresford Station often saw the odd express train from London when repair works blocked the main line. From the 1920s the long decline in traffic on country railways set in, as first buses and later lorries took to the road.

Now that the age of steam has passed the sight of engines, great and small, has again a powerful fascination. The purchase of the line in 1975 followed only two years of disuse, but a period of chronic inflation nearly defeated the preservationists' hopes. Since the first trains ran again in 1977 the service has become a highly successful tourist attraction and this almost entirely through the dedication of an army of volunteers who drive and restore the engines, staff the stations and have recently relaid the long section to Alton. This has restored the link with British Rail Services which many believe should never have been broken. It is now possible to board at Alton or Alresford, with intermediate stations at Ropley, Medstead, and Four Marks,

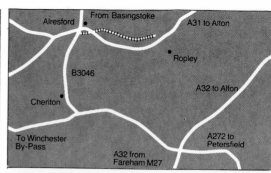

'HOW TO GET THERE'

Station in centre of New Alresford sign-posted off A31 Winchester to Alton road. From S.E. Hampshire and M27 take junction 10 and A32 to West Meon Hut, turn left (A272) and right, through Cheriton on B3046. Mid-Hants Railway uses Platform 3 of B.R. station at Alton.

1. Deliveries of watercress to Alresford.

2. End of the day at Ropley Workshops.

3. Bodmin - one of the great express engines.

4. Watercress line engine driver.

5. Bodmin leaving Alresford.

2 + 5 Mike Esau.

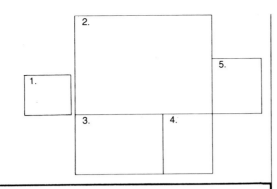

though parking at these stops is limited.

The ten-mile journey to Alton brings back every detail and nostalgic thrill of a trip on a 'real' railway with the sight of a powerful engine, the gleam of pipework, the roar of fire and steam, the eager wait for the signal and the guard's flag and whistle. Out of the station the delight of a journey is in the succession of fleeting impressions; glimpses of ivy-covered quarried chalk in deep cuttings and then the contrast of distant views across unspoilt downland farms, the savouring of coal smoke and the musical rhythmic beat of an engine hard at work, climbing all the way. For a growing number of adults it is a step back to a much-loved past, and for generations of young a new experience of the engaging world of the country railway.

In many a country station the porters and signalmen created gardens and Ropley was always celebrated for topiary, so even the trees have been reworked to their original shapes. It is well worth visiting the yard and modern workshop at Ropley where the sad wrecks of engines, after countless thousands of man-hours, are restored to working condition and their polished liveries. No small part of the fascination of railways lies in the incredible variety of design of steam engines from the earliest to the latest, and guides are often on hand to explain about the different locomotives in use on the line.

Perhaps the biggest surprise is that even the fireman on a train has to take a driving test which lasts all day! In this age of expensive energy we can better appreciate his skill in coaling the fire and maintaining the pressures of steam huge enough to haul the heavy trains up slopes as steep as those 'over the Alps', as the journey along this line was often described.

123

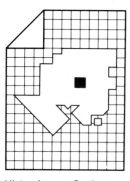

Hinton Ampner Gardens
(National Trust)

Hinton Ampner,
Near Alresford
Telephone enquiries
Bookham (0372) 53401

Price Guide - C

Car Parking
Free

Handicapped
Not very suitable yet for
visiting in wheelchairs,
because of garden steps

Party Visits
Welcome at normal times
Enquiries to the telephone
no. above

Where to Eat
Local pubs, Cheriton village
green, or Alresford

Time to allow
1 hour

Open
Early June - end of September
Wednesday to Sunday
afternoons

Nearby Attractions
Beresford House Museum

NEW ALRESFORD
& HINTON AMPNER GARDENS

Now renowned for its antique shops, New Alresford (said Awls-ford) grew up because it was near sheep country and water. Its streams are so abundant that there were no less than nine mills in the town at the time of the Domesday Survey, while a century later a dam was built to make a huge mill pond, Old Alresford Pond, which once covered 200 acres. Now a privately owned bird sanctuary, it has shrunk to a mere 25 acres. The dam was built in about 1200 by the bishop of the day and lord of the manor, Godfrey de Lucy, to bring wealth to the medieval equivalent of a 'new town'.

In addition to milling, Alresford grew fat on wool, which was probably taken by barge down the Itchen to Southampton. The downs to the north and east of Winchester are ideal for sheep and made Alresford one of the top ten wool markets in the country. Large quantities of cloth were also woven locally and finished in fulling mills. One of Alresford's fulling mills, now a private house, is passed on a beautiful riverside walk that starts at the foot of Broad Street at Ladywell Lane.

Despite the medieval origins of New Alresford, which followed an earlier Saxon settlement, the town's buildings are almost all Georgian. This is the consequence of a massive fire which the town suffered in 1689, said to have been started by 'a wandering band of Irish', which raged for three hours and destroyed 117 houses, the church and the market place. The town was burnt on several other occasions, including a minor blaze started after the famous Roundhead victory of 1644 at Cheriton nearby, when Royalists had to flee Alresford.

The author Mary Russell Mitford was born in Alresford, in 1787 at No. 27 Broad Street. She was prolific in her output - largely to keep her gambler father - but is best known for *Our Village*, based on Three Mile Cross, near Reading. She later wrote 'Alresford is, or will be, celebrated for two things; the first - to speak modestly - is my birth; the second is cricket'. In a way she was right, for the broadcaster and writer John Arlott lived for many years at The Old Sun, on the corner of Sun Lane and East Street.

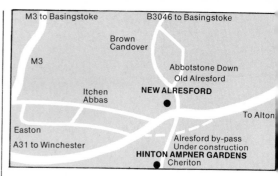

In the 1870s Alresford became the centre of attention when the Tichborne Claimant, Arthur Orton, set up house at No. 23 Broad Street to pursue the title and wealth of the Tichborne family, whose estates were nearby. After two of the most celebrated trials in British legal history, the wiles of the butcher from Wapping and Wagga Wagga, Australia, were uncovered and he was obliged to spend ten years in prison.

HINTON AMPNER GARDENS

A glimpse of a stone nymph at the end of an avenue of yew, a lovely terrace, its worn paving stones decorated with moss and creeping plants, a view of rolling parkland stretching as far as the eye can see . . . Some of the delights of a garden described by Christopher Bricknell, Director General of the Royal Horticultural Society's Gardens at Wisley as "although of relatively modern design, one of the best I have seen."

From June 1986, visitors will be invited to enjoy this garden, part of an extremely generous gift from Ralph Dutton, the eighth and last Lord Sherborne. When he died in April 1985, Lord Sherborne left Hinton Ampner to the National Trust which will hold the core of the 1640 acre estate for preservation. There is no endowment, so some outlying parts of the estate may have to be sold off to finance the upkeep of the main part.

The importance of Hinton Ampner", says Martin Drury, the Trust's Historic Buildings Secretary, "is that it is the creation in the first half of the twentieth century of a squire whose family had been established on the same estate for 300 years, a squire furthermore in the eighteenth century tradition, with a deep appreciation of the history of English architecture, decorative arts and gardens."

The house has been rebuilt twice since 1930, so cannot lay claim to national historic importance, but it has great charm and Lord Sherborne's collection of furniture, paintings and objets d'art will be of considerable interest to connoisseurs. Full opening of the house is impossible because of lack of funds, so the Trust has decided to leave it, for at least 5 years, to a sympathetic individual or organisation who will allow access on at least 30 days each summer. It is hoped that some rooms will be open from 1987.

The house and its contents will be kept largely intact and the situation as regards opening will be reviewed at the end of five years.

Alresford Pond

Tony Nutley

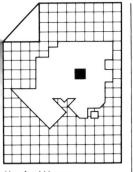

Alresford House
(P.G. Constable Maxwell)

Old Alresford,
Hampshire.
SO24 9DY
Telephone
(096273) 2843

Price Guide - D

Car Parking
Free
Coaches welcome

Handicapped
Grounds only suitable

Party Visits
By prior arrangement
Guided tours

Publications
Leaflet
Briefing Notes

Where to eat
Cream teas

Time to allow
½ - 1 hour

Other Activities
'Pick-your-own' soft fruit
and vegetables in season

Open
Grounds and museum:
mid-May to Mid-September,
Wednesday-Sunday and
Bank Holidays, 2.30-5.30.
House open throughout
August at stated times or at
any time of year for booked
groups. PYO open all day in
season

Public Transport
To New Alresford, 15-20
minutes walk away.
Bus Services -
Alder Valley buses on week-
days every hour from
Guildford, Alton and Farnham,
every half-hour from
Winchester. Every two hours
on Sundays.
Rail Services -
Alresford Station, New
Alresford. Summer steam
services operated by the mid-
Hants Railway between Alton
and New Alresford, telephone
(096273) 4200 or 3810.

Nearby Attractions
Beresford House Museum
The Watercress Line (Mid-
Hants Railway)
The Grange
Avington House

Moundsmere Manor Gardens,
Preston Candover
(Moundsmere Farming
Company)

Extensive gardens around
'Wrennaisance house built
in 1910
Open
By appointment, contact
Mr. Andrea
Telephone Preston Candover
(025 687) 207

Photo: Barry Shurlock

OLD ALRESFORD
& ALRESFORD HOUSE

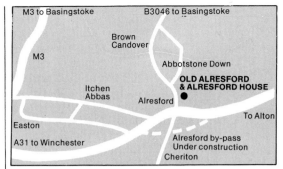

Before New Alresford grew up in the 13th century the main part of Alresford was to the north, across Bishop de Lucy's dam at the foot of Broad Street. London traffic on the Winchester-Alton road used to pass through Old Alresford, Abbotstone and Avington until the coming of the turnpike (now the A31) in the 18th century, which isolated the old village. Today it is a quiet corner of Hampshire with some particularly interesting historical connections. The Georgian church, itself a rarity, is often sought for a memorial on the south wall which records that it was at Old Alresford in 1875 that the Mothers' Union was founded by Mary Sumner. Her husband was the rector for many years and the rectory where they lived, now used as a retreat, still stands near the church.

Opposite the Mothers' Union tablet is a splendid marble memorial set up by the famous 'pre-Napoleonic' admiral, Lord Rodney, as a memorial to his wife Jane, who died in child-birth in 1767. Lord Rodney is also buried at Old Alresford. They lived at Alresford House, which stands immediately to the east of the church, and is now open to the public.

an eagle discharging 'thunderbolts', an allusion to Rodney's first command, the *Eagle*. After completing the house Rodney extended his estate by purchasing several local farms and acquiring Alresford Pond. He was particularly fond of animals and said he wanted the 'opportunity of showing mercy in not suffering the poor birds to be shot at'.

Later, election expenses (we would now say bribes) forced Rodney to escape his creditors in France and he was even offered a command in the French navy! He declined, saying: 'Pecuniary difficulties, it is true, have driven me from my country, but no temptation can draw me from her service'. Rodney's career was in fact crowned by defeating the French, in an action against Admiral de Grasse in the West Indies in 1782.

ALRESFORD HOUSE

George Brydges Rodney was a man who made his fortune from prize money gained by capturing enemy ships during the War of Austrian Succession in the late 1740s. With it he bought an estate at Old Alresford and replaced an existing pile with the present elegant redbrick country house. This brought Rodney the sort of life his father had known before becoming bankrupt in the South Sea Bubble. Not only was this a personal disaster but it meant that his son had to be brought up by his godfather, George Brydges, who lived at Avington, only a few miles from Alresford.

Alresford House is no longer owned by the Rodney family, though several links with the admiral remain. The centrepiece of a fine plaster ceiling in the morning room, for example, depicts

The cannon captured at the time still stand on the terrace at Alresford House, which was owned by successive generations of the family until the 1870s.

Some of the present treasures of Alresford House were acquired by art collector Dr. C.F.G.R. Schwerdt and include splendid French oak pannelling in the dining room and a rare carved marble roundel (a tondo) by Rossellino, who trained in the workshops of Leonardo da Vinci.

In 1939 the house was purchased by Wing-Commander Gerald Constable Maxwell, a distinguished fighter pilot who fought in both world wars. He and his son William are commem-orated by a small Catholic chapel built about 30 years ago and a museum. They are decorated with a trompe l'oeil designed be Pietro Annagoni as a favour - for help in securing a commission to paint HM the Queen.   BS

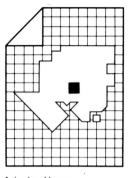

Avington House
(J.B. Hickson)

Avington Park,
Winchester,
Hampshire,
SO21 1NJ
Telephone
Itchen Abbas (096278) 202

Price Guide - D

Car Parking
Free

Handicapped
Ground floor only

Party Visits
Party tours available
throughout the year by
arrangement

Publications
Guidebook and leaflet

Where to eat
Tea bar - Sundays and Bank
Holidays
Picnic area in open space
across lake (Avington to
Easton Road)

Time to allow
1 hour

Open
May - September 2.30-
5.30pm Saturdays, Sundays
and Bank Holiday Mondays
(occasional Saturdays
closed)

Public Transport
Bus Services -
Alder Valley buses every hour
from Guildford, Alton and
Winchester, to Itchen Abbas,
every two hours on Sundays.
Also buses from
Southampton.
Rail Services -
Winchester Station

Nearby Attractions
Hinton Ampner Gardens
The Grange
Itchen Valley Walk

AVINGTON HOUSE

Avington, one of Hampshire's smallest villages, remains also one of the loveliest. Even 150 years ago William Cobbett, the radical itinerant journalist, described a sense of well-being which was uncommon in the impoverished southern counties of his day. Today it is an ideal place for long walks around the Park and through the valley. At summer weekends the great house is open to visitors, many of whom go on to the lovely church a particularly fine Georgian building.

The house, which once looked out across a landscaped park with a lake that has sadly become dried out, has a spectacular facade and rooms once as lavishly decorated as those of Broadlands, though Avington is much older. The present building was remodelled to please King Charles II who often lived in the Close at Winchester towards the end of his life. To meet the objections of senior churchmen, Nell Gwynne his mistress stayed at Avington.

Later Avington was owned by George Brydges, a kinsman of the Duke of Chandos to whom he left the estate. At the end of the 18th century the ownership passed, by the marriage of the last Duke's only daughter and heiress, to the Marquis of Buckingham who often welcomed his friends the Prince Regent and Mrs Fitzherbert, to enjoy country celebrations in this idyllic park. The Marquis and his wife (he was later to be created Duke of Buckingham and Chandos) were very generous to the people who worked on their estate, as the Duchess's memorial in the church testifies.

The estate was sold in 1848 to Sir John Shelley, younger brother of the poet, and in 1952 was sold again. Now part of the house is let as apartments. The tour visits the state rooms, including the ballroom, the drawing room and the library; beyond are the delightful Victorian orangeries where cream teas are served.

St Mary's Church, a short walk from the park, is one of the most perfect Georgian churches in the country, completed in 1771. The original box pews and an impressive three-decker pulpit are well preserved.

Near the lake is a picnic area where a country walks leaflet is available with a selection of routes, from one to several hours in length, on footpaths near the banks of the Itchen. The tracks can be muddy so boots are often necessary. The free leaflet can also be obtained by sending a stamped addressed envelope to the County Recreation Department in Winchester.

THE GRANGE

Some half-million pounds have been spent by the Government to save this "startlingly beautiful" building, which is one of the most important in the history of architecture for it was the first country house in Europe to be designed on classical Greek lines.

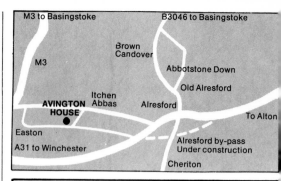

The Grange is more, however, than a unique piece of architecture; it is a sobering advertisement of the tragic fate which can overtake the very finest buildings in the land, for much of the interior has been left to rot during recent years of indecision though at one time the house, together with a millionaire's art collection, was offered to the state. The shell which remains has an extraordinary history and an archaeology all of its own. In this superb composition of building and landscape, the Greek temple and a pastoral park epitomise the two great English contributions to civilisation: the Greek revival and the Picturesque - one a hardheaded belief in reason and progress, the other a romantic desire to realise the painter's imagination.

The architectural history of the Grange was revealed by the demolition men: a house lay inside the outer skin, its inside walls hidden behind later interior panelling added like sets in a theatre. This was the first, four-storey brick house built in 1670 by William Samwell, a most ingenious gentleman-architect who created a mansion typical of the 18th century some thirty years in advance of the period. The north front has been restored to its original condition, before the revolutionary classical Greek redesign of 1804.

Before this happened, however, the grounds were landscaped in the 1760s with a winding lake, probably by Capability Brown, and the Prince of Wales was reputed to have set up a harem in the house. In 1804 the Grange came into the hands of

**'HOW TO GET THERE' –
AVINGTON HOUSE**

From Winchester take
Kingsworthy Road, cross
by-pass onto B3047. At Itchen
Abbas turn right.

**'HOW TO GET THERE'
THE GRANGE**

Take B3047 or A31 to Alresford
and turn north up Broad Street.
Two miles north of Old Alresford
continue left on B3046 to
Swarraton. The Grange is sign
posted to the left.

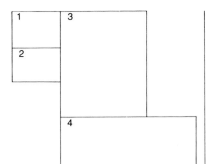

1.   West front of Avington
       House
2.   Colonnade on north side
3.   The Orangery tea room
4.   The Grange buildings
       seen across the lake

4.   *Hampshire County
       Planning Department*

an 18 year old dandy, Henry Drummond, who had
just returned from his grand tour and found a
like-minded relative and architect, William
Wilkins, to create a unique home in the form of a
temple. In the next ten years this was achieved
to dramatic effect by building up a platform which
buried the old ground floor. To this new building,
surfaced in roman cement, he added the huge
Doric portico overlooking the lake on the east.
The original fourth floor was hidden and the
servants living at the top were left without
windows for some seventy years!

Soon disappointed, Drummond sold the
property - "a temple, not a house" - and
continued his eccentric life as a mystic in
Switzerland. The next owner, another banker, was
Alexander Baring who negotiated the sale by
France of most of North America to the newly-
born United States in 1803: the Louisiana purchase
was probably the world's biggest land deal. Baring
had the house extended enormously but all that is
left of his additions is the Orangery. This also
was a brilliant classical temple in the delicate
Ionic order, a distant echo from the Parthenon in
Athens where the two orders were also used
together. Even this conservatory was an architectural milestone, one of the earliest cast-iron
and glass buildings in Europe; in it were grown
bananas, figs, peaches, melons and nectarines.

With restoration complete and the scaffolding
down this splendid pair of temples stand
like beautiful follies on their podia above the
lush Hampshire countryside, itself sculptured so
finely. As Cockerill, the designer of the Orangery,
said: "Nothing could be finer, more classical or like
the finest Poussin. It realises the most fanciful
representations of the painter's fancy of the poet's
description... There is nothing like it on this side
of Arcadia."

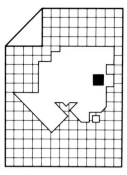

The Oates Memorial Library and Museum and the Gilbert White Museum
(Oates Memorial Trust)

The Wakes,
Selborne,
Alton,
Hampshire,
GU34 3JH
Telephone
Selborne (042050)275

Price Guide - C

Car Parking
Free parking nearby, behind Selborne Arms

Handicapped
Much of the museum and garden is suitable

Party Visits
By arrangement

Publications etc.
Leaflet and guidebook
The Wakes Garden - A Short Guide
Displays
Day courses with country walks

Where to eat
Pubs, hotel, cafe and licensed restaurant/bar in village

Time to allow
1 - 2 hours for museum
Entry ticket valid all day

Open
Main season - any day but Monday (open Bank Holiday Mondays)
Out of season - Wholly closed (can open for parties booked in advance)

Public Transport
Bus Services -
Alder Valley buses from Alton or Petersfield, five journeys a day, Monday - Friday, three journeys on Saturday. No Sunday service.
Rail Services -
Alton

Nearby Attractions
Jane Austen's House
Curtis Museum and Allen Gallery, Alton

Romany Folklore Museum
Selborne
Open daily throughout the summer, 10am - 5pm
Price Guide - B.

Top	The Wakes from the Plestor
Centre:	18th century engraving of the Plestor
Bottom:	Gilbert White's gravestone
Centre:	*The Gilbert White Museum*

SELBORNE

At about the age of ten Gilbert White came to live in The Wakes, across the village street from the church and the rectory where he was born in 1720. The Wakes remained his home until he died there at the age of 72.

To the original house, dating from the 16th century, Gilbert added a great parlour and later owners created a rambling mansion by further extensions which are explained in an illustrated architectural guide. In the 1950s the house and grounds were purchased as a memorial to the remarkable achievements of this clergyman. The greater part of the fund came from R.W. Oates and there are displays here about Captain Lawrence Oates who joined Scott's unfortunate 1911 Antarctic Expedition, and his uncle Frank, a 19th century naturalist and one of the explorers of 'Darkest' Africa. Captain Oates was the brave man in charge of the ponies, who on the desperate return from the Pole walked out of the tent in a blizzard with the words: 'I'm just going outside. I may be some time'. His frost-bitten and gangrenous feet were slowing the progress of the party, who were soon to die in their tent.

The Wakes has two furnished rooms and there are splendid family portraits in the great parlour, but sadly no authentic painting of Gilbert White himself is known. There are numerous rooms with exhibitions including a fine one about White's contribution to British natural history and the local environment which he explored and studied. There is a small display of finds recovered by excavation from the Priory of Selborne, a mile and a half east of the village which was closed down in 1486 after a struggle for survival which lasted for two hundred and fifty years. Much of the village and countryside were then granted to Magdalen College, Oxford.

Behind the Wakes is the garden once tended by Gilbert White, where many of the flowers he mentions in his "Garden Kalender" are now grown. White's own sundial, ha-ha and part of his fruit wall are still there. The museum staff run the Gilbert White Field Studies Centre, mostly for Hampshire school children, and there are also day courses for adults on a variety of topics. The countryside where 200 years ago the humble curate discovered a new approach to the study of nature, has become familiar to people all over the world through his writings.

It is due to gifts by Magdalen College and a local landowner that there are numerous delightful walks around the village, across the common, by the village 'hanger' or through the 'lythes'. These are mainly woodland walks among the beeches which grow on the hills and are a charming feature of the East Hampshire countryside.

Copies of a leaflet about these local walks, "The National Trust in Selborne" can be bought in the village. The visitor should not miss the pleasure of a stroll around the village, or a look around the church with its massive yew. Signs direct the visitor to the simple grave of Gilbert White at the back of the church.

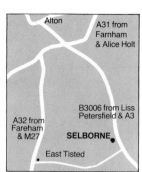

'HOW TO GET THERE'
From Winchester A31 to Alton, turning off by-pass as if for the town. Turn right then onto B3006. Village 4 miles. From Portsmouth follow directions as for Jane Austen's House.

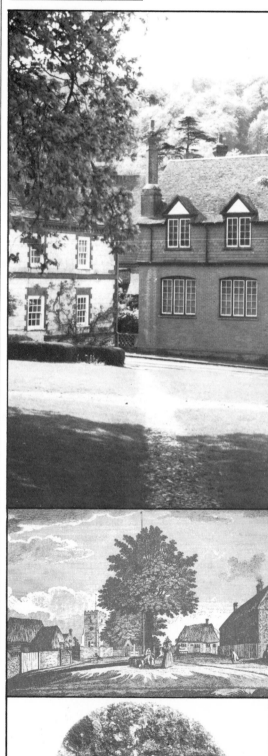

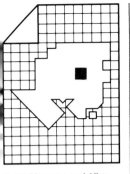

Curtis Museum and Allen Gallery, Alton
(Hampshire County Museum Service)

(Museum) Crown Hill
High Street
Alton
GU34 1BA
Telephone
Alton (0420) 82802

Price Guide
Free

Car Parking
Nearby

Handicapped
Ground floors of museum and gallery accessible to visitors in wheelchairs

Party Visits
By arrangement
School holiday activities arranged

Publications
Leaflets

Where to eat
Cafes and tea rooms in Town nearby

Time to allow
1 - 2 hours

Open
All through year
Museum Monday - Saturday
10am - 5pm
Gallery Tuesday - Saturday
10am - 5pm

Public Transport
Bus Services
Alder Valley buses hourly from Winchester and Guildford, every two hours on Sunday. Additional buses from Basingstoke and Southampton, Monday - Saturday.
Rail Services
Alton Station ½ hourly service from Waterloo

Nearby Attractions
Watercress Line
Jane Austen House
Selborne
Birdworld
Alice Holt Forest

Top: Skewering a surplice of hops at Amery Farm, Alton, 1880

Bottom: The Mechanics' Institute (now the Curtis Museum) and Cottage Hospital at Crown Close, Alton, 1882.

Photos: Hampshire County Museum Service

THE CURTIS MUSEUM
& ALLEN GALLERY

Now more than 125 years old, the Curtis is one of the County's longest established museums, and can be found in one of the prominent group of buildings at the northern end of Alton High Street. Just across the road in two old cottages is the Allen Gallery. Both foundations owe much to the inspiration and generosity of the well-known and long-established Curtis family of Quakers in Alton, one of whom was a famous botanist.

In a town with such a long tradition of brewing, surrounded by countryside celebrated to this day for its hops, the 'Curtis' naturally has many fascinating items connected with beer making. On show are photos of hop pickers; rakes and horse-hair cloths used to dry the hops on the kiln floors; and large "pockets", marked with the local sign of a lion, for sending the hops to market. There are stilts used in the hop gardens and displays on the main breweries, including Halls, who used to

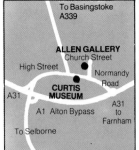

'HOW TO GET THERE'
From Winchester on A31 continue past roundabout junction with A32 from Farnham then take second turning to left into town. Continue down Anstey Road to Normandy Road. Car parking, near Turk Street or off Church Street.

produce 20,000 barrels a year before being taken over in 1903 by the London firm of Courage.

The Curtis is undergoing extensive changes which will transform the displays and bring to life the story of Alton and its surroundings. A colourful display of children's toys, dolls and games has already been completed and gradually the rest of the museum will be renovated and redisplayed. The growth and development of the area will be traced from its foundations in the landscape, through the railway era and right up to the present day, when this part of rural East Hampshire is being affected by discoveries of oil.

The Allen Gallery also contains other items which should not be missed by any visitor to the town. The highlight indeed of all the County's collections is here. This is a unique set of spoons made in 1592. These were given later to a member of the Tichborne family from near Alresford, who in 1657 was Lord Mayor of London. Sir Robert Tichborne was, however, soon imprisoned in the Tower because he had signed the death warrant of King Charles I. Each of the twelve spoons bears a figure. There are three Jews, including King David, and three Pagans, including Julius Caesar. Three

Christian Knights include King Arthur, and then there are also Christ, St Peter and Queen Elizabeth I. These have been called 'perhaps the most famous English spoons in existence'.

The Allen Gallery is, however, for the most part taken up by a large display of English pottery. This forms a splendid chance to admire ceramics of every kind from Medieval Bellarmine bottles to Toby Jugs, "Willow patterned" plates and the multi-coloured pictorial printed lids of pots which once contained bear grease hair dressing. Although simply a ceramics exhibition, it shows as well changing ideas on design across the centuries, through to the 1980s with modernist studio pottery.

The Gallery downstairs has more room for travelling exhibitions, and outside there is a charming garden with seats for the public, an oasis of peace in the middle of the town.

129

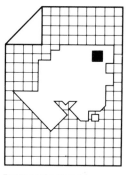

Basingstoke Canal
(Hampshire County Council,
County Recreation
Department)

The Canal Manager,
Ash Lock,
Near Aldershot,
Hampshire.
Telephone
Aldershot (0252) 313810

Price Guide - Free

Car Parking
Colt Hill Bridge, Odiham
Barley Mow Bridge,
Winchfield
Chequers Bridge, Crookham
village

Handicapped
Difficult access to towpath
Suitable toilet at Colt Hill
Bridge, Odiham

Party Visits
Boat trip by arrangement, for
booking telephone (0252)
519619

Publications
Guide book available from
H.C.C. Recreation
Department,
North Hill Close,
Andover Road,
Winchester. Price 60p
plus p.&p. 20p

Where to eat
Many pubs along the canal
Refreshments are available
on boat

Time to allow
1 - 3 hours

Open
At all times

Boat trips for public
Sundays and Bank Holidays
2.30
Seat bookings, Fleet (02514)
5694

Nearby Attractions
Basing House
Willis Museum, Basingstoke
Ghurkas Museum, Church
Crookham
Odiham Pest House
King John's Castle
Military museums, Aldershot

Farnborough Abbey
(St Michaels Abbey)

Mausoleum of the Emperor
Napoleon III and the
Empress Eugenie
Tours at 3.30pm every
Saturday
Telephone Farnborough
(0252) 546105

BASINGSTOKE CANAL

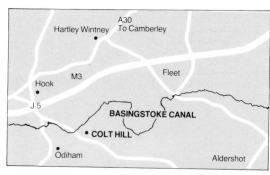

In 1914 the last barge to make the complete journey from Aldershot through to the now weed-clogged western end of this canal reached Basingstoke after a trip which took three months! For a little more than a century the small market town had its own route to the London docks, 71 miles and usually only 3 or 4 days' journey away. Although the restoration of the waterway which started in 1973 is unlikely ever to allow the final seven miles to be reopened, it will enable craft and walkers along the towpath to travel from Odiham to the Wey and from the Wey to the Thames, thirty-three miles further on.

The reopening of the towpath, and more gradually of the canal, is a superb achievement of the two neighbouring County Councils, Surrey and Hampshire, who purchased the virtually useless waterway, for the Canal Society who campaigned for its protection and have provided an army of volunteers. Without their dedication and skill the estimated million-pound cost would have been several times that amount. A great deal has also been achieved by trainees on Government schemes. The most complex task of the project is the re-building of many locks in Surrey which raised the barges on to the summit level near the county border at Ash. The surveyors of the late 18th century were able to select a route for the next 22 miles which needed no locks, by building embankments and creating two tunnels.

Along the towpath today can be found typical canal-side inns and traces of the old wharves as well as the many bridges which were built to keep peace with the local landowners. There are nature reserves along the banks and many historic features.

Odiham makes a most attractive starting point to explore the canal in Hampshire. Footpaths from the High Street cross the fields to join the waterway as it swings through North Warnborough. Nearby it passes King John's Castle and enters the Greywell Tunnel, the partial collapse of which sealed the commercial fate of the western end. To get through this broad tunnel, which had ten foot head-room, the bargees had to push with their feet on the brick sides for nearly three-quarters of a mile. Meanwhile the horses were led over the hill to be re-hitched at the opposite portal.

King John's Castle, recently excavated by Hampshire Museum Service, is a most attractive octagonal tower surrounded by moats which were cut through by the canal. The archaeologists very surprisingly found that the building may be late thirteenth century, a century after King John had founded here one of the most expensive castles of his reign. From this site, if not from the building, he rode to Runnymede to sign the Magna Carta. The castle is known to have been besieged by the French Dauphin, and later in the century it belonged to Simon de Montfort's wife, whose daily account books survive to give one of the very few detailed pictures of the life of medieval nobility.

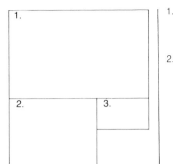

1. *John Pinkerton* the Canal Society waterbus on canal near Odiham.

2. Barge crews just after the First World War, when goods were still being carried to Aldershot.

3. King John's Castle ruins beside the canal and the River Whitewater near Greywell.

1, 3: Hampshire County Recreation Department

2: Tony Harmsworth

way, became "The Camp" - military Aldershot, with its vast training grounds. To the north of the canal is the long landing strip of the Royal Aircraft Establishment at Farnborough, where the extraordinary American showman Samuel Cody made some of the first military airship journeys and the first officially recorded airplane flight in Britain.

To the south is the enormous area of former ranges stretching down to Farnham; Long Valley, which includes Beacon Hill, Caesars Camp and many other features well remembered by generations of ex-soldiers who have been on exercises and manoeuvres here. As long as warning flags are not flying one can walk across these former heathland commons.

Once past the barracks and the playing fields of Aldershot the waterway crosses the Blackwater Valley on a large embankment, before beginning the long descent through a series of locks. Seeing the work which has been involved in restoration it seems incredible that the canal could have been built in just six years without the aid of modern technology. Its fortunes only rose in time of war when the competing coastal trade was diverted onto the canal's broad boats, after carriage across country to the wharf at Basingstoke.

The steady return of water down the canal, from springs in the Greywell Tunnel, to the limits of excavation of accumulated mud will naturally have an effect on the ecology: the silted-up habitat was ideal for dragonflies and to help their preservation the Greywell stretch is left free of power-boating. The tunnel is a valuable environment for bats which can be seen emerging at dusk, and its dark water, cold in summer, warm in winter, is said to have its own large and colourless pike. The canal is stocked with many fish including tench, carp and perch, all well suited to slow-moving shallow freshwater. On the surface the waterfowl most commonly seen are moorhen, coot, and dabchick; walkers with sufficient stealth may be rewarded with a sight of these birds but they are wary of people, quickly scrambling out of sight or taking shelter among the reeds.

The flowers of the canal are particularly interesting. There are water-plants such as yellow waterlily and crowfoot and, growing along the banks, the large reed-mace, yellow iris and the tiny forget-me-nots. The frequent changes of setting add especially to the interest of the canal for ornithologists, but there are few people who will not find pleasure and interest in discovering London's beautiful "lost route to Basingstoke."

An attractive and informative guide book has been published by Hampshire County Recreation Department: 'The Basingstoke Canal, the Western Length'.

To the east of Odiham there are very pleasant outings to be enjoyed from Colt Hill, either along the towpath or in rowing and motor boats, for a small boat yard has craft for hire. Colt Hill is also the base for outings on the *John Pinkerton*, the Surrey and Hampshire Canal Society's very successful cruising narrow boat, which usually heads west for the castle. However, east of Colt Hill the navigation passes through woodlands on a long detour around the former park of Dogmersfield where Prince Arthur, brother of Henry VIII, first met his wife to be, Catherine of Aragon. Beyond this pleasant countryside the waterway crosses the heathland which, sometime after the canal's business had been lost to the rail-

131

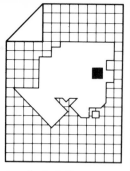

JANE AUSTEN'S HOUSE
CHAWTON

Not long ago heavy traffic between London and Winchester streamed around the sharp bend which skirted Jane Austen's house in Chawton Village. Today the village street has returned to the blissful peace visible in old photographs, which even Jane herself would recognise if she could return.

The house in which she lived for eight years until, with her fatal illness she retired to Winchester, was once a large roadside ale-house. Jane and her brothers and sister grew up in the manor-house rectory of Steventon some twelve miles away, near Basingstoke. After her father's death Jane, her sister Cassandra, and her mother came here after one of her brothers, who changed his name to Knight, had been left the estate of Chawton Park. The house and garden have been brought back to the simplicity and state of those early 19th century years, and the walls of its rooms display a wealth of documentary and illustrative material about Jane's life, her homes, her family and her books.

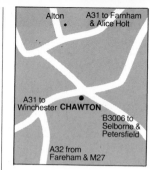

HOW TO GET THERE'
Chawton village is sign-posted off roundabout junction of A31 from Winchester and A32 from Fareham. From Portsmouth A3 to Sheet, turn left onto A325 through Liss and fork left onto B3006 to Alton via Selborne. Just before Alton turn left into Chawton.

CHAWTON VILLAGE POND, AS IN JANE AUSTEN'S TIME

There is furniture that belonged to Jane, a patchwork quilt she made and even a small dress of hers. Upstairs one can visit five of the bedrooms, with their creaky floors and their many exhibits, but it is downstairs that one feels closest to the writer who here composed, or rewrote, some of the greatest masterpieces in English literature, including *Pride and Prejudice* and *Emma*. In the dining parlour Jane laboured in secret, although with the knowledge of her family, writing the books which were published anonymously.

As one knows from her novels Jane led more than a home life. Indeed, with the rewards of success she enjoyed visits to London and journeys to friends and relations until, tragically, at the age of 42 she wasted away from a rare disease. Just behind her home there still stands the little bakehouse with its chimney and oven built in and its boiling tub for washing, and here can be seen the little donkey cart which Jane used during her final months in 1817, her health failing rapidly.

The garden nearby, as well as the house are a delightful memorial to her life and a mark of the pleasure given to countless millions through her books.

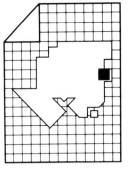

BIRDWORLD

Birdworld
Bird Park and gardens
(R.T. Harvey)

Holt Pound
Farnham
Surrey
GU10 4LO
Telephone
Bentley (0420) 22140

Price Guide - D

Car Parking
Free

Handicapped
Special toilets, concrete paths with ramps

Party Visits
Welcome
Educational resources available
Set meals on request

Publications
Guidebook

Where to eat
Cafe
Picnic tables on site

Time to allow
2 - 3 hours

Open
All year every day
In Autumn and Winter closes at 3.30

Public Transport
Bus Services -
Alder Valley buses every two hours from Petersfield, half-hourly from Aldershot, Monday - Saturday. Limited service on Sunday.
Londonlink Service from Victoria Coach Station, London
Rail Services -
Aldershot on Waterloo - Alton line

Nearby Attractions
Alice Holt Forest and Visitors Centre
Farnham Museum
Frensham Ponds
Jane Austen's House
Military Aldershot

'HOW TO GET THERE'
From Alton take A31 up to roundabout junction with A325 on the outskirts of Farnham. Take A325 south and Bird World is two miles, on the right.

Literally next door to the Alice Holt Forest, close to Farnham but still within the Hampshire county boundary is the large and colourful Birdworld, a rapidly developing zoo park. Birdworld began in 1968 and is the result of the energy and enthusiasm of one family who are dedicated to birds and to share their pleasure have built up one of the most comprehensive collections in Britain.

The success of their efforts has enabled the gardens and aviaries to be expanded year by year in ever more ambitious ways. Not only are there the bird gardens but an excellent aquarium, while the most imaginative part is a recreated sea shore aviary, complete with beach and waves.

plovers and shag, oyster catchers and curlew as well as Tufted Ducks who are especially well adapted, staging many displays for visitors. In this clever but necessarily artificial environment even coastal birds have been breeding quite happily.

The aquarium is also an impressive achievement showing about a thousand tropical,

The variety of birdlife in the world is astounding, their beaks and feet, wings, size and plumage in every case adapted to exploit the habitats and food of so many different kinds of environment. To wander round the many acres of paddocks, lawns and parkland enjoying the brilliant rainbow colours of the Macaws, the astounding beaks of the Toucans, the charm of the Penguins, as well as eagles, peacocks, geese and storks is to appreciate zoological expertise as well as our good fortune that the birds survive our climate and can even be enjoyed throughout the year.

Even winter has its own special attraction for then the waterfowl put on their true colours. As well as providing enjoyable outings Birdworld is invaluable for schools in helping to teach the importance of preserving specific environments to protect the way of life of birds and breeding stock in captivity to replenish species which are threatened with extinction.

The sea shore walk is surprisingly successful in this regard for within a high caged enclosure a beach and cliff has been created complete with waves, where you can walk amidst

fresh water and marine fish and invertebrates, all displayed in tanks carefully furnished with tropical plants and literally tons of rocks and shingle and coral. One can watch a Nurse shark and a very big grouper which can apparently be an even more dangerous creature. One can quite safely stare piranhas and the beautiful Moray eels in the eye. Apart from such dramatic fish and eels there are many small and colourful ones that are delightful to watch, as well as crab, sea horses and sea urchins.

One of the clearest signs of how well Birdworld and 'Underwater World' have been prepared for visitors is the consideration paid to handicapped people who will have no difficulty enjoying any part of the site or the aquarium.

In recent years great emphasis has been placed on developing the gardens, where many shrubs are now maturing into beautiful specimens. In season there is also a wealth of colour, from fuschias, pelargoniums and exceptional baskets of flowers which seem to be growing out of the wall.

Rhea Family
Photo: Birdworld

133

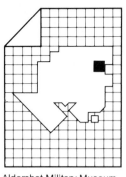

Aldershot Military Museum and Visitors Centre
(Aldershot Military Historical Trust)

Queens Avenue,
Aldershot,
Hampshire,
GU11 2LG
Telephone
Aldershot (0252) 314598

Price Guide - B

Car Parking
Free

Handicapped
Suitable

Time to Allow
1 - 2 hours

Open
Daily
March - October, 10am-5pm
November - February,
10am-4.30pm

Airborne Forces Museum
Browning Barracks,
Queens Avenue
Telephone
Aldershot (0252) 24431
Ext. Montgomery 619

Price Guide - B

Open
Every day including
weekends (except Christmas
Day) 10am-12.30pm,
2.00-4.30pm

Royal Corps of Transport Museum
Buller Barracks,
Alison's Road
Telephone
Aldershot (0252) 24431
Ext. 2417

Price Guide - Free

Car Parking
Free

Handicapped
Suitable

Open
Weekdays only, 9-12am,
2-4.30pm. Groups at week-
ends by arrangement.

Royal Army Medical Corps Museum
Keogh Barracks
Ash Vale
Telephone
Aldershot (0252) 24431
Ext. Keogh 212

Price Guide - Free

Handicapped
Full facilities

Open
Weekdays only, 8.30am-4pm.
Closed over Christmas and
on Bank Holidays.

Other Museums
For information on other
military museums in and
around Aldershot contact
The Visitor Centre.

MILITARY ALDERSHOT

Probably the most surprising place described in this volume is Aldershot, a Victorian town with few distinguished buildings and to its north, on a plateau, the Army Camp, a large area of barracks and depots, playing fields and hospitals. Signs warn that on the Government-owned roads traffic may have to give way to marching soldiers and before parking visitors may be asked for their driving licences, for security has to be taken seriously. Despite these qualifications Aldershot should not be missed by visitors, for the 'Home of the British Army' has more museums packed into a smaller area than any other of the County, and on the way from one to another can be seen monuments and features preserved from the days of the Victorian Army.

It is difficult to believe that until 1854 Aldershot was a small settlement lost among vast heath-land commons, with two inns and nine hundred villagers. Its transformation, much encouraged by Prince Albert, resulted from the need for perman-ent training areas for the Army and Militia. The commons, with a railway nearby, were ideal for practising manoeuvres, and a good site to keep a force which could speed to defend the coast against invasion.

The first occupants bivouacked in tents but in 1855 two camps of wooden huts, which later became the home of many regiments returning from the Crimea, were erected north and south of the Basingstoke Canal. Initially designed for summer use only, there were no roads in the camp, the huts were "neither wind nor rainproof" and winter conditions were appalling. Wives and children occupied spare huts, with blankets hung from rafters as partitions between families. These camps were replaced in the 1890s and virtually all of these brick-built barracks have also now gone, for the last two decades have seen another generation of barracks rise in their place.

The army which returned from Crimea was of course very much a horse-borne, or horse-powered one and the buildings at Aldershot included very large cavalry barracks with rooms for the cavalrymen above their horses. One of the enormous indoor riding schools survives, as does the Royal Army Veterinary Corps which has a small museum. Nowadays though, only some 700 horses are retained by the Army compared with as many as a third of a million during the First World War. Victorian officers were expected to lead the life of a gentleman, riding and hunting, and one of the generals even said that for his staff, ability to ride well was more important than to think: a good 'seat', was preferred to a good head!

One amenity which was established by the Prince Consort for officers was a beautiful library, which still stands and can be visited by prior arrangement. The Royal Pavilion on a nearby hill where Victoria and other members of the Royal Family often stayed has been swept away for the modern headquarters of Queen Alexandra's Royal Army Nursing Corps, who have a fascinating exhibition. Visitors will not fail to notice the fine Cambridge hospital of 1879 overlooking the town.

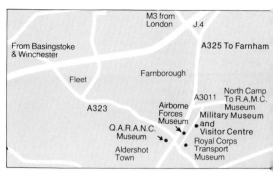

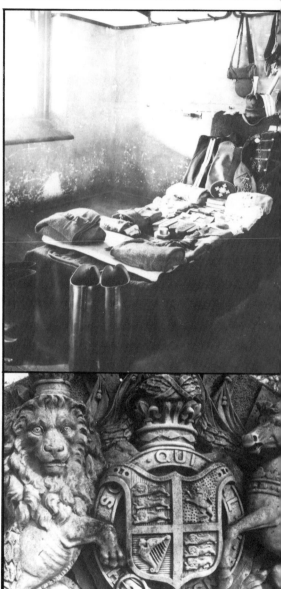

'HOW TO GET THERE'

From M3 (Junction 4) follow A325 through Farnborough. By Queens Hotel roundabout turn left into A3011 (to North Camp and Ash Vale) and soon turn right into Queen's Avenue. Continue down Queen's Avenue and turn right into Alison's Road for Airborne Forces Museum. From Portsmouth, A3 to Sheet, then left onto A325 to Aldershot.

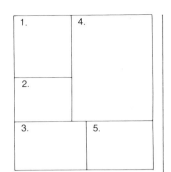

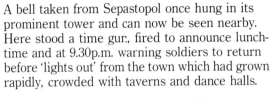

1. Kit Inspection, 13th Hussar at the turn of the century

2. Fine sculpture saved from the old Blenheim Cavalry barracks, now outside the Prince Consort's Library.

3. Royal Wagon from the Napoleonic War days.

4. Transport during the First World War, part of the Royal Corps of Transport Museum display.

5. A tricky exercise with collapsible canvas boats on Frensham Pond. c.1904

A bell taken from Sepastopol once hung in its prominent tower and can now be seen nearby. Here stood a time gun, fired to announce lunchtime and at 9.30p.m. warning soldiers to return before 'lights out' from the town which had grown rapidly, crowded with taverns and dance halls.

The full story of the camp is told in the Aldershot Military Museum and Visitors Centre. Housed in the last remaining Victorian barrack block it relates 130 years of change in the life of the soldier, with many photographs, models and displays. One end of the block has been furnished just as it might have looked at the time turn of the century, complete with the telescopic beds that were needed to allow room for a central mess table.

Aldershot was also the birth place of British military aviation and in the large military cemetery can be seen the grave of the pioneer aviator and eccentric American, Samuel Cody.

The museums of the Royal Corps of Transport and the Royal Army Medical Corps illustrate army history from well before the establishment of Aldershot. Both give fascinating insight into the practicalities of war: keeping the army on the move, getting food, fuel and soldiers to the front and the wounded out again and back to health. The Medical Corps Museum is at the training depot just across the Basingstoke Canal at Ash, which is just in Surrey. The Royal Corps of Transport Museum, which includes displays on the Royal Engineers Transportation and the Royal Army Service Corps, can be found in South Camp close to an enormous artificial ski slope. Also near here is one of Aldershot's largest museums, that of the Airborne Forces. While the first parachute jumps were made from planes in World War One the new organisation (whose emblem is Pegasus the Winged Horse) was formed on the orders of Churchill after the capture of Crete by the Germans who strangely, but fortunately, never used this tactic again. The museum's impressive displays contain many models used to plan the invasion of the Normandy countryside on D-Day, hundreds of examples of ingenious light-weight designs of equipment and even examples of the dummy parachutists used to create diversions.

There are numerous other museums to visit and sights to be seen at Aldershot. Full details on them and the Military Town Trail will be found at the Aldershot Military Museum and Visitors Centre, open daily on Queens Avenue. Further displays are being developed to cover the Second World War, when Aldershot was the H.Q. of the Canadian Army Overseas, and post-war events. There is also a small local museum which can be seen by visitors to Aldershot Library.

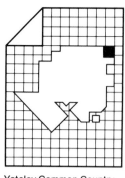

Yateley Common Country Park
(Hampshire County Council, County Recreation Department)

The Ranger's House,
Cricket Hill Lane,
Yateley,
Camberley,
Surrey.
Telephone
Yateley (0252) 874346

Price Guide - Free

Car Parking
Free

Handicapped
Suitable

Party Visits
Tours available

Publications etc.
Trail leaflet

Where to eat
Picnic tables on site

Time to allow
1 - 2 hours

Open
At all times

Fishing
Fishing by permit from Rangers, telephone number as above

Public Transport
Bus Services -
Hourly services from Aldershot and Reading. Half hourly from Camberley by Alder Valley Bus Services, in each case every two hours on Sundays.
Rail Services -
Sandhurst

Two Countryside Rangers look after the Common and are pleased to be able to offer help and advice to visitors

Nearby Attractions
West Green House near Hartley Wintney (National Trust)

Typical charming small 18th century English House with delightful walled gardens.

Open
April to end of Sept.
Garden - Wed, Thurs, and Sun. 2-6pm
House (three rooms) by written appt. only Wed 2-6pm
Contact Lord McAlpine of West Green, 40 Bernard Street, London WC1N 1LG

YATELEY COMMON COUNTRY PARK

"The wind was a torrent of darkness on the gusty trees
The moon was a ghostly galleon tossed upon cloudy seas
The road was a ribbon of moonlight across the purple moor
As the Highwayman came riding, riding, riding up to the old inn door."

An excerpt from *The Highwayman* by Alfred Noyes, a poet of the late nineteenth and early twentieth centuries, these beautiful lines embody the character of a heather-filled landscape where the dramatic effect of wind and moonlight create the atmosphere of a romantic wilderness which we look back on with nostalgia.

With the ever-increasing pressures of modern urban society, and its insatiable appetite for land, such heathland commons are becoming few and far between. Yateley Country Park is Hampshire's largest common, yet it is merely a small fragment of a heather moor which covered a vast triangle between Stratfield Saye, the Thames at Windsor and Farnham. While large commons survive in Surrey, only 500 acres are left here, mostly to the north of the old main road between the West Country and London. It was traditionally known as the Hartford Bridge Flats, after the river-crossing nearby at Hartley Wintney. The road was repaired by Highland Troops of the notorious 'Bloody Butcher', the Duke of Cumberland, after Culloden in 1746.

The area had its share of highwaymen as well as smugglers, for casks of spirits were hidden on the heath at Brandy Bottom. The flats were known for the breakneck driving of the coachmen, who found it the fastest stretch in the country; they were able to cover five miles in twenty-three minutes. In the 1830s there were as many as 60 coaches each day on the road, among them being Quicksilver, the Devonport Mail, the Regulator, and the Cornet.

The sufferings of the shaken passengers was watched with great amusement by the villagers, whilst working on the common. They cut furze and turf for fuel, and bracken for bedding and litter, and their cattle grazed the heather. The old parish records show how the common was occasionally whittled away, being taken over for cart-sheds and pigsties. Claims to new lands were even based on the siting of clothes posts and other convenient markers! In 1826 a large piece of land where the annual Black-water fair was held was lost by the parish, despite the employment of two common-keepers as well as the haywarden, who lived in an ancient isolated cottage in the middle of the heath, built as a refuge for the plague victims.

The common is only half its pre-war size due to the construction of a war-time light bomber aerodrome and a private airfield. The runways at Blackbushe Airfield, as it was called were on both sides of the main road and traffic had to be stopped as the bombers taxied for take-off. Civil use continued until 1960 and in the fifties

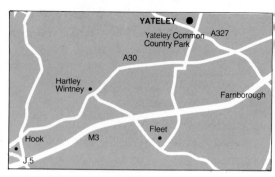

'HOW TO GET THERE'

From M3 (Junction 5) at Hook join A30 towards Camberley. Country Park on left beyond Hartley Wintney. Picnic areas signed off main road and further car-parks off Vigo Lane (turning to left into Yateley).

Top	Coach crossing Yateley Common in the 1820s.
Lower Right	R4D-8 'Super Dakota' US Navy. Typical of daily visitors to US Navy installation at Blackbushe during late 1950s.

N. Cullingford

purple which contrasts with the subtle shades of yellows, oranges and browns, as the birch and oak change colour.

Left to itself the heather would not survive since trees, especially the Scots pine and birch, readily take over if not arrested. Heather moors were the result of large-scale woodland clearance in prehistoric times; since then mineral salts and humus have been washed down through the porous sandy soil. As a result of a chemical reaction they accumulated as a hard layer or pan several feet below the porous surface. On this poor acidic soil, dried by the sun and blown by the wind, few plants can grow well unless able to endure drought. This is why one finds that the heathers with their tiny leaves, are able to survive as well as broom and gorse. The bracken vigorously colonises any open ground, especially after the heathland fires, but being poisonous to livestock it was traditionally kept in check by cutting.

The common has a nature trail, around Wyndham's Pool, and there are a variety of pools and bogs in the hollows and valleys. In the surrounding wet-heath habitats cotton grass can be found, as well as the insect-eating sundew, the pretty yellow-flowered bog asphodel and the cross-leaved heath, which likes the damp.

Endowed with tall woodlands, water, gorse and heath it is not surprising that Yateley is good territory for bird-watchers. The Dartford Warbler, our only resident warbler, which is seldom seen outside Hampshire and Dorset, breeds here, while another bird, the Hobby, can sometimes be seen perched in a tree watching for prey - a dragonfly or perhaps a swallow or swift. Woodlarks, like the Dartford Warbler, are also dependent on such heathlands.

For many people a picnic, perhaps by one of the ponds, will be enough to enjoy but the car parks of the Country Park are a good starting point for walkers equipped with the Ordnance Survey Map (Sheet 175) to explore further afield. There are footpaths across Hawley Common to the South of the A30 main road, passing a sadly-named spot called Starve Acre, as well as the attractive Hawley Lake. In another direction is a path across the airport which continues through the extensive woodlands which surround Bramshill. Although this important Jacobean house cannot be visited it can be seen from a distance at Hazeley Heath. There is a consoling thought for anyone who ventures through the seemingly endless coniferous plantations which have taken over the original heath: James I of Scotland is said to have planted the first fir in England here at Bramshill, which is small comfort for the conservers who are trying to weed them out from the open spaces of the Country Park!

it was described as the country's second largest airport. Historic aircraft can be seen gathered there nowadays.

The main attraction of today's common is its great beauty, despite the development along much of its northern edge. With its typical mixture of areas of open heather, gorse thickets, oak and birch woods, ponds and bogs, the landscape is invariably a pleasure to the eye. This is especially true during late summer and autumn when the heather is in full bloom, providing a carpet of

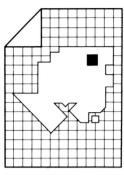

Basing House Ruins
(Hampshire County Council
County Recreation
Department)

Old Basing,
Basingstoke,
Hampshire RG24 0HB.
Telephone
Basingstoke (0256) 467294

Price Guide - B

Car Parking
Free

Handicapped
Suitable

Party Visits
By arrangement
Educational resources and
tours

Publications
Guidebook and variety of
publications
Displays
Trails and Guided walks
available
Tape recorded guides

Where to eat
Cafe opened on Sundays and
Bank Holidays
Suitable picnic area

Time to allow
1 - 2 hours

Open
2pm - 6pm
April, May and September
Weekends and Bank
Holidays only.
June, July and August
Daily (except Monday and
Thursday)
Out of Season - Parties by
appointment only.

Public Transport
Bus Services -
Hourly from Basingstoke,
Monday - Saturday.
Connections at Basingstoke
from Salisbury, Andover, Alton
and Aldershot
(B.S. Redbridge Lane)
Rail Services -
Basingstoke, 2 miles

Nearby Attractions
Willis Museum, Basingstoke
The Vyne
Stratfield Saye
Basingstoke Canal
Silchester
Pamber Forest

BASING HOUSE

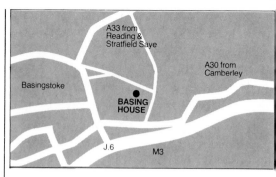

The ruins of Basing House are all that remain of the largest private house of Tudor England, a castle dating back to the Norman Conquest which was the scene of an epic siege in the Civil War. It was withstood by the Paulet family against the Parliamentary troops for two years.

Sadly their defeat became inevitable and the forces of Cromwell destroyed the palatial buildings which had commanded the local country-side. What can be seen now is the result of the archaeologists' digging: the foundations and cellars, the wells and the ovens. All this in the strangely lovely setting of powerful mediaeval earthwork fortifications. The Tudor garden walls still stand and even the dovecote towers.

A Victorian lodge on site has an exhibition telling the story of the 17th century fighting. One can hire a cassette tape-guide made by recording the lively conversation of experts on archaeology, the Civil War and the garden history, as they explored the ruins.

The whole episode of the siege of Basing House is an amazing testimony to the scale of the buildings. The first arrivals were horrified at having to attack it ..."as large and spacious as the Tower of London". Two years later, after lengthy bombardment the place was still described as "fit for an emperor's court". Its garrison was reduced however by religious differences and disease to 300 men who could hardly hope to protect defences which extended for a mile and a half!

Basing has a second fascinating side which helps to make it such a superb place to discover history, for what kind of man was it who could build up such an immense estate? The answer is that he was one of the most enigmatic characters of the 16th century: William Paulet, a statesman who served each Tudor crown and not only kept his head but made his fortune, used to raise two immense buildings side by side here, which made Basing larger than most of the royal palaces. Across the village is a Tithe Barn which is the oldest building from the time of William Paulet. Miraculously it was not destroyed in the artillery barrages or the hand-to-hand fighting when the original farm was burnt. Although smaller than the one at Titchfield, it is still immense with huge brick walls rising 43 feet to support a spectacular roof. The building has been called one of the finest, if not the best, of all late mediaeval barns in the country.

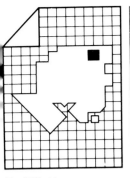

The Willis Museum
(Hampshire County Museum Service)

Old Town Hall,
Market Place,
Basingstoke RG21 1DP.
Telephone
(0256) 465902

Price Guide - Free

Car Parking
Surface and multi-storey car parking nearby

Handicapped
Not suitable, but plans for lift in hand

Party Visits
By arrangement preferred

Publications
Visitors Guide to Old Basingstoke

Where to eat
Pubs and eating places nearby

Time to allow
1 hour

Open
All year, Tuesday - Friday 10-5, Saturday 10-4

Public Transport
Walking distance of bus and railway stations. Frequent buses from all parts of Basingstoke. Hourly service from Andover and Newbury, Monday-Saturday, every two hours on Sunday from Andover only.

Nearby Attractions
Basing House
Basingstoke Canal
The Vyne
Silchester

Photo: Mike Englefield

THE WILLIS MUSEUM BASINGSTOKE

Even at the height of the Industrial Revolution few places can have matched the growth experienced by Basingstoke in recent years. In response to the 'London overspill' policies of central government the population of this once-small Hampshire town has rocketed from 17,000 in 1950 to more than 90,000 today. In the 1960s change was so rapid that important historical artefacts were often rescued from the advancing developer's bulldozer! Yet within the encircling carriageways that have led some to refer to the town as 'Doughnut City' there remains a working Market Place which was once the heart of the old town. Here, in the former Town Hall, are the galleries of the Willis Museum, named after George Willis (1877-1970), the watchmaker who founded it in 1931. The building itself dates from 1832 and is of interest in its own right: it was here, for example, that X-rays were first demonstrated in Basingstoke. It was one of the events witnessed by Willis during a long life that obliged him to see the town he loved developed out of all recognition.

The Willis Museum has recently moved from an earlier site and its exhibits have been completely redesigned and set out in modern display units. There is an extensive section on local prehistory with many artefacts, including a mammoth's tusk three feet long, discoverd on the banks of a stream near Odiham. An intriguing letter from O.G.S. Crawford, the first Archaeological Officer of the Ordnance Survey, to George Willis is also on display. He asks if Willis could help out by photographing hitherto unknown barrows that he has just spotted from the train!

At Domesday, the manor of Basingstoke was held by the King, while nearby Basing was the most important of the 55 Hampshire manors held by Hugh de Port. He probably built a castle close to the present ruins of Basing House, on a site called Oliver's Battery.

One interesting relic of Basingstoke's medieval history featured in the museum is the Chapel of the Holy Ghost, whose picturesque ruins can be seen beside the railway station. It owed its origins to a papal ban on the use of churches for marriages or funerals during the period 1208-13. As a result, burials were carried out to the north of the town, an area which was subsequently consecrated and furnished with a fine chapel whose painted roof and stained glass windows later became famous. It was associated with a Guild or Fraternity of the Holy Trinity, a sort of friendly society. Lord Sandys, the owner of The Vyne, built another chapel alongside the original structure in 1524.

Much later, in the 1880s, Basingstoke achieved notoriety for the Massaganian Riots, detailed in the museum, when the efforts of the Salvation Army to bring temperance to the town were violently opposed by a drunken rabble. The Massaganians at first followed members of the Salvation Army 'blowing trumpets, rattling potlids and singing obscene songs', but later started to attack them with clubs. Temperance sympathisers,

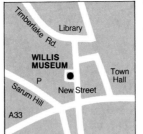

'HOW TO GET THERE'
Follow signs to Town Centre. The museum is in Old Market Place, at the intersection of Church Street, Wote Street, Winchester Street and London Street.

of which there were many, had their door handles torn off. The rioters were eventually prosecuted and sent to Winchester Gaol for a two-week sentence. But after their release they returned to a celebration dinner and were each given a silver watch, for the brewers of the town viewed them as heroes!

Victorian Basingstoke produced a number of industries which have become household names, including Milward's the shoemakers and Burberry, the coat which owes its origins to the observation of a local man that shepherds' clothes acquire a natural weatherproofing from the grease of the sheep. Basingstoke was an important manufacturing town during World War I, when the local firm of Thorneycroft produced more than 5,000 Model J lorries for military use. And in the 1930s the town's future was further assured when the pharmaceuticals company Eli Lilly set up a factory.

The Willis Museum in its new premises is now a major attraction with more than a purely local appeal. One of its prize exhibits is a fascinating post box which dates from the early nineteenth century and is probably the oldest in the country.

BS

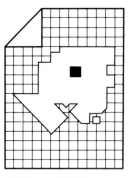

Whitchurch Silk Mill
(Hampshire Buildings Preservation Trust Ltd.)

Winchester Street,
Whitchurch,
Hampshire.
Telephone
- Mill (025682) 2065
- Trust (0962) 54411

Price - C

Car Parking
Free Nearby

Handicapped
Suitable only to view weaving room from outside

Party Visits
By arrangement only
Guided tours

Publications
Leaflet

Where to eat
Pubs locally

Time to allow
½ - 1 hour

Open
Easter - October:
Monday - Friday,
10am-4.30pm
(closed 12-1pm)
Saturday and Sunday and
Bank Holidays, times on
application
Shop open at any time of year
during working hours

Public Transport
Bus Services -
Hourly service from Andover
and Basingstoke, every two
hours on Sunday. Additional
services from Oxford,
Newbury, Southampton
and Winchester
Rail Services -
Station at Whitchurch, one
mile to north of mill

Nearby Attractions
Andover Museum
Hawk Conservancy, Weyhill

WHITCHURCH SILK MILL

When London QCs 'take silk' they don robes made from silk woven beside the River Test at Whitchurch. Elsewhere, many a university don wears Whitchurch silk on ceremonial occasions, while Army flags and Royal Standards are also quite likely to have originated in this small Hampshire town. In an age when the silk industry is dominated by foreign companies it is a miracle that this legacy of 19th century rural industry has survived and continues to function, albeit with only a handful of weavers. It has achieved this by specialising in high-quality, short-run materials and looks forward to a healthy future in the fashion world. The mill was recently acquired by the Hampshire Buildings Preservation Trust, who are preserving it as a working business.

The mill building with its distinctive pediment and elegant cupola has stood on its beautiful site on Frog Island since about 1800. The clock was added in 1815 to commemorate the Battle of Waterloo. In a wooden extension at the west end is a large undershot mill wheel which provided all power until the last war: the cast-iron machinery is still in place.

The mill was originally a brushmaking factory and then for a while was used for staymaking, a substantial local industry, and handweaving of wool. It only became a silk mill in about 1830 but within a few years employed more than a hundred people, including 39 children under the age of thirteen. Almost all the workers were women. Despite the removal of duties on imported silk in 1860, Whitchurch Silk Mill survived during a period when nationally the workforce in the industry, most of which was in Macclesfield and the Manchester area, fell by two-thirds. In about 1890 power-looms were installed and although none of these exist the oldest looms still used date from the turn of the century. Much of the silk woven at Whitchurch was 'raw' silk used for electrical insulation, though linings for Burberry raincoats, first manufactured in Basingstoke, were also woven, from 'spun' silk, which is made from cocoon 'waste'.

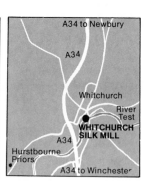

'HOW TO GET THERE'
Turn off the A34 Newbury - Winchester road into Whitchurch. The mill lies on the left-hand side of the approach from the south, just before crossroads in the centre of the town.

It is fascinating to see the old mill at work at Whitchurch, still using techniques that have changed little since the last century. It is a process that demands incredible patience and at the mill they reckon to tell within a month whether a new recruit has the necessary qualities. The skills involve the 'three w's' of winding, warping and weaving. As many as 500 bobbins, each containing 12 miles of thread, must first be wound before the warp (lengthways thread) of the material can be set up, rolled around the beam, a wooden cylinder a few inches in diameter. This is then transferred to a loom, where shuttles fed by pirns (thin bobbins) zip to and fro to insert the weft (crossways threads). The mill weaves ottomans for legal silks, taffetas for dresses and linings and fine striped materials, ideal for cravats, shirts and scarves. But it is a remarkably slow process: a standard 'cut off' of 55 metres usually takes a full seven or eight days to make. Perhaps the most demanding task comes at the end of a run, when the four or five thousand threads of the old warp have to be individually joined to the threads of the new warp. This is carried out by hand by one person at the rate of about a thousand twists an hour, a process which may leave the weaver with a permanent dent in one finger.

After seeing the workings of the mill, visitors may purchase some of its products at the Mill Shop, or look around the small town of Whitchurch, once an important staging post. A popular venue is The Silver Shop, where three generations of Potters, silversmiths, make cutlery and other pieces of silverware to traditional Georgian patterns. The premises are on Newbury Street, which runs from the crossroads in the centre of the town. All Hallows Church in Church Street is well known for its Saxon tombstone, which was found walled up during a 19th century restoration. One regular member of the congregation is Lord Denning, former Master of the Rolls, a lifelong inhabitant of Whitchurch who started his education at the local school. BS

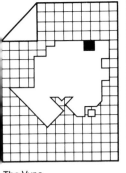

The Vyne
(The National Trust)

Sherborne St. John,
Basingstoke,
Hampshire,
RG26 5DX.
Telephone
Basingstoke (0256) 881337

Price Guide -
House and Garden - D
Garden - B

Car Parking
Free

Handicapped
Ground floor is accessible to
visitors in wheelchairs.
(2 nine inch steps to stone
gallery entrance)

Party Visits
By arrangement

Publication
Guidebook (French, Dutch
and German versions
available)

Where to eat
Cafe/tea-room on site

Time to allow
1 - 2 hours

Open
April - end October 2-6pm
(except Monday, Friday)
(Oct. 2 -5.30pm)
Open Bank Holidays
11am-6pm (Closed Tuesday
following)

Public Transport
Bus Services -
Hourly from Basingstoke to
Sherborne St. John Monday -
Saturday (1¾ mile walk)
Rail Services -
Bramley Station 2½ miles
away

Nearby Attractions
Basing House
Willis Museum and Art Gallery
Stratfield Saye
Pamber Forest

Top:	Staircase added in the 18th century
Centre:	The Chapel
Lower:	The Tapestry room with its oriental scenes

| *Top and Centre:* | *Jeremy Whitaker* |
| *Lower:* | *Basingstoke Gazette* |

THE VYNE

The National Trust house of The Vyne was
built in the decades after 1500, and is an
elegant Tudor mansion lovingly adapted by different owners until today one can enjoy a virtual
treasure-house of the different styles and tastes of
each passing century. It has been discussed as
"one of the most rewarding houses in Hampshire,
both visually and historically". As one would
expect at a National Trust house there are also
delightful grounds, for The Vyne slopes down to
the placid waters of a tributary of the River
Loddon artificially broadened into a fine lake to
enhance the surrounding parkland.

The house was built for one of Henry VIII's
courtiers, William Sandys, who became Lord
Chamberlain and also gained possession of
Mottisfont Abbey. Shakespeare portrayed him in
Henry VIII as 'Lord Sands'. One gets a good
impression of his house in the upstairs long
gallery, sparsely furnished and decorated with
carved heraldic arms on the fine linenfold panelling. The great hall was turned to a new use in the
18th century to house a superb classical staircase.

The best known feature of The Vyne is perhaps
the great classical portico built on the lakeside front in the 1650s, one of the first of its kind
added to any English country house. Indoors are
many small rooms for dining and withdrawing,
furnished largely with the exquisite work of 18th
century craftsmen and artists. In 1754 the house
was inherited by John Chute who became part of
the circle with Horace Walpole, the celebrated
letter-writer and great enthusiast for decoration
and design in the gothic style. Despite Walpole's
pressure the exquisite house-chapel was
fortunately left unspoilt. The group had a frivolous
fad for catholic 'enjoyment' with incense and Mass
books. The beautiful chapel merely had a large
canvas of trompe l'oeil fan tracery added above the
stalls which was later moved to the chapel gallery,
and in the next room a grand tomb (containing no
body) was built as a memorial to Chute's great-
grandfather, dead a hundred years earlier! He had
been a barrister and Speaker of the House of
Commons during Richard's Cromwell's short
protectorate, and is sculpted in the robes of his
appointment on the traditional straw mat. In the
chapel there is more fine wood panelling, delight-
fully carved figures on the stalls and 16th century
stained glass windows, said to have no match in
England, with portraits of Henry VIII, his sister
Margaret, and his first wife Catherine.

Upstairs the long oak gallery is arrived at by
way of a library of 19th century books and
through another room decorated with tapestries
woven in London in the 1720s showing imaginary
scenes of the Orient.

The Chute family continued to live at The Vyne
until the 1950s when the house was gener-
ously bequeathed to the Trust: much restoration
work had to be carried out. Part of the house is
still occupied, divided off into flats. A National
Trust shop has been opened for the sale of their
great range of excellent gifts which are so useful
to buy as souvenirs of a memorable visit or in
preparation for Christmas.

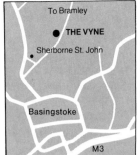

'HOW TO GET THERE'
From M3 (Junction 6) follow
Basingstoke ring-road to 4th
roundabout. House well sign-
posted. Turn onto A340,
Tadley - Aldermaston road.
Turn right following signs into
Sherborne St. John and out of
village on road to Bramley.
House mile and a half on left.

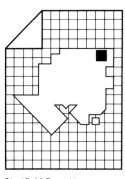

Stratfield Saye House
(Duke of Wellington)

The Wellington Office,
Stratfield Saye,
Reading,
Hampshire,
RG7 2BT
Telephone
Basingstoke (0256) 882882

Price Guide - F

Car Parking
Free

Handicapped
Suitable

Party Visits
Tours and Educational
resources

Publications etc
Leaflet and guidebook
Displays
Trails on site

Where to eat
Tea-room and licensed
restaurant/bar
Suitable picnic area on the
side of the car park

Time to allow
2 - 4 hours

Open
11.30am-5.00pm
Easter Saturday, Sunday and
Monday, weekends during
April and daily (except Friday)
1st May - 28th September

Wellington Country Park

(Duke of Wellington)
Riseley,
Near Reading,
Hampshire,
RG7 1SP
Telephone
Heckfield (073583) 444

Price Guide - D

Car Parking
Free

Handicapped
Suitable

Party Visits
Available
Educational resources

Publications etc.
Leaflet and guidebook
Displays
Trails on site

Where to eat
Cafe/tea-room on site
Picnic tables on site

Time to allow
2 hours - all day

Open
Main Season - Every day
November - February
Weekends only (other times
open for parties by
arrangement)

Public Transport
Bus Services -
Alder Valley services every
three hours from Aldershot
and Reading on Sundays.
Weekday buses hourly to
Wellington Monument on A33

STRATFIELD SAYE
& WELLINGTON COUNTRY PARK

It may come as a surprise that the Duke of Wellington's home, a grateful nation's reward to its greatest hero, should only be the size it is, for even though one of Hampshire's largest houses it is truly domestic in comparison with Blenheim, or indeed many Victorian country houses.

Stratfield Saye reflects the personality of the Iron Duke who, disliking grandeur and unnecessary expense, rejected plans to pull down the 200 year old house and erect a more suitably spendid domed palace elsewhere in the park. Instead, Wellington concentrated on making his home more comfortable, almost pioneering oil lamps, steam baths and radiators, and applying his own fad, still unusual at that time, for water closets and drainage. The Duke travelled greatly but kept more than 40 servants at Stratfield Saye. Today, the 8th Duke has carefully brought the house up to date as a family home, while preserving the unique atmosphere created by his great-great-grandfather.

The newest attraction at Stratfield Saye is an exhibition around the amazing funeral carriage of the Duke, built from the bronze cannons captured at Waterloo and recently brought from the crypt of St Paul's, the resting place of both Nelson and Wellington. It is 18 tons in weight and 17ft high and, pulled by 12 horses, was used in the most impressive funeral of the modern age, in 1852.

Another exhibition area illustrates the life of the great Duke from the time he left his family home in Ireland for the years of military service in India, and covers the campaigns to clear the Peninsula of the French invaders, the battle of Waterloo and his political career. An interesting part of the display is the collection of clothing, remarkably preserved after nearly 150 years, part of a large cache discovered in trunks at Apsley House. On show are indoor, outdoor and ceremonial clothes; even the Duke's underclothes are perfectly preserved.

The tour through the house is restricted to the ground floor. The front door leads directly into the stately hall richly draped in French Tricolor while the stone floor incorporates Roman mosaic pavements discovered in the excavation of nearby Silchester. Next follows the library which includes books that belonged to Napoleon. In this room, with its richly gilded ceiling, the Duke was painted at play with his grandchildren. The picture, on ivory, hangs in the small drawing room. Beyond is the music room with paintings of Copenhagen, the favourite charger who carried the Duke at Waterloo and whose gravestone can be seen in the grounds.

There are many other rooms: the grand drawing and dining rooms, the print-lined gallery and the Duke's billiard room with its beautifully painted table. Among the treasures on display are superb pieces of Sèvres and Meissen porcelain, fine French Boulle furniture, portraits by Lawrence and Hoppner and many personal items used by the Duke of Wellington during his campaigns.

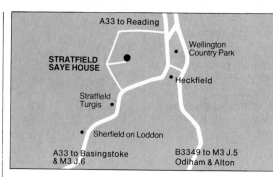

'HOW TO GET THERE'

From M3 (Junction 6) follow signs for A33 to Reading. Past Sherfield-on-Loddon turn left at Wellington Arms. House well sign-posted.

For Country Park follow directions as for Stratfield Saye House but continue north on A33 (or A32 from Hook).

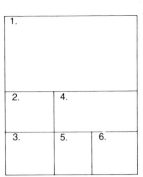

1. Stratfield Saye House
2. The Duke of Wellington, part of the Exhibition
3. The grave of the horse Copenhagen
4. The lake in the Country Park
5,6. The National Dairy Museum display in the Park Centre

1: *The Basingstoke Gazette*
2-6: *Wellington Enterprises*

WELLINGTON COUNTRY PARK

Up on the Hampshire/Berkshire border between Basingstoke and Reading, and straddling the Reading to Alton (B3349) road, is The Wellington Country Park landscaped around the banks of a modern man-made lake. Since it was opened in 1974 the woodlands and meadows have gained a reputation as an excellent centre for activities and family visits and, unique among Hampshire country parks, has space set aside for visitors' caravans and tents.

The lake, formed after gravel pits had been dug, has been well stocked with coarse fish, and has such a winding outline that there is room for anglers as well as sunbathers and others who want to watch wildfowl. You can hire a rowing boat or a canoe, windsail or launch your own boat. In the woods there are Roe Deer and Fallow Deer, and a selection of nature trail paths.

For children there is a small farm with domestic animals, crazy golf, an adventure playground, and most recently introduced, a miniature steam railway. An exciting new feature is the Thames Valley Time Trail, which traces the evolution of life over 4,500 million years and includes life-size models of dinosaurs and Neanderthal man.

There is no lack of opportunity for anyone wishing to keep fit. The walk around the lake is a full mile in length and jogging enthusiasts are unlikely to find a more pleasant setting than this, either in the north of Hampshire. Anyone who enjoys a challenge may like to try the fitness 'assault' course which has been designed for all ages. There are also facilities for riding in another part of the park, amongst the trees and heath west of the Alton Road, though it is advisable to make a telephone booking. The riding school can be reached from the Basingstoke to Reading Road (A33).

During the winter months not every facility is always available so it may be worth 'phoning the Country Park Centre for information. There are each summer special events in the Waterloo Meadow, a tree-studded showground created from an overgrown heathland wilderness.

Another attraction is the inclusion in the Park Centre of the small but colourful National Dairy Museum. The real novelty to enjoy here are the occasional demonstrations of butter sculpture.

By the waterside is an attractive refreshment pavilion, and there is also an area reserved for barbecue parties. Overall, a visit to Wellington Country Park makes a superb day out for all the family.

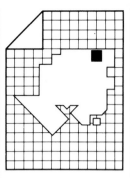

Calleva Museum
(Trustees of the Calleva Museum)

The Secretary,
Sawyers Lands,
Silchester,
Reading,
Berkshire,
RG7 2NG
Telephone
Silchester (0734) 700362

Price Guide - Free
Contribution appreciated

Car Parking
Free, nearby

Handicapped
Museum not suitable

Party Visits
Tours by arrangement

Publication
Guidebook and leaflet

Where to eat
Suitable picnic area nearby
at Silchester Common or the
pond by Silchester Church

Time to allow
1 - 2 hours

Open
Museum and Site: all year
round during the hours of
daylight

Public Transport
Bus Services -
Hourly from Reading bus
station

Nearby Attractions
Stratfield Saye House
Wellington Country Park
The Vyne
Blackwater Valley
Pamber Forest

Reading Museum
Monday - Friday,
10am-5.30pm
Saturday, 10am-500pm
Closed Sundays

Top,1　　Some of the
　　　　Victorian
　　　　excavators at
　　　　Roman Silchester

Below, 2　Bird's eye view
　　　　impression of
　　　　Roman Silchester
　　　　by Alan Sorrel

1:　　　Reading Museum
*2:　　　Department of
　　　　Environment,
　　　　Crown Copyright*

SILCHESTER

C lose to the border with Berkshire are the visible remains of the tribal capital of the Atrebates, the tribe who fled their homeland to escape from the Romans after Caesar's conquest of Northern France. After the invasion of Britain, Calleva Atrebatum gradually developed into a fully romanized town. The octagonally-shaped settlement was later given a substantial wall of flint and bonding stone, nearly 10 feet thick and 20 to 25 feet high. Strong gates defended the roads to Winchester, London, Dorchester-on-Thames and westwards towards Bath. No other Roman town in Britain survives with such extensive walls, nor has any been completely excavated as this was over many years from 1864 to 1909. Modern excavations continue during the summer.

A mong the many discoveries within the 107 acres enclosed was a great forum and basilica in the centre of the town. The forum was a large square surrounded by shops, offices and the town hall. The shops provided a rich variety of goods for sale to the town's inhabitants, many of whom farmed the land outside the walls. There were also public baths (similar to Turkish baths) and at

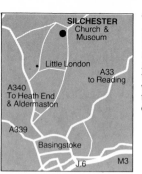

'HOW TO GET THERE'
From M3 (Junction 6) at Basingstoke follow ring-road round to A340 to Tadley and Aldermaston. At Pamber End turn right to Little London, where fork left, following signs to Silchester. Museum on right of Green, signed near school.

least half-a-dozen temples. An outstanding find was the small Roman Christian church, one of the earliest signs of the acceptance of Christianity in this country.

A very complete picture of life in the town can be built up, though sadly today the streets and walls, foundations and gardens are covered with soil and farmed. However, as a scheduled Ancient Monument, its preservation is assured for future generations.

A t Silchester village there is an excellent interpretive site museum, where copies of an informative guide book are available. From here an ancient track crosses the fields to join a footpath through the middle of the site, emerging at the isolated church of St. Mary's, Silchester. From Wall Lane the amphitheatre outside the town can be seen and the road continues, closely following a long stretch of the northern wall.

W hen planning a journey to explore Silchester it is worthwhile to consider also visiting Reading Museum. Two of the decorated pavements discovered by the Victorian archaeologists can be seen at Stratfield Saye, the home of the Duke of Wellington, but most of the discoveries are housed in the museum.

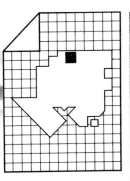

SANDHAM MEMORIAL CHAPEL

Hampshire's largest work of modern art may well be Britain's most unique war memorial and is certainly Hampshire's strangest church. Stanley Spencer's experiences in a World War One military hospital, where he served as an orderly, and his life with the Army Medical Corps in the mountains of Macedonia (now Southern

Sandham Memorial Chapel
(The National Trust)

Burghclere,
Near Newbury,
Berkshire.
Telephone
Burghclere (063527) 394
or 292

Price Guide - B

Car Parking
Limited space on road verge

Handicapped
Suitable (2 small sets of steps)

Publications
Leaflet available

Time to allow
Half an hour

Open
All year (except Good Friday,
Christmas Day and New
Year's Day)
10.30am - 1pm & 2 - 6pm

Public Transport
Bus Services -
Alder Valley buses from
Newbury, three journeys per
day, Monday - Saturday
Rail Service -
Newbury Station 4 miles away

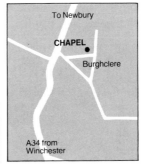

'HOW TO GET THERE'
From Winchester, follow A34 Newbury Road. Beyond Beacon Hill watch for turning on right into Burghclere (n.b. not Old Burghclere). Chapel on left. From Basingstoke or north Hampshire, follow A339 to Kingsclere Village. Watch for signs to Sydmonton, and beyond it turn right to Burghclere.

Jugoslavia), were the inspiration for these murals which cover the three principal walls of the Sandham Memorial Chapel.

The chapel was built for the Behrends family of Burghclere who had met Spencer in 1922 and been impressed by his ideas for a set of murals. The chapel had to be designed to house the artist's scheme, while on either side were built a pair of almshouses. It was later dedicated to the memory of Henry Sandham, Mrs. Behrends' brother, who died of illness contracted in the Macedonian fighting. The chapel was given to the National Trust in 1947.

The design and paintings took ten years to complete. From 1927 to 1932 Stanley Spencer lived in the village and worked in the chapel, painting on large canvases which were fixed to the walls.

In none of the pictures is there the least portrayal of violence: we see the sorting of piles of linen, the filling of tea-urns, the preparation of kit for inspection, all the daily humdrum life of the hospital. Even at the battle front there are scenes showing lessons in map-reading, or camp litter being collected. The biggest and most impressive painting is on the central wall: the resurrection of soldiers, who help each other out of their graves and gather around Jesus while the mules wander, freed of their loads. A lady visiting the chapel was overheard saying to her daughter, "My dear, the Resurrection is not in the least like that"!

Nowadays, services are seldom held here but the key to the door can be obtained from a neighbouring caretaker. This key was used by Spencer when he needed to paint a bunch of keys, which the sharp-eyed visitors may like to discover.

Illus.:   Soldiers drinking
from a fountain

The National Trust

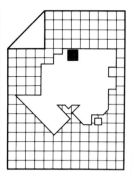

Beacon Hill
(Lord Porchester)

Managed by Hampshire County Recreation Department
On A34 Winchester - Newbury Road
Burghclere
Telephone (Office)
Winchester (0962) 64221

Price Guide - Free

Car Parking
Free at foot of hill

Handicapped
Unsuitable, very steep slope

Where to eat
Picnic tables on site

Time to allow
1 - 2 hours

Open
At all times

Nearby Attractions
Watership Down, Whitehill, Kingsclere
Sandham Memorial Chapel
Kennet and Avon Canal
Newbury Museum

The Temple, Highclere Park
(Highclere Estate)

A splendid folly on a remote knoll overlooking a lake created by Capability Brown. The focal point of the park thought to be one of the finest in the country.
Grounds surrounding the Temple only.

Open
April to September

Car Parking
By London Lodge on A34

Photo: Beacon Hill, seen from 'Seven Barrows' where the Wayfarer's Walk crosses the Newbury - Winchester road

Beacon Hill
Burghclere

For anyone keen to escape to the high downs or to enjoy the strange communion between earth and sky which the hilltop crests bring, there is fine walking country in the north of Hampshire. These steep slopes gained a sudden international fame as the countryside setting of Richard Adams's saga about rabbits, *Watership Down*. Watership (the strange name probably comes from a dew-pond for the sheep flocks) is real and is crossed by the ridgeway path to Ladle Hill from White Hill above Kingsclere. There is a prehistoric fort at the top of Ladle Hill; across the vale stands Beacon Hill in curious isolation.

Beacon Hill dominates not only the modern A34 road from Newbury to Winchester, but also many of north Hampshire's views. It is no less a landmark now than in the days when travellers across the open downland pastures simply rode towards it as if to a signpost for Newbury.

The climb to its summit is hard but rewarding. From here the traditional beacons sent warnings as far afield as the Midlands. From the slopes some of the earliest British airplane flights were made by Geoffrey de Haviland in 1909. On the hilltop is another Iron Age fort, probably the most strategically placed of all Hampshire's many camps. Another connection with archaeology is the simple grave (not open to the public) of the discoverer of Tutankhamen, the fifth Earl of Carnarvon, who died in Cairo in 1923 to the reputed accompaniment of strange phenomena, the city lights going out and a pet dog dying here in England. Highclere Castle below to the north is still the family home of his descendants and is one of the truly great Victorian mansions. It was restyled by Barry, who designed the Houses of Parliament.

A ridgeway path skirts south of Beacon Hill and continues for several miles further on into Berkshire to Pilot Hill. Just beyond, Walbury Hill (974 feet) provides a marvellous background for the lonely, unspoilt and perfectly-named hamlet of Combe, set in a dramatic chalk bowl. The villagers played their part in a curious story of two lovers and a murder, so long ago that the tale must begin "once upon a time". The two lovers were taken up to the narrow ridge and hanged on a gibbet high above the adjoining parishes. The macabre spectacle of the gibbet post, renewed from time to time, is kept as proof of the story. More prosaically, the gibbet commemorates the hanging in 1676 of a man and a woman for the murder of two of her children.

'HOW TO GET THERE'
To Beacon Hill from Winchester, take Andover road B3420 to join A34 Newbury road. Picnic area and car parking sign-posted off main road.

146

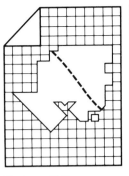

Wayfarers Walk

The route begins at Emsworth, follows the coast round to Bedhampton and after crossing Portsdown Hill, passes through Denmead, and Droxford, then across the downs via Exton to Alresford. Beyond Dummer it climbs the North Hampshire downs near White Hill, turning west to end at Inkpen. There are car parks at many places along the route, including Langstone, Portsdown, Denmead, Droxford and Alresford, Abbotstone Down and White Hill.

The maps needed for the walk are the Ordnance Survey 1:50000 sheets 174, 185, 196, 197.

A guide to the walk is available from the County Recreation Department, North Hill Close, Andover Road, Winchester, Hants. SO22 6AQ, telephone Winchester (0962) 64221. This includes information on accommodation and public transport.

THE WAYFARER'S WALK

Hampshire's first long-distance walk has been created by linking footpaths and bridleways across the heart of the county from one corner in the south-east to its north-westernmost point. Along the 70 miles in between these two points the Way follows the coast, leads along ancient trackways, crosses valleys and rises to high chalk

Follow the Country Code

Keep your dogs under close control.

Photo: Walkers on The Wayfarers Walk *(Hampshire County Recreation Department)*

downland. It is clearly signposted from its start at Emsworth to its end several miles inside Berkshire at Inkpen Beacon, some 1,000 feet up, with commanding views across into the Midland Counties.

From the mud-flats and ancient coastal ports to the highest hill-top of Southern England the Wayfarer's Walk opens a new door to the Heart of Hampshire, a landscape with much to delight both the spirit and the eye of anyone who wishes to explore and enjoy it.

A helpful guide has been published by the County Recreation Department which will help keen walkers to cover the whole journey at an easy pace in seven days. The new guide contains an extensive list of all accommodation which can be used by individual walkers. It is also quite possible to explore the walk in parts since there are car parks in many places, and public transport wherever it can often be used to reach the path. Much of its course though is fairly isolated, only occasionally passing small villages or lonely farms. Much of the charm of the route is the opportunity to come upon these settlements, perhaps after walking along a mediaeval track, along a stream-side path, or even through a deep beech hanger; a refreshing change from the usual quick flash seen from a car window as one drives by on the road.

The Wayfarer's Walk is an invitation to slow down and explore ancient villages such as Droxford and Cheriton, Preston Candover and Hinton Ampner as well as small towns like Emsworth and Alresford; to discover their churches and pubs and see something of their life. After walking on the heights and enjoying splendid views it is delightful to descend into the valleys for rest and refreshment. The easiest way to use the route is with two families sharing transport, leaving a car at a suitable stopping place to be collected later.

The whole route is a cross-section of Hampshire farming, so one must expect large cultivated fields and not many sheep. There are few woods and not many of the chalk herbs - thyme and kidney vetch and salad burnet - on which butterflies feed. In such a densely populated country we need intensive farming and the new agricultural landscape certainly has its own impressive character, which can be appreciated better perhaps because scattered islands of downland have been preserved as country parks and nature reserves as well as open spaces, while the villages are safeguarded by careful planning.

LIVE ENTERTAINMENT

Hampshire and its hinterland is one of the richest areas outside London for live entertainment - theatre, dance, variety, classical and pop music - all these are on offer somewhere throughout the season, while opera and ballet make regular appearances on tour. Several of the theatres in the region have distinguished repertory companies which present a varied programme of West End successes, classics and new plays.

Most major shows are presented at venues along the M27/A31 'South Coast corridor', from the nationally famous Chichester Festival Theatre to the Bournemouth International Centre.

The Mayflower Theatre in Southampton, formerly the Gaumont, is the foremost centre in the South of England attracting international pop and variety stars and staging spring and autumn seasons of full-scale opera and ballet.

The main centres for live entertainment in Portsmouth have for many years been the King's Theatre and the Guildhall, while in Southampton visitors also seek the Nuffield Theatre or the Turner Sims Concert Hall, both on the university campus, or the Guildhall in the Civic Centre.

In the centre of the County the newly-furbished Theatre Royal, Winchester, offers varied programmes and operates a ticket agency for local, regional and London productions. Further north, Basingstoke is fast becoming a major centre for theatregoers and at Farnham the well-known Redgrave Theatre has a long record of memorable productions.

Chamber concerts, organ recitals and lunch-time concerts are performed regularly during university terms in the Turner Sims Concert Hall, which lies on the university campus on the northern outskirts of Southampton. Alongside is the Nuffield Theatre, a major centre which has gone from strength to strength in recent years, following a policy of presenting new plays and interesting revivals. Several productions originated by the resident rep have later gone to the West End, notably 'Daisy Pulls it Off' and 'A Month of Sundays' starring George Cole. An adventurous programme at the Nuffield is further spiced by occasional touring shows and amateur productions.

Southampton Guildhall presents a varied programme of concerts, recitals, and pop shows. Nearby, the Mayflower Theatre is the region's leading venue for opera, ballet, variety and pop concerts. The Theatre will reopen in 1987 after an extensive programme of refurbishment which will restore it to its original glory, complete with gold leaf and ornate balustrades. Behind the Mayflower Theatre is the Gantry, Southampton's recently opened arts centre, which presents an exciting programme of alternative theatre, workshops, and community arts.

A few miles along the coast the King's Theatre, Portsmouth, presents a popular programme of touring London shows and amateur productions -

theatre, ballet, opera and variety. For major concerts, choral events, variety or one-night stands by pop groups, visitors should seek the programme of the Guildhall, Portsmouth, which i in the centre of the city. This is also the home

of the renowned Music in Portsmouth Series, which as well as presenting concerts by the leading British orchestras, in particular the region's own orchestras, the Bournemouth Orchestra and Sinfonietta, promotes concerts by many of the world's leading orchestras. Just along the road from the Guildhall is the Theatre Royal, probably Hampshire's finest Victorian theatre, which is currently being restored. The Dress Circle Bar, already reopened, provides an ideal setting for a lunchtime snack or pre-concert supper. Elsewhere in the city, the Hornpipe Arts Centre provides a regular programme of touring theatre, contemporary dance and other arts activities.

The Chichester Festival Theatre usually presents a summer season of four plays, but this will be extended to five in 1986 to celebrate its Silver Jubilee. At other times of the year the theatre's superb custom-built auditorium is used for concerts, ballet, opera and touring drama, while each October it plays host to the Chichester Jazz International.

Just outside Hampshire, to the west, Bournemouth and Poole have a number of venues where a wide variety of entertainment is presented, particularly during the summer months. Most significant of these are the Bournemouth International Centre and the Poole Arts Centre.

Salisbury and Winchester, so similar in many ways, present interesting contrasts in their theatres. The Salisbury Playhouse is a long-established theatre with a modern purpose-built auditorium and its own rep. Productions of the classics are popular and in recent years memorable productions of 'Far From the Madding Crowd' and 'A Tale of Two Cities' have been performed. Winchester has recently experienced a resurgence of interest in the performing arts and much local effort has gone into saving the Theatre Royal, built in the early 1900s as a cine-variety theatre. A recent refurbishment and development programme has brought the city an ideal venue for a regular programme of 'theatre for all', including dance, drama, jazz, folk, classical concerts and children's shows.

In the north of the County Basingstoke's Haymarket Theatre has created a strong following for a varied programme of mainly popular plays performed by its resident company. In a theatre located in one of the town's old markets, the Horseshoe Theatre Company have had great success with many productions, including Keith Dewhurst's two plays 'Lark Rise' and 'Candleford', based on Flora Thompson's famous trilogy.

For visitors to the north and east of Hampshire, Farnham's Redgrave Theatre is readily accessible. Productions cover a wide range of entertainment, including, classics, musicals, farce, modern drama and children's plays.

Drama and art centres in Aldershot, Basingstoke, Bordon, Havant, New Milton and Romsey all provide an extremely varied programme of live entertainment. From contemporary dance to alternative theatre, folk and jazz concerts, film video, and a wealth of opportunities for the resident and visitor alike to participate in the arts.

Details of current programmes should be obtained from the theatres themselves.

Tickets for both local and London theatres can be purchased from the box office of the Theatre Royal, Winchester, and other agencies, including some Tourist Information Centres.

Many theatres offer facilities for dining before the show, and most accept credit cards.

Entertainment centres in Hampshire and surrounding counties.

Full listings *arranged alphabetically by place*

ALDERSHOT

WEST END CENTRE, Queens Road, Aldershot, Hampshire GU11 3JD
Telephone: (0252) 330040   Seats: 100/180
Facilities: Bar, coffee shop, restaurant, wheelchairs
Parking: Public car park opposite
Transport: 5 minutes walk from BR station
Type of programme: Theatre, poetry, dance, weekly concerts, film

ANDOVER

CRICKLADE THEATRE, Charlton Road, Andover, Hampshire SP10 1EJ
Telephone: (0264) 65698   Seats: 270
Facilities: Bar for professional shows, coffee shop, restaurant - Tuesday, Thursday and Friday - wheelchairs by prior arrangement
Parking: At theatre
Transport: 10 minutes walk from BR station, 5 minutes walk from bus station
Type of programme: Professional and student theatre shows

BASINGSTOKE

HAYMARKET THEATRE, Wote Street, Basingstoke, Hampshire, RG21 1NW
Telephone: (0256) 465566   Seats: 438
Facilities: Bar, coffee shop, restaurant, wheelchairs - two spaces by arrangement, hard of hearing loop
Parking: Public car park in New Road and multi-storey nearby (free after 6pm)
Transport: 10 minutes walk from both BR and bus stations
Type of programme: Repertory (September - May), touring professional dance, children's theatre, amateur plays and musicals

CENTRAL STUDIO, Queen Mary's College, Cliddesden Road, Basingstoke RG21 3HF
Telephone: On the night, (0256) 20861; Other bookings, (0256) 465566   Seats: 130
Facilities: Coffee shop, wheelchairs by arrangement
Parking: Free at Queen Mary's College
Transport: Not readily accessible by public transport. 30 minutes walk from BR and bus stations
Type of programme: Modern theatre, mime, music, film and art exhibitions

BOURNEMOUTH & POOLE

BOURNEMOUTH INTERNATIONAL CENTRE, Exeter Road, Bournemouth BH2 5BH
Telephone: (0202) 297297
Facilities: Bar, coffee shop, restaurant, wheelchairs, hard of hearing loop
Parking: Own car park
Transport: Frequent bus services
WINDSOR HALL   Seats 3,900
Type of programme: Light entertainment popular music
TREGONWELL HALL   Seats: From 500
Type of programme: Summer season revue

PAVILION THEATRE, Westover Road, Bournemouth BH1 2BX   Seats 1,500
Parking: At theatre
Transport: Frequent bus services
Type of programme: Classical concerts, plays, ballet, pantomime

PIER THEATRE, Pier Approach, Bournemouth BH2 5BH
Seats: 850
Facilities: Bar and cafeteria (in season), wheelchairs by arrangement
Parking: Public car parks near theatre
Transport: Buses from BR station
Type of programme: Summer shows and popular plays
Season: May - September

WINTER GARDENS, Exeter Road, Bournemouth, BH1 2BX
Seats: 1,600
Type of programme: One-night shows, concerts
POOLE ARTS CENTRE, Kingland Road, Poole Dorset BH15 1UG
Telephone: (0202) 685222, Credit Card Bookings (0202) 674234
Facilities: Bar, coffee shop, wheelchairs by arrangement, hard of hearing loop, many local restaurants
Parking: Multi-storey car park opposite
Transport: Bus station opposite, 5 minutes walk from BR station
TOWNGATE THEATRE   Seats: 600
Type of programme: Touring repertory theatre, opera, ballet
WESSEX HALL   Seats: 1,463
Type of programme: Concerts of classical and popular music

CHICHESTER

CHICHESTER FESTIVAL THEATRE, Oaklands Park, Chichester, West Sussex PO19 4AP
Telephone: (0243) 781312   Seats: 1,374
Facilities: Bar, coffee shop, restaurant, wheelchairs by arrangement, hard of hearing loop
Parking: Adjacent to theatre. Space limited for matinees
Transport: Short distance from both BR and bus stations. Bus from BR station
Type of programme: Festival Season, May - September Classical and jazz concerts in Spring and Autumn. Winter ballet, opera and pantomime. Touring theatre.

FAREHAM

FAREHAM AND GOSPORT DRAMA CENTRE, Osborn Road, Fareham, Hampshire PO16 7DX
Telephone: (0329) 235161   Seats: 120
Facilities: Bar, coffee shop, snacks (performance times only), local restaurants nearby, wheelchairs
Parking: At Drama Centre and also public parking nearby (free after 6pm)
Transport: 15 minutes walk from BR station, 10 minutes walk from bus station
Type of programme: Theatre, dance, mime, classical music concerts, folk and popular music, theatre and dance workshops
FERNEHAM HALL, Osborn Road, Fareham, Hampshire PO16 7DB
Telephone: (0329) 231942   Seats 1001
Facilities: Bar, restaurant, wheelchairs by arrangement
Parking: Large car park and multi-storey adjacent (free after 6pm)
Transport: 15 minutes walk from BR station, 10 minutes walk from bus station
Type of programme: Theatre, dance, opera. Military bands, cinema, wrestling, dancing, to TV stars, variety artistes, popular light entertainment Amateur and professional shows

FARNHAM

REDGRAVE THEATRE, Brightwells, Farnham, Surrey GU9 7SB
Telephone: (0252) 715303   Seats 362
Facilities: Bars, coffee shop, restaurant, wheelchair by arrangement, hard of hearing loop
Parking: Car parking nearby in South Street and Dogflud car parks
Transport: BR station nearby. Alder Valley buses
Type of programme: Repertory theatre, Sunday jazz concerts, studio theatre, foyer exhibitions. Theatre talks and tours by arrangement.

HAVANT

HAVANT ARTS CENTRE, East Street, Havant, Hampshire PO9 1BS
Telephone: (0705) 472700   Seats: 130
Facilities: Bar, wheelchairs by arrangement
Parking: Free at Old Town Hall adjacent
Transport: 10 minutes walk from BR and bus stations

Type of programme: Wide range of plays, dance, mime and music. Touring professional and amateur. Children's theatre

PORTSMOUTH

THE GUILDHALL, Guildhall Square, Portsmouth PO1 2AD
Telephone: (0705) 824355. Credit Cards (0705) 756566
Seats: 2,017
Facilities: Bar, coffee at performances, wheelchairs by arrangement
Parking: Ample parking nearby
Transport: Close to BR station with frequent bus services
Type of programme: Concerts, one-night shows

THE HORNPIPE, 143 Kingston Road, Portsmouth PO2 7EB
Telephone: (0705) 817293   Seats: 300 maximum
Facilities: Bar, coffee shop, wheelchairs by arrangement, many local Indian restaurants
Parking: Street parking nearby
Transport: Buses from BR station (nos. 740 - 749 inclusive, and 347)
Type of programme: Theatre, dance, folk music, rock bands, entertainers, film (Rendezvous Cinema),
(0705) 833854

KINGS THEATRE, Albert Road, Southsea, Portsmouth PO5 2QJ
Telephone: (0705) 828282/811411   Seats: 1,780
Facilities: Bar, coffee, wheelchairs by arrangement
Special accommodation rates at Crest Hotel and Holiday Inn
Parking: Street parking
Transport: Frequent bus services from the City Centre (nos. 17 and 18)
Type of programme: Theatre, ballet, opera, one-night variety shows. Also amateur shows

NEW THEATRE ROYAL, Guildhall Walk, Portsmouth, PO1 2DD
Telephone: (0705) 823729
Facilities: Morning coffee, light lunches and afternoon teas. This is an historic theatre which *does not currently present performances,* though may do so in the future. Live music, mainly jazz or folk, is presented each Thursday evening
Parking: Ample parking nearby
Transport: Close to BR station. Frequent bus services

SALISBURY

SALISBURY PLAYHOUSE, Malthouse Lane, Salisbury, SP2 7RA
Telephone: (0722) 20333   Seats: 516
Facilities: Bar, restaurant, wheelchairs by arrangement, hard of hearing loop
Parking: Large free car park nearby
Transport: Close to BR and bus stations
Type of programme: Monthly repertory, throughout the year with exception of month of June
SALBERG STUDIO   Seats: 100
Type of programme: Repertory season (September - May) with many visiting drama companies

SALISBURY ARTS CENTRE, Bedwin Street, Salisbury, SP1 3UT
Telephone: (0722) 21744   Seats: 160 - 400
Facilities: Bar, coffee bar, restaurant - Egon Ronay listed, vegetarian menu available, wheelchairs, hard of hearing loop
Parking: Car parking in Salt Lane and College Street
Transport: Bus station nearby
Type of programme: Dance, mime, modern and classical music, touring theatre. Rock music on Thursdays

SOUTHAMPTON

THE GANTRY, Blechynden Terrace, Southampton SO1 0GW
Telephone: (0703) 229319   Seats: 300 maximum
Facilities: Bar, coffee shop, wheelchairs by arrangement
Parking: Street parking and central car parks nearby
Transport: Easy walking distance from bus and rail stations
Type of programme: Professional and amateur drama Children's workshops, music and literary events

THE GUILDHALL, West Marlands, Southampton SO9 4XF
Telephone: (0703) 32601   Seats: 1,486
Facilities: Bar, coffee shop, restaurant, wheelchairs
Parking: Public car parks nearby
Transport: Close to BR and bus stations
Type of programme: Live shows, concerts, classical and popular music

MAYFLOWER THEATRE, Commercial Road, Southampton SO1 0GE
Telephone: (0703) 229771   Seats 2,251
Facilities: Bar, wheelchairs by arrangement
Parking: Car parks in city centre nearby
Transport: Close to BR and bus stations
Type of programme: Touring companies - ballet and opera. Major West End productions - variety and pop concerts

NUFFIELD THEATRE, University Road, Southampton SO9 5NH
Telephone: (0703) 555028   Seats: 506
Facilities: Bar, restaurant, wheelchairs by arrangement, hard of hearing loop
Parking: Free adjacent to theatre and in street
Transport: Bus services 10,20 and 6 pass by theatre, while 4 and 11 (from Civic Centre) stop nearby in Burgess Road
Type of programme: Repertory theatre (September - May). Touring and amateur, including dance, March - July

TURNER SIMS CONCERT HALL, University of Southampton, SO9 5NH
Telephone: (0703) 555028   Seats: 461
Facilities: Coffee shop, restaurant bar, (at Nuffield Theatre nearby) wheelchairs by arrangement, hard of hearing loop
Parking: At rear of concert hall and in University Road
Transport: Bus services 10, 20 and 6 pass close by the concert hall, while 4 and 11 (from Civic Centre) stop nearby in Burgess Road
Type of programme: Open to the general public, but held only during university term times. Professional evening concerts of chamber music, organ recitals, lunchtime concerts on Mondays and Fridays

WINCHESTER

THEATRE ROYAL, Jewry Street, Winchester, Hampshire SO23 8SB
Telephone: (0962) 63210. *The Box Office also acts as an agency for London and regional theatres*
Facilities: Bar, wheelchairs by arrangement, hard of hearing loop, combined theatre/dinner tickets with Elizabethan Restaurant nearby.
Parking: Public car park adjacent (free after 6pm)
Transport: Close to BR and bus stations
Type of programme: Theatre, variety, classical and jazz concerts, dance. Occasional amateur performances.

INDEX